High and Dry

High and Dry

Antonia Hunt

Ashford Press Publishing
Southampton
1988

Published by   Ashford Press Publishing 1988
                1 Church Road
                Shedfield
                Hampshire SO3 2HW

British Library Cataloguing in Publication Data

Hunt, Antonia
    High and Dry.
    1. England. Hunt, Antonia. Biographies
    I. Title
    942.085 092 4

    ISBN 1-85253-067-7

Printed by Hartnolls Limited, Bodmin, Cornwall
Typeset by Words&Spaces, Rowlands Castle, Hampshire

Contents

Foreword

I'm writing this by torchlight – curled up in my sleeping bag in a small tent, with the rain lashing down outside, during a 1,000 mile walk round Wales in winter – working with some difficulty!

However, it somehow seems appropriate that the foreword for such a courageously-written story as *High and Dry* should not be composed among the easy comforts of a desk and typewriter.

High and Dry is a book I have natural affection for, because of my own years of living in a small boat and sailing round the world with nappies flying from the rigging instead of ensigns. Antonia's account of her storm-tossed honeymoon – hurricane force winds and the many other adventures and near disasters she describes – confirms my opinion that sailing in the Channel and round the coast of Britain can be just as challenging, and sometimes more so, than voyages across thousands of miles of ocean.

Her life on board both *Pat* and the *Elsa* as a young wife and mother, during those traumatic four years leading up to the Spithead Review, gives a fascinating insight into life afloat during the difficult post-war period. It is all particularly interesting because sailing was never one of Antonia's dreams. Like many famous sailors thoughout history she was more or less 'press-ganged' on board – in her case by fate and James!

I particularly liked the account of her 'mutiny', when she jumped ashore on Portland breakwater on the southern arm – stretching out endlessly to sea with nowhere to go – and had to climb ignominiously back on board; also her poignant description of the preparations for the Spithead Review. Most of all I loved her stories about that colourful character, who was perhaps, after all, the real boss on board – Tilly the cat.

However this is much more than just a book about sailing. It is a story of love, fear and vulnerability. The same tremendous courage which must have helped Antonia survive during her years as a young girl alone in Nazi occupied France, shines through in *High and Dry*, even though she doesn't recognize

it herself, and helps her cope with many very difficult situations, I would say most magnificently. But after all she went through when very young, I think I can understand why Antonia was more vulnerable when it came to loving somebody, than she ever seemed to be facing purely physical dangers.

Anyway, fear has many forms. I thank God that I have never had to undergo Antonia's ordeals. But I do know that fear, whether of man, or the elements, is not something you become inoculated against, or immune to, like some virulent disease – just because you have endured it once!

I remember crouching in the tiny cabin of 17 ft *Fiesta Girl* during a bad storm, while on a solo transatlantic voyage from Pembroke to New York in 1983. Water kept welling through the portside shroudplate fittings, which had worn loose in previous gales, and the whole plywood hull seemed to give a little more each time a wave thundered into the side of the little boat. At any moment I knew the whole thing could give and the sea would rush in with incredible speed. I felt utterly, totally paralysed by terror. My heart was pounding in my stomach, in my legs, in my brain itself; cloned in every part of my body, except where it should be. America was still 900 miles away. The nearest 'land' was the seabed, at present marked on the chart as about 2,000 fathoms below the hull.

All I could think of was, 'I may never see a tree again. . . never again hear the sound of a human voice. . .be hugged by those I love. . . .' Even little things like the fact that I might never again taste a cup of coffee in my life panicked me. I tried desperately to calm myself, knowing that unless I did so, I couldn't act and do whatever little might be possible to try and help *Fiesta Girl*.

Strangely enough, what worked best for curing the worst of my terrible fear was actually imagining the water forcing its way into my mouth and lungs, telling myself it might not really be such a bad end; that being drowned couldn't last and hurt forever; and that at least my skeleton might finish up in some interesting unexplored part of the seabed!

Anyway, in the end, I pulled myself together and somehow the little boat and I saved each other. After that I thought, 'I'll never be frightened of anything ever again, after this. . . .' Oh – how wrong I was!

There was the time more recently when I lost my two horses and everything I had in a thousand miles of pitiless, waterless Atacama desert, after a sandstorm. There were the occasions later during the same journey down Chile, from the Atacama to Cape Horn, when I had to swim terrifying

rivers holding onto my horses' tails; the time when I was trying to cross one of those fragile swaying bridges, such as are seen in westerns, and my horse caught his foot in one of the missing slats and panicked and the whole bridge swung like a skipping rope and the horses and I very narrowly escaped being flung into the ravine 200 feet below. . . .

There are many more occasions when I have felt total terror – that I don't even want to remember!

So – my heart goes out to Antonia and I wish her very entertaining new book all the best of success. It certainly has been a privilege to write this foreword, especially because Antonia writes as though all her readers are her friends; as I am sure they will become – myself amongst them.

Rosie Swale

Prologue

High and Dry is the sequel to *Little Resistance* – in which I described the eventful period between 1940 and 1945, when I was mistakenly left behind, at the age of 14, in what was to become Nazi-occupied France. Those vulnerable teenage years, when I survived escape and arrest, imprisonment and torment, left an indelible impression on me, but luckily had no lasting physical effects. This book is the story of a later part of my life, after the war. Though differing widely from my first book, it again highlights one of the most basic human emotions: fear. This time it is fear of the elements – the wind and the sea – rather than fear of Man.

High and Dry recalls experiences which culminated in a four-year spell between 1949 and 1953 with my husband and family in a small sea-going boat. Living afloat in those days was a great deal more hazardous than it is today, when modern navigational facilities, such as efficient ship-to-shore radio communications and long-term weather forecasts, considerably reduce the risks involved.

High and Dry recounts briefly my year in the WRNS (Women's Royal Naval Service), my marriage in 1946 to a naval officer, and my first encounter with the ex-RNLI lifeboat called *Pat*. The next era took place on board another slightly larger boat, the 50 ft Dutch Boeier (barge) called *Elsa*. There followed the tumult of the raging, unquiet sea on many risky sailing trips both abroad and round the coast of Britain. Admittedly it has not the panache of a single-handed round-the-world cruise, nor the daring of Atlantic Ocean racing, but the English Channel is capable of as much devious wickedness and cunning as most of the watery world.

I have endeavoured to be as correct as possible in my sailing terms, hopefully being neither pedantic nor wildly inaccurate. For personal reasons I have changed the names of some of the characters, except in the case of dear Sarah, to whom the book is dedicated.

ACKNOWLEDGEMENTS

Acknowledgements and grateful thanks are due to the following people: Mr Paul Ridgway, Public Relations Officer at Trinity House, Tower Bridge, for his encouragement and help with my research, advising me to whom I should write for correct details and data; Mr Brunton-Reed, of Reed's Almanac, for his letters enclosing many invaluable photocopies of the harbours and ports mentioned in the book, between 1949 to 1953; the Meteorological Office, for publications and verification of certain important factors; Mr David Hastie, Public Relations Officer of the Port of Manchester, for the information he sent me, including the comprehensive publication on the Manchester Ship Canal and a splendid chart of the Mersey; Mr Terry Jenkinson, Dock Manager of Weston Point Docks, for the Photocopies and plans of the Weaver Navigation; the Danby family; and finally to Sarah, without whose sense of humour and encouragement I would have 'sunk without trace'.

CHAPTER ONE
The Spithead Review

Despite the cold, grey choppy Solent of that June weekend in 1953, an air of intense excitement and anticipation prevailed. This was a royal occasion eagerly looked forward to by the Navy and small boats alike, for those lucky enough to draw a place in the anchorage provided would participate in a unique celebration of the Queen's Coronation – the Spithead Review. Our Dutch Boeier *Elsa* had been lucky enough to draw one of the carefully marked anchorages on the chart. Perhaps I was the only person among the thousands present among the bobbing, tossing craft, who could not join in the joyousness of the occasion. But my inner pain would not, *must* not intrude on the thrill and majesty of such an event. This was history. It was also, I now knew, *Elsa's* swan song – and mine too.

James was coming back from HMS *Ariel* for the two days of the Review, with the Captain's elderly secretary and Ted. Did either the secretary or Ted know? I must at all costs appear normal. That weekend was the English June at its worst; cold, bleak and blustery with the inevitable squally showers. The regulations stipulated that we all had to be at our anchorage at least the day before, so the three from HMS *Ariel* arrived on Saturday 13 June to give us time for a sail on Sunday before the Review on the 15.

My heart missed several beats as I saw James again. Conflicting emotions tore me apart yet had to be kept hidden. Most heart- rending of all was the boys' unbounded delight at seeing their father after nearly a month's absence. He was friendly – even relaxed. How was I going to live through the next two days? The Captain's secretary was understanding, kind and sympathetic. There was no need for words. She knew anyway.

We only spoke about the boat and I dared to ask for his

approval of my efforts to enhance the lovely *Elsa*, asking: 'Have you got the flags to "dress her overall", for the Queen?' He nodded. Tense and numb with grief and longing, for once I was not seasick, though Spithead was rough enough. Our exact position was marked off on a vast chart, among quite a few other yachts, but with plenty of room to swing to our anchors as the tide turned.

The excitement and anticipation of the great day on the morrow helped enormously to reduce the tension. It was fascinating to watch the remaining boats arrive and position themselves with less and less room to manoeuvre as time went on. In the distance we could see the ships of the Royal Navy; ships too from visiting navies, including Russia; and biggest thrill of all, not too far away from us, the breath-takingly beautiful *Amerigo Vespucci* with a crew of cadets lining the yard arms. Our two boys were just old enough to be interested in all the ships, snatching the binoculars from each other. The wind freshened and as the tide turned, some yachts dragged their anchors, one bearing down on us at an alarming rate before her crew got her under control – not before we had hung out all our fenders!

James had decided that with the perfect sailing conditions for *Elsa* we could actually sail up and down the entire lines of assembled ships, thus doing a review of our own, which would – and did – make the occasion indelibly unforgettable.

In order to ease the electric atmosphere James and Ted rowed ashore on Sunday morning to get the Sunday papers, leaving the Captain's secretary with the boys and me. I was too shy to say anything, for there was no point. She had Sarah's old cabin and Ted was on the settee in the saloon – so James had to sleep in our bunk. Though I longed with all my shattered, aching soul to hold him, to lie in his arms, we lay there, carefully not touching – like strangers.

Sheer exhaustion allowed me the blessed drug of sleep at last. My red eyes were a giveaway in the morning.

After an early lunch and a glimpse, no more, of the sun before massing grey clouds covered it for good, we prepared to sail up and down the lines. It was an impressive turnout and as we sailed, close hauled between the assembled navies, we had the impression that *we* were the inspecting craft taking the salute.

Several of the ships were known to us; the frigate HMS *Battleaxe*, the minelayer *Apollo* and the submarine *Sea Devil*. At the end of the line lay the Russian aircraft carrier and flagship *Sverdlov*; admittedly looking like any other ship

and as we drew near, to the boy's great excitement a helicopter, fairly rare in those days, prepared to land on her decks. Simultaneously, a horrendous twenty-one gun salute crashed deafeningly around us, causing Peter, the three year old, to fling himself down covering his ears with his hands. We presumed it must have been Bulganin and Khrushchev, regretting that we should have mistimed our inspection to include such a barrage.

Back we sailed to our anchorage to await Her Majesty's inspection in the Commander in Chief's Mediterranean dispatch vessel, the converted frigate HMS *Surprise*. Sadly she was miles away from us, her route obviously near to HMS ships, but not taking into account – how could it – the myriad small yachts all intensely loyal and eager to show their allegiance. To us, she appeared as a small, fragile white dot and we waved and cheered ourselves hoarse for a long time.

My eyes strained to see her, the tears of devotion and loyalty masking my own dumb misery. Tears too remembering her father, King George VI, whose dedication, courage and kindness had inspired me as I struggled through a lonely exiled war, left behind in France by mistake at the age of fourteen in 1940, and not returning to Britain till 1944 after many horrendous adventures.

Queen Elizabeth II would now inherit all that surge of devoted admiration from her millions of subjects. I could not help contrasting her happy, secure future with my own stark emptiness. Though we could only just see the tiny far-off figure, I imagined her tall, handsome and protective husband beside her, taking care of her through the years, with her children and a loving family, as well as a constant reassuring background of all her subjects. Apart from the two boys, from now on I had no one – not even anywhere to go. I must not think of it until I was alone again.

Later that evening, in an atmosphere of anticlimax, we sailed back to our berth in the Hamble. James returned to HMS *Ariel* with Ted and the Captain's secretary. I did not see him again.

During the week that followed, the supreme betrayal to *Elsa* was advertising her for sale. She had not only been our home, she was somehow part of my family, for we had been through so much together. We had been happy and we had nearly sunk without trace. If the boys and I went on living on board alone, I would never be able to sail her and she would become a mere houseboat. Such humiliation would not become her, so instead the three of us would buy a cottage in Devon. During the daytime, the boring daily chores had to be

done, the water tank filled, the shopping done (by bus, for I had no car), the boys cared for. Tears had to be hidden from them, but fell, impossible to check, when during long evening hours I recalled both sweet and bitter memories of four years afloat.

Perhaps I could exorcize the four wasted years by reliving each incident, each year; encapsulate them then bury them for ever. After all, I had successfully managed that for the four teenage years spent drifting alone around France, in and out of the clutches of the Germans. But then, that exorcism had been easy with newfound and ecstatic happiness in married life – at first. Once I had moved to the little village of Lustleigh in Devon another era must start afresh, untrammelled by masochistic memories or reliving the past, or indulging in bouts of heartbroken nostalgia. That sort of mother would be useless to the boys. I would tell them their father had gone to sea again and behave accordingly, or at least I would try, while giving them all the love and security I was capable of. That was far more important than any tragedy that could happen to me. I would survive. Witness the war – solitary confinement in a Gestapo cell in Paris aged eighteen, four teenage years without my parents in occupied France. . .this was nothing, or so I tried to tell myself – merely an episode. My present world had ended but in years to come another one might start.

Each day, for that last week before leaving dear *Elsa*, I remembered, the early happiness causing as much pain as the recent devastating misery. Like touching a sore place or aching tooth to experience an acute pain as a contrast to an unbearable ache – I remembered. It all flooded back so vividly, in minutest detail. Oh! if only the actual physical pain of losing him would go. Surely it must fade – wounds heal, they say. But they do not – really – ever.

I recalled my homecoming in 1944 which was so anxiously anticipated and yet also turned out to be an anticlimax. Travel weary and lost, having flown back from a front-line hospital in war-torn France, in a Mosquito, I reached Glasgow eventually in the dark. I had wandered up and down the platform searching for my mother and we must have passed each other several times in the gloom unable to recognize each other. She was in WVS uniform and so much smaller than I remembered. Finally, we were the only two left on the platform. At that moment, in August 1944, apprehensive and feeling like an alien in my own country, with my entire worldly possessions in a small battered case, I had at last returned. . .home? My mother had spent those years in a

hotel in Ayrshire, so that there was no 'home' to go to where I could lick my mental and physical wounds in seclusion.

As we drove to the Bellisle Hotel in Ayr from the station, we talked like two strangers. When my mother had last seen me I was a fourteen-year-old schoolgirl, now I was nearly nineteen. I told her of my engagement to a wonderful French boy, my own age, she told me about her father's death – we were poles apart. As soon as I was fit I bicycled into Ayr daily to take a Pitman typing course and applied to join the WRNS (the Women's Royal Naval Service). I was accepted as a trainee and invited to join the establishment at Mill Hill.

Naturally, by now, my one ambition was to get back to 'la douce France', so, buoyed up by dreams of becoming an interpreter, I gladly undertook the fortnight of arduous initial training. Despite my present troubles I could not help smiling as I thought back to that life.

To begin with, the huge dormitories with double bunks reminded me of a German prison camp. The shouted orders and exhausting chores were hard to bear, for new recruits had to rise at 5 a.m., scrubbing acres of stone or linoleum corridors, before a huge breakfast which was followed by endless drilling and marching. The boring lectures, of which I hardly understood a word, sent me either to sleep or into a state of near panic as I knew *nothing* about the Navy, nor the strange language that went with it.

The interview with the WRNS Officer in charge of allocating careers was disappointing.

'There aren't many jobs vacant now, no drivers or boat crew – but then I don't suppose you drive do you? Would you like to be a cook or a steward? Plenty of vacancies there.' I shuddered.

'Well Ma'am, I don't know how to cook either, but I do speak French as I've only just got back from France, and I *would* like to be an interpreter and go to Paris.' The poor flabbergasted officer exploded, thinking I must be making fun of her.

'Don't talk such nonsense girl, don't you know there's a war on? No one is allowed to travel to Europe.'

I could see she did not believe me and there was no point in insisting I was being truthful, or pursuing my ambition – to argue with an officer was an act of insubordination, a criminal offence, and the punishment very severe. I blushed, bit my lip and said nothing. The officer relented.

'Perhaps you could be in Signals, would you like that?' Maybe my voice had been clear, possibly I did not look like a good cook or steward. Though I had no idea what 'Signals'

entailed, and could only conjure up a picture of someone waving flags, it sounded much the best alternative, so I meekly replied. 'Yes, please Ma'am.'

The house that all the Wrens lived in near the base at Bo'ness in Scotland had been a large private manse standing in parkland; the dormitories quite small, only six girls to a room. In fact, as was so often the case, the LCT base had not been expecting another signaller to arrive for a week or so. This proved a great help, as I was able to find my way round the dockyard and the strange glass box-like room which was the SDO (Signal Distributing Office). This was situated at one end of the vast hangar where all the sailors slept in their hammocks; the building was very dark, so the light in the SDO had to be on all the time, and once installed, one was unaware of the hollow darkness around it, or the men, off watch, who were sleeping there. Inside was a telephone, a typewriter and an antiquated duplicating machine. The duties, on the surface, were simple: on a special pad, one took down the message over the telephone, adding the time of dispatch and arrival. After typing it on a special carbon, this was put into the duplicator and the required number of copies churned out by turning a handle. The machine was temperamental, filled with a bright mauve ink which spluttered everywhere, covering hands and white uniform shirts indiscriminately. Then, the complicated part started. Firstly, working out who the message was for and, secondly, where to find them, for little offices were tucked away in odd corners all over the base. There were two signallers, who did 'watch on' and 'watch off' as the SDO had to be manned night and day, a nightmare for me as I could not keep awake. Most of the time I failed to understand the broad Scottish accents over the telephone and drove people to distraction asking them to repeat what must have been fairly simple straight-forward messages. Next, I would be merrily turning the handle of the purple-spraying duplicator when the phone would ring again; the signals would pile up – and panic set in. As I never knew who might be interested in some obscure communication, I distributed them gaily to everyone I could think of. The offices in charge of the various departments soon tired of this, complained, and subsequently became somewhat annoyed when some relevant signal never reached them. In civilian life I would not have lasted five minutes.

Occasionally there would be two free hours in the afternoon, so, buying a packet of Smith's Crisps, with the little twist of blue paper containing salt, I would go for a walk

in the lovely country near Bo'ness and sit and write my daily postcard to my fiancé Pierre.

It was now nearly a year since I had returned from France, and though I loved him as much as ever, the anguish and pain at being separated from him had lessened. There was so much to do, no time to think and I was tired, though healthy, for the naval food suited me, as did the straightforward if rough behaviour of my fellow Wrens, restoring a sane balance to my war-troubled mind. The love for France, the memory of Pierre were slowly being superseded by an active new life. Without realizing it, all my Mother had wished for was being achieved painlessly and without a word written or spoken overtly against my proposed marriage to a Frenchman.

Later on that spring, one signal came through that revived all my excitement and hope of getting back to France. It was a long-awaited, expected signal nevertheless marked 'Top Secret'. The message stated simply – 'Splice the mainbrace' – for the following day, VE day!

We were all assembled the next morning and told of the cessation of hostilities in Europe. The Germans had surrendered. I was in the SDO on duty when the order to 'Splice the mainbrace' was carried out. A sailor brought me a large tot of the strong, sweet dark rum in a mug: my first taste of rum or any alcohol for that matter for months.

Work in the SDO slackened off. The LCTs (Landing Craft Tanks) were still going out to the Far East, but the pressure was easing. Finally, the day came when the base was reduced to a skeleton staff: signallers were no longer needed and, along with several others, I was sent on leave, with instructions to attend a writers' course at Wetherby in Yorkshire after the summer. My pay, of 10 shillings (50p) a week had only just caught up with me, so that I had a few pound notes to return to Ayr with.

With the possibility of my father's return to England in the not too distant future, my mother thought of moving south, to another hotel though, for I still could not persuade her to buy a cottage. She proposed a visit to old friends:

'Tonia, there are so many of my friends I haven't seen for years, who've been asking about you during the war. Now that you're home for a nice long leave let's go and visit one or two of them.' This was an exciting thought, though I could not remember any of them:

'Who were you thinking of?' Surprised, she answered, 'Surely you remember the Rentons? Aunt Grizelda and Uncle Robert in Catterick when we were all stationed there. Not a

real uncle and aunt, but we knew them so well and you used to play with their children, when you were nine and ten.' Suddenly it came back to me.

'Yes, there was Celia – quite a lot older than me – and James. They were very good at riding, and always daring me to jump streams and things. I was a bit frightened of them but I liked James. I think he wrote to me once from school – just before the war.' I paused before going on and risking an unpopular idea. 'Though I would love to come with you, do you think it would be possible for me to try and go back to France – and see Pierre? It's over a year since I've seen him. Postcards and letters don't help much.' My mother was adamant.

'No. There is no question of civilians crossing the Channel for months – if not longer. You'll just have to wait and, anyway, I don't really want you to go back there.' It was hopeless. The die was cast.

Mrs Renton was written to in Dorset and replied enthusiastically. We would have to stay in a small hotel in Bridport for she had no help in the house and not enough food rations, but she was longing to see us, would book two rooms for us, adding that her son, James,was home on leave from his submarine and, 'Wouldn't it be fun for the "children" to meet again?'

I had never been to Dorset and the view from the train of the gentle rolling hills, green, peaceful and comforting, unchanged for centuries, helped to soothe my sadness at not being able to go to France.

We went straight to the old Bull Hotel on the main street in Bridport. The floors in our rooms sloped crazily, giving the impression of being at sea in rough weather; there was not a straight line anywhere; the walls dipped and bulged, curving entrancingly. The whole atmosphere was warm, glowing and very welcoming; curtains and chairs covered in a soft blend of faded colours. I relaxed and felt happier than for a very long time indeed.

Mrs Renton telephoned to say they would come and pick us up for tea. I put on my prettiest dress. I possessed few clothes and had worn uniform almost continuously for months. My short dark-brown hair had auburn lights in it and shone in the sunlight; apart from a little lipstick, I wore no make-up and, to be honest I was not pretty, though high cheekbones and a pointed chin did what they could to redeem my face, helped by slanting brown eyes and a wide mouth. Yes, I was excited at the thought of meeting a young Englishman, for the first time for over a year.

There was a knock on the door of the little sitting room, followed by Grizelda Renton who kissed us both warmly,

exclaiming over the changes in me. In a lull of affectionate greetings and exclamations a very tall young man with intensely blue eyes slipped round the door. I met his eyes and quickly looked away, for I could not believe the impact of what I felt – an electric shock, a bolt of lightning. In short, a breathtaking 'love-at-first-sight'. I found myself unable to speak, for I thought anything I did say would sound so foolish it would give my feelings away.

Our conversation in the back of the car was stilted. We let the grown-ups talk, entering into general conversation about the war, rationing, etc. We were only staying in Dorset for a couple of days, so Grizelda suggested that James might like to show me the famous high cliff called Golden Cap on the Dorset coast. Events had been taken out of my hands.

The next day he picked me up in his parent's car and we drove in awkward silence to Seatown, not far from Bridport. Tentatively, I asked him, 'How long have you been in the Navy? It must be awfully claustrophobic in submarines. Have you had an awful time?'

I realized too late that, no doubt, everyone asked the same questions. His reply was offhand and matter of fact, 'Well, I went straight from school to Brittania Royal Naval College – and I *like* submarines. We went aground off North Africa after attacking an Italian convoy, and were taken prisoner by the Italians which was boring – didn't last long. We were released by the Desert Rats – winning back what Rommel had taken.'

My emotion heightened. Here, at last, was someone who had been a POW too, who would understand my strange experiences. It was too soon to talk about them though, and a shame to spoil this beautiful isolated afternoon, walking up the lovely cliffs overlooking the whole spectacular beauty of Lyme Bay. That afternoon the sea looked so idyllic, so calm and friendly, its treachery masked.

Being 1945, the coast was still deserted, no holiday-makers had invaded the West Country and we had Golden Cap to ourselves, except for hundreds of bobbing and scuttling rabbits and the lazily swooping gulls. I had no head for heights and drew back from the edge of the cliff at the top with a gasp, before we sat down on the springy turf and heather; presently James lay down and slept. He was only twenty-one, and the exertions of war had exhausted him. I watched him sleep, knowing that I would love him deeply and for ever. First, I would have to write to Pierre; he would be bitter and hurt. It occurred to me that James might already have a girlfriend, and not be in the least bit interested in me.

Even if he felt nothing for me, a possibility that made me shiver with apprehension, I knew I must not continue a charade of loving Pierre; it would be dishonest.

Quite a long while later James awoke, stretching lazily: 'Heavens! I must have dropped off. What's the time? Why didn't you wake me? Race you down to the bottom!' We set off in long, leaping ungainly strides down the steep slope, scattering rabbits to right and left, whilst the loose sole of James's shoe flapped furiously, and his old tweed coat billowed behind him; our laughter, natural and unforced echoing around us. Our silence after that afternoon was an easy, companionable one, but both our mothers were a bit upset at 'the children not getting on very well'. Shaking her head, Grizelda told my mother, 'They hardly spoke to each other.'

James and I met once more before leaving Dorset. He picked me up in the old car that last evening to go to the cinema in Lyme Regis – very Victorian with red velvet seats, with double ones in the back row – where we sat side by side, though not holding hands, nor even touching shoulders. I hardly dared to breathe for fear of breaking the enchanting spell, as we watched Judy Garland in *Meet me in St Louis*. He seemed relaxed and happy, kissing me gently on the cheek in a brotherly way when he left me outside the Bull Hotel.

I remembered very little of the rest of our short holiday visiting other old friends, trying to sort out my confused feelings. My mother admonished me, 'Really Tonia, you weren't very nice to poor James – you might have made more of an effort to talk to him and be friendly – it seemed a bit ungrateful.'

Soon after our return to Scotland, my official posting came through, requesting me to report to Wetherby in Yorkshire to attend a writers' course. It was already bitterly cold and the Wrens' quarters were in old Nissen huts with no heating! I threw myself into my work in a frenzy to make up for having been such an unsatisfactory signaller, knowing too that the most interesting jobs would go to the most successful. Before the final exam, we were given a long weekend and I travelled up to Scotland to find a letter waiting for me – from James. My fingers shook as I opened the envelope, eager to read the short but friendly letter in which he told me that his submarine was going to be stationed at Plymouth and he hoped he might see me again one day. . . . Surely he would not have written unless he felt attracted, yet there was no suggestion of any feeling stronger than friendship in the letter.

The last days of revision were hectic, but luckily for me the

first questions on the exam papers concerned points of Naval Law which I had read very carefully. I came second, which pleased me for I had had no schooling to speak of. However, as there was no job for me to go to, it was decided to send Wren Smith to a holding depot near Dunfermline, after a short period of leave.

Once again, the Rentons asked us to visit them to see their new house, 'Jackmoor'. I thrilled at the idea and my eyes lit up as I asked how soon we could go. My mother gently asked me 'Tonia, what have you done about Pierre? Have you written to him yet?' Guiltily I replied, 'No. How can I? I can't bear the thought of hurting him, and I don't know how James feels about me.' She was rightly annoyed and urged me to write as soon as possible.

The Rentons were at the station to meet us and James was with them, obviously delighted to see me again; a shy grin started in his eyes, curving his wide mouth into a lopsided curl. He teased me about the results of the writers' course, 'It must have been a pretty low standard of English if you came second!' I was so supremely happy, he might have been paying me the most elaborate compliment and I laughed with him as I told him we could only stay for two nights as I was being sent to Dunfermline. He smiled into my eyes, merely saying, 'Never mind. I don't know what our respective parents are arranging but I expect we'll be spending most of tomorrow together. Won't that be fun?' By now I was nearly certain he more than liked me, and when we were dropped off at the Bull I ran to my room to relive everything he had said, experiencing the huge joy of letting myself fall irrevocably in love with the tall good-looking submariner whom I had known as a boy, when he was eleven and I was nine.

Next morning I wore a new grey suit and green blouse; I felt transformed and wondered if it showed. 'Jackmoor' was a most entrancing old, thatched house. A short tree-lined drive led up to it, with lawns and a rather untidy garden surrounding the house and a very large pond, or tiny lake overhung by weeping willows. Behind the house was a stable yard and a coachman's cottage. The whole property had a romantic, dreamlike quality which enraptured me. The old oak door was nearly hidden by wisteria and virginia creeper that had been allowed to climb and intermingle over the soft pink of the old bricks, whilst roses reached the bedroom windows. The house was low, with leaded windows encased in mullioned stonework; inside, warm colours and lamp light, framed by old beams seemed the ideal, the perfect setting. Having no home, living either in Wrens' quarters or impersonal

hotels I had forgotten how comfortable and cosy a house could be. The Rentons' furniture was old and lovingly cared for, well polished, with gleaming brass handles on the chests of drawers. Indian and Persian rugs, shaded lamps, old and faded chintzes completed a harmony in each room. In the big open fireplace flames leapt and glowed. The last rooms to be seen were James's and his sister Celia's, on the top floor with steeply sloping ceilings up to the eaves under the thatch.

To my dismay, I saw, on top of his desk, a silver frame with a large photograph of a serenely beautiful girl. The shock of realizing what I had secretly feared, that there was indeed a girl in his life, made me feel shaken and sick. I wanted to leave but knew we would have to stay to tea and talk and behave naturally as though nothing had happened. Somehow, I managed to conceal my feelings, letting everyone talk around me, without appearing to be distressed. James looked at me enquiringly once or twice when I merely answered yes or no to his eager and friendly questions.

I could not bring myself to look into James's very expressive blue gaze as the two families said goodbye. He was puzzled and a little hurt, not understanding, as yet, the reason for my sudden withdrawal.

For two or three days, back at Camberley, I was in despair, knowing full well that whether James liked me or not, I should write to Pierre straightaway. His letters to me were full of plans, hoping to arrange a passage to England on one of the very first civilian ships, and he was saving money for our future. I suffered appallingly from guilt and remorse as well as shame at my own indecision.

Then, on the day before I was due to catch the train to Glasgow, a letter came from James. The letter was fairly casual, but one sentence might have been written in red ink or capitals. It merely said that he no longer had room for the photograph on his desk and had taken it down. He had finally understood my silence and distress that day. He would like to hear from me when I got back – suddenly everything was absolutely wonderful!

The Wrens' quarters in Dunfermline brought me back to earth with a bump; the buildings were cold, grey and bleak, no one expected me but eventually a bed was found for me in one of the dormitories. There was nothing much for us to do apart from attending a few lectures or taking over the switchboard for the odd day – but I only achieved a hopeless muddle. I wrote a short pathetic letter to Pierre which sounded better in French. It would take ages to get a reply and, in the meantime, his faithful, loving, tender pages,

written in his rather childish writing kept arriving each day, moving me to tears. My depression and anxiety deepened as I waited for his reply. I became thin and ill, finally spending a week in the sick bay. When it did arrive I was feeling stronger, luckily, for he was desolate and inconsolable, though he urged me not to grieve overmuch for him, imploring me to go to him should I need help.

My conscience eased a little and my days were taken up by a new activity. The Naval Motor Transport Instructor gave me an intensive course, at the end of which I passed my test in hilly Dunfermline. This included an extra test taken in a ten-ton lorry, which had its dramatic moments such as when I was told to back it up one of the steeper hills on the outskirts of the town. The examiner must have been feeling particularly tolerant that day, as my zig-zag backward course was fairly hair-raising!

During that fortnight James wrote to me again, so that in one swift half hour my distress see-sawed back to dizzy delight. He wanted to see me and his submarine was going to be in the Clyde for a while. He asked if I could meet him in Edinburgh one weekend. This completed my happiness and I sought permission from my Wren Officer for a weekend pass. I phoned my mother excitedly; 'Everything is sorted out, I've written to Pierre – and James wants to see me.' She interrupted me, 'How do you mean? Where? You can't go and see him on your own.'

How strange that sounds now – in the permissive society of the 1980s. But it was all important then. I was determined, 'Don't worry Mother – he is on board his submarine and I shall stay in a little hotel.' I looked up train times and found I could leave early on Saturday, not having to be back till 11 p.m. on Sunday, which meant two whole days together. When James telephoned from the submarine base it took all my willpower to disguise the tremble in my voice. He explained, 'I've borrowed a little car and I've got the weekend off too. What time is your train?' I stuttered, unwilling to appear too anxious, 'Would 9.15 a.m. be all right?' 'Yes. That's fine. I'll be there.' Such a bald , plain conversation, but the most thrilling one of my life.

We shook hands, smiling widely. Both of us ridiculously carefree and happy, not knowing what to say. James spoke, 'We'll take your case to a quiet little hotel – then we can explore. I don't have to be back on board till 11 p.m., so we've got the whole day, isn't that fun?'

The day took on an elusive, unreal quality. It was a dream, or else I had died and was in heaven! We walked up to King

Arthur's seat, talking, of all and nothing, laughing at anything. As we sat on a boulder, overlooking the magnificent,
romantic view of the Castle and Edinburgh itself, I jokingly
said, 'I suppose you'll fall asleep now, like the day we were on
Golden Cap – do you remember?' But James said nothing.
His eyes smiled and looked into mine with so much love, I
was certain he felt the same and I waited for him to say
something to confirm my thoughts. Instead he countered
with, 'It's too cold to go to sleep – but I could race you down
to the bottom like we did on Golden Cap!' As we were both
in uniform this would have been impossible, but such a
delightfully ludicrous idea made us both laugh outright again.
He took my hand, 'No, we'll walk – slowly – and remember
every minute of today.'

We walked back all the way, hand in hand. Darkness came
early in the northern winter. We stopped and bought *The
Times* on the way back, choosing a quiet secluded corner of
the lounge on our return. He did some of the crossword, but
I was hopeless. Even under normal circumstances I was
unable to get more than three or four of the obscure clues, but
at that particular moment, all coherent thinking had
exploded in a brilliant kaleidoscope. We dined early, dreading
the moment when James would have to drive back to the
submarine. We sat, close together, pleasantly exhausted from
the early start, the physical and mental exertions of the day.
James spoke, 'There's a clue here – a quotation: "Journeys end
in lovers" . . .' leaving it to me to complete. I knew that verse
by heart, murmuring: 'Lovers' meeting'. Blushing at the word
'lovers', James put down the paper.

His thoughts and plans must have been difficult to put into
perspective. Like all young men of his age, he had gone
straight from school at eighteen, into the Services, in his case
the Navy, and to war. The future in 1946 was still unsettled,
and he had no idea where his submarine might be posted, or
when the next 'pierhead jump' (a sudden posting) might be
announced. I could only guess at his confused thoughts,
somehow communicated to me telepathically. First of all, his
pay was hardly adequate, as a lieutenant, in those days, to
support a wife; and if we *did* marry, where could we live? He
would never be able to afford a house or cottage, and naval
quarters were non-existent then.

He leant forward, and took my hands. No one else was in
the room, which gave us an illusion of privacy. 'Antonia –
will you marry me?' Quickly, too quickly, I said, 'Oh! James,
yes,' and in the same breath, 'But you don't even know me
properly.' He smiled, 'We can start now. I expect you wonder

why I didn't ask you this afternoon on top of King Arthur's Seat.' I admitted that the hotel lounge was a bit. . . James spoke the word, 'Unromantic!' and went on, 'I think that's probably why – it was *too* romantic, too idealistic in that perfect setting. It means much more here – in this boring, practical hotel. And you've said yes – and now we're engaged. How tremendous!' I could say nothing, but sat beside him, thankful that I was sitting down as the room spun and whirled about me. He kissed me, rather experimentally at first, and then wholeheartedly and very passionately indeed. 'Oh Antonia – I hope you won't mind, but I'm very inexperienced – there's been no time to be involved with girls.' I wondered why on earth I *should* mind. Then, 'Heavens! I must get back to the sub. Walk to the car with me. I'll pick you up tomorrow after breakfast, and take you back to the sub. and we'll play some records on my old wind-up gramophone.'

The night was frosty, clear and except for the stars, very dark. We stood and kissed each other till James gently said, 'I must go now, darling, or I will want to stay too much.' I felt like waking everyone up to tell them I was engaged to the most extraordinarily wonderful young man in the world, and was too happy and excited for sleep.

On board the submarine next day, we had the minute wardroom to ourselves as the other three officers were ashore. James played Tchaikovsky's *Symphonie Páthétique* on his gramophone, and we listened in blissful, idyllic contentment, despite having to wind it up between each of the five or so records.

When we rang them with the news, our respective parents were both delighted and surprised. It was decided that I should go and stay with the Rentons at Easter, during my leave, and James added, 'You must meet Celia again, my sister. She's married now, you remember her don't you?' Unbidden, unexpectedly, I experienced the slightest pang of jealousy. As children, Celia and James had been inseparable; but I concealed the unworthy thought, replying, 'Yes, of course, I'm longing to meet her again. When we were children at Catterick I can remember her daring you to kiss me!' James laughed: 'And did I?'

We promised to write to each other every day – and the poignant misery of our parting was very bitter, coming so soon after two such memorably happy days.

Back at Dunfermline, I had no time to pine or be too depressed; a posting had come through for me, as a 'writer' at Queen Anne's Mansions in London. Not a very exciting job,

merely looking after and up-dating Wrens' Service Records. London was nearer to Portsmouth, Plymouth and Chatham though,which were all probable bases at one time or another for James's submarine. I wrote to him immediately with this exciting news, wondering when we might meet up again . . . .

By now it was late and I ought to go to bed or else I would be unable to drag myself through another nightmarish day. I lay down in the lonely bunk, hugging those precious memories, willing myself to sleep but I could not, for now all the complications prior to the wedding forced themselves into my memory flashing past so fast, so fast, half dreams. Back again to 1946.

In principle, Naval officers were not encouraged to marry before they were twenty-five, receiving no marriage allowance. However, during the war this had been relaxed, as in all the Services, and even very junior officers married when they managed to snatch some leave. If we did not marry in June of 1946 we would have to wait three endless years. We both longed for a home after the upheaval of the disturbed and distressing war years.

I settled into new Wren quarters in 'The Boltons', travelling by underground in the dark of the blackout, to Queen Anne's Mansions for my work as a writer. I lived for James's letters, until at last, in March I learnt that his submarine was coming to Portsmouth, when he could get a long weekend and meet up with me in Camberley, where my parents were staying in a small guest house. Having got a lift from the station, I noticed a little old Austin 7 parked in the drive, but paid no attention to it, thinking that as it was still so early James could not have got here yet. He was waiting for me and we kissed and held each other close. 'I've been here since before dawn, darling. I didn't want to miss a moment of the day.' The word 'darling' was new and very special to me. He tried to sound casual, 'Did you see my car outside?' Together we admired our first possession, and he asked, 'What shall we call her? Ships always have a name – our car must have one too. I know. We'll call her William-and-Mary, it'll make her feel important, having a long name like that – make up for her being so small.'

There was a lot to discuss and James related the naval ruling over marriage. My father exploded; 'But you *can't* get married so soon – it's only three months to June – and you hardly know each other. You don't know where you'll be stationed. No. It's madness. Far more sensible to wait a few

years and see what's going to happen.' I was distressed and looked appealingly at my mother, who gently said: 'I think we ought to find out what James's parents think, but I'm afraid they'll agree with your father – it does seem so sudden.' To us it did not seem sudden at all. It had all begun in the Bull at Bridport, months and months ago; but that was very private and secret, how could our parents understand.

We got into the Austin 7 feeling like millionaires. Shyly I put my hand on his knee; he held it for a moment before putting it to his lips and telling me not to distract him from his driving! 'I've been thinking, darling, somehow we must make them understand how important it is for us to be married this summer. We mustn't waste years living apart – it would be too cruel.' I agreed, adding: 'Especially after such a lonely and horrible war.' James went on: 'If we had somewhere to live half their objections would go. I've had an idea about where we might live – or rather what we might live *in*. What do you feel about living in a boat?'

I was enchanted with the idea, although I knew nothing of boats or sailing. The last and only time I had been out sailing was at the age of ten or eleven, off the coast of Brittany. Then the sea had been cerulean blue, the day hot, with just the right breeze to speed the boat along. My imagination pictured us both sailing over an ever- blue, ideally calm ocean. 'What a marvellous idea – but where will you get one, and won't it be dreadfully expensive?' James reassured me: 'We'll do some sums on the back of an envelope – but I reckon it will *save* us money – no rates, no furniture – and, think of it, I'll be the only sailor to have "a wife in every port" – my own wife!' I interrupted his enthusiastic flow, 'But James, I haven't any money at all – how can we buy one?' He thought for a moment, 'I have £1,000 saved from my pay while I was in the Italian POW camp. We're bound to get quite a big boat for that. Celia is living near Ramsgate. When we're on leave at Easter, we'll go and stay with them and look for one. I'll also look at the ads in *Yachting Monthly*, and other sailing magazines.'

I breathed a sigh of utter content, as all our problems seemed to melt away with this sublimely simple solution. One small nagging fear crept into my mind: 'James, I might be seasick – I am on big liners, and I was in the aeroplane flying back from France.' He reassured me, 'Darling, its *quite* different on small boats and there are pills you can take now – anyway most of the time we'll be in harbour. We can explore at weekends – in our own home – it'll be perfect.'

Aunt Grizelda, James's mother wrote an affectionate letter,

saying that I was exactly the sort of girl she and her husband had always wanted for him, adding that we could discuss the future at Easter.

His sister Celia wrote, too, delighted at the idea of us living in a boat, reminding us to ask her to crew, for she loved sailing and assured us she was *never* seasick. She promised to make some enquiries about boats in Ramsgate.

At last, our leave started and James collected me in the Austin 7 looking crestfallen; 'Darling – my father *is* against our getting married until I'm twenty-five. He got so angry – kept saying it was all for my own good – and yours – but I *know* it isn't. I'm determined to find a boat and to marry you even without his permission.' Poor dear James; I knew how upset he must be. Three long years of waiting hit me with a physical blow, a sickening hollow in my stomach. I tried to comfort him, 'I love you James, we'll find our boat and persuade them. I'm sure we'll be together very soon.'

The little car did not go fast and it took several hours to reach Broadstairs, tired and ravenous. Celia and her husband Martin hugged us both and, while the two men admired the valiant, overheated car, Celia put her hands on my shoulders and looked at me with the clear blue eyes which were so like her brother's, 'I am so glad he has fallen in love with you, you're just right for him; remember the fun we had at Catterick when we were children?'

During supper we talked 'boats' and Celia told us of two or three in Ramsgate harbour, 'They're a bit neglected and dirty but nothing that a coat of paint can't put right. Anyway, it's the only answer – there just aren't any houses at all – none were built during the war.'

After supper, she challenged her brother to a game of chess – another surprise for me; I was unaware that he played it. He gently refused though, for he was tired, suggesting that we finish off the crossword. Inwardly I groaned, for I was hopeless at that too!

Next morning was a blustery, cold spring day and we wrapped up warmly before going down to the harbour. James kissed my cold nose affectionately, 'You look as though you're ready to go to sea at once in that nice warm duffel coat. It would be fun to sail away to the Caribbean and hot, hot sun – and never come back wouldn't it?' Cheerfully I nodded, remembering mackerel fishing off the Brittany coast, 'Yes – we wouldn't need any money – we'd live off fish and pick fruit off any passing island!'

Down by the jetty, a few boats lay alongside, filthy and covered in coal dust. No one had had time to sail during the

war and the few abandoned yachts tied up, bobbing up and down, looked sad and neglected, their paint flaking off. I sniffed, the curious smell of a harbour, compounded of sea, oil, fish and rubbish, which was to become so familiar. We asked one or two fishermen sluicing down the decks of their trawlers, if they knew which of the yachts were for sale; they directed us to the Harbourmaster's office at the other end of the harbour. He told us that the only one definitely for sale was an old RNLI converted lifeboat, lying alongside; no one was on board, so we could look over her if we wished.

The tide was in, so she lay nearly at the same level as the jetty. Unmistakably a lifeboat with the rubbingstrake from stem to stern, there she swayed, a battle-scarred old veteran, the name *Pat* painted on the stern; looking old and scruffy to me. The pale blue paint of her hull was streaked and flaking, the white rubbing strake likewise. James was entraced and spoke warmly; 'Think, Toni, how safe she'd be, unsinkable – perfect for us, and lots of room.' We examined her carefully. She was ketch-rigged, with her mainmast for'ard, between thirty and forty feet tall; the mizzen-mast was just abaft the well-deck, with a foresail and staysail too. James could not wait, 'Let's go aboard and look at her properly, darling.' We jumped on board. Her wheel was fixed to the after bulkhead of the well-deck, where a brass compass, suspended in gimballs swung gently; badly needing polishing. A catwalk ran fore and aft on either side of the raised cabin deck, and James swung himself expertly along it. The hatch over the ladder leading down into the main cabin slid back and we went down the three steps into a tiny saloon. I gasped as the smell of bilge water, damp bunks and old ropes hit me; however, I could not say anything to upset James's enthusiasm. It ws too low to stand up fully in the saloon except under the skylight, and as this was directly above the fixed table, one could only stand up with a bent neck, expecially James, at six-foot-three! The table had flaps fixed to the bulkheads which when raised could be reached from the bunks on either side. These stretched the entire length of the cabin, about seven feet. In other words, it was *minute*.

A little old-fashioned black stove was fixed just in front of the table, and by it hung a brass oil lamp. Facing for'ard, a low opening, necessitating ducking, led into a galley, where only one person at a time could stand; there was a small washbasin on the left – the only washing place – and beside it a flap about two foot long and one foot wide which let down on a chain as a working surface. An old rusty gas cooker stood on the right, with two burners; not in gimballs, but with a little

rail round it. The anchor chain filled up the remaining space in the sharply pointed bows. It was all depressing, dirty and dark; my heart sank, but glancing at James, realized he was as happy as a sandboy.

'Let's go and look aft,' he suggested. We had to bend double in order to squeeze along under the catwalk which ran along the port side of the boat, This tiny cabin, with even less headroom than the saloon, appeared to be empty, till we saw what seemed to be a double mattress strapped to a flat wooden board, itself hooked onto fittings on the bulkhead. When we let it down, it rested on two wooden legs which swung out, and practically filled the available space. 'A double bed – how splendid!' said James. I was appalled, filled with dismay at the filth, the smell and the discomfort of it all – but knowing that if we had no home we could not possibly marry for years, I bravely agreed – that it was all splendid! An even lower opening led into a very small space in the pointed stern, and there stood a loo, with no door or privacy. James was exultant. 'Let's see if it works.' He pumped away at the lever which both flushed away, and brought in fresh sea water. It *sort* of worked. A muddle of ropes lay coiled around this black hole. 'I wonder if there's a decent engine?' James asked. We went back up to the well-deck, and lifting the hatch immediately behind the wheel, saw what appeared to be a huge engine, taking up a lot of space. 'It looks all right, but it will need an engineer to get it started and running again after all these years standing idle.' He said thoughtfully: 'It must have been added when she was converted to a yacht.'

To my horror, I discovered that I was beginning to feel distinctly unwell, and could not believe it was due to the small but undeniable movement of the boat, putting it down to the pungent smell. 'Darling, she's so dirty – we couldn't live in that mess.' It was the nearest I could bring myself to criticism; James reassured me, 'No, of course not – we'll paint her up, inside and out, and she'll be snug and dry. She must be quite a museum piece, from the days before steam, when lifeboats had sails. Did you see the shackles on that loose-footed lugsail?' I thought I must have misheard, or that James had broken into a foreign language; 'What *are* you talking about, darling?' He explained, 'Sorry, Toni, but sailors have a jargon of their own – you'll pick it up in no time – much easier than French, which I know you speak like a native.' Then, noticing that I was not exactly dancing up and down with glee at the prospect of making *Pat* our future home and life together, went on explaining, 'Do you realize how much a modern sailing boat with this amount of room

would cost? It would be way out of our reach. I think she's built of teak too — the hardest wood there is. She's a bit of history.'

I tried really hard to feel as enthusiastic as he obviously was, 'My love — I love you — and would live in a tent or a cave in order to be married to you, you know that.' Secretly, I reckoned that at least those habitats would not make me seasick. I added, 'You do know, don't you, that not only do I not know the first thing about sailing, but I have another confession. As we've had no home since I came back from France two years ago — I can't even cook — I don't know anything!'

Self pity overwhelmed me. James, so sensitive, was immediately loving and sympathetic, 'Toni — you are you and I love you. I adore you. What's more, I cannot and will not live without you. Let's find the owner and ask how much he wants for her. It's our only hope of marrying now and having a home,' I melted, not having the heart to explain how much my whole being rebelled at the idea of living on board a cramped, dirty, evil-smelling, swaying lifeboat!

Next day, we composed a suitably moderate letter to the owner; if we showed too much enthusiasm the price might well be increased. Celia had to be invited on board and James proudly showed his sister everything, already visualizing himself as the skipper of *Pat*. She was delighted — but then she was not going to have to live on board — and promised us pillows, sheets, mugs, a kettle and kitchen utensils. At a time of such acute shortage, when bed linen and blankets required coupons and china was virtually unobtainable and only white, her generosity was much appreciated.

During the long drive to Dorset we talked of little else — getting *Pat* ready for sea. The Rentons gave me a wonderful welcome, then Aunt Grizelda took me up to the beautifully furnished spare room with its leaded windows looking out over the garden, golden in the setting sun. A huge bunch of daffodils lit up the room, and I revelled in the luxury of the thick pink carpet, matching chintz curtains, the polished antique dressing table and little swing mirror — all the comfort of such a home. Ungratefully, I wished we could live in a similar cottage.

Over dinner, conversation was general and, knowing that his father was against an early marriage, James talked about the Navy and submarines in particular. Two or three days slipped by in sheer contentment, happy to be able to talk and make plans instead of the previous, few, snatched hours. Then came a phone call from the owner of *Pat*. Eventually, he

accepted James's offer of £1,000 – the total of his savings. We had a home, and James told his father straight away, 'We've bought a boat – to live in. You see, we do so want to get married this summer and as I won't be entitled to marriage allowance for two or three years – it won't matter if we have a boat – it won't cost anything living on board.' He stopped, expecting his father to explode. He spoke carefully: 'You know how I feel about this. I think you are both too young, but I'm so very pleased it's you he's chosen, Tonia, and you are both so determined I can't really behave like a Victorian parent and forbid it. I'm not so sure about the boat. Does Tonia know what she's letting herself in for? But on the whole I give you my consent and blessing.'

I hugged my future father-in-law rapturously and heard myself saying the boat was a marvellous idea, like a naval caravan; no rates to pay and that it would enable us to moor wherever James's submarine was lying, etc. Grizelda, too, was happy, starting to make wedding plans and to discuss dates. She decided on June, promising to organize it all; a great relief to my parents as they were living in a small hotel in Folkestone. I had no proper home.

We explored Folkestone harbour, finding it very exposed to the south-east, with a few boats alongside the jetty, surging back and forth on long mooring ropes. Next to visit was Dover, still badly damaged, with sunken wrecks in the mouth of the entrances, and vast. By now I had accepted a future life afloat, reflecting how adaptable and chameleon-like women had to be. The end of the Easter leave did not seem as shattering as other partings, for in a few months we would be together, 'setting up house' in *Pat*.

Back in London I applied to be demobbed from the WRNS. The girls at Queen Anne's Mansions sighed in romantic appreciation at the rightness of a Wren marrying a young Naval officer. Submariners had an extra special appeal of their own. Presents, consisting mainly of decanters, started to arrive – after all there was little choice, and I viewed the saucepans with apprehension, never having used one! With some of my clothing coupons I bought a pretty wedding dress.

James had been hoping to organize his summer leave so that we could spend our honeymoon settling into the boat, cleaning her up a bit, and painting the tiny kitchen – or 'galley' as I kept telling myself I must call it. With any luck, perhaps a week's sailing might be squeezed in as well. Unhappily, naval matters took precedence and all that could be arranged was a long weekend for the wedding, postponing the honeymoon and fortnight's leave till

August. With this we had to be content.

We only saw each other for one weekend prior to June, when we travelled to Dorset to meet the Vicar of Symondsbury – old, frail and full of love and kindness. James's parents booked us into a little guest house in Charmouth for our two-day actual honeymoon, and all plans fell into place as if by magic, allowing me to inhabit my daydream, which always stopped short of the boat.

Some friends of my parents, the Martins, living near Symondsbury, had invited us all to stay with them for the night before the wedding and it was late afternoon before we arrived. The scent of roses was intoxicating and my heart beat fast thinking that by this time the next day I would be Antonia Renton. I could not sleep. The night seemed magical and full of promise. The Elizabethan house was surrounded by a walled garden, from which the hot June sun had drawn out all the scents from flowers and fruit alike, sending them drifting up to the window where I sat, perched on the window seat, hugging my knees. It was natural and simple that I should be overawed. I adored James with every part of me, but we had never made love; no one had ever made love to me. In those dim, distant days, it was quite natural for a twenty-year old to be a virgin. I knew and felt him to be one too. A war at sea left little time for seductions. Unconsciously I was saying farewell to my old self and ardently praying and hoping that I would be a good sailing wife. 'Please God, don't let me be seasick!' I added fervently before finally falling asleep.

There was too much to recall in the evenings alone; during the day too, I must remember, remember; while my body automatically does the sea-wifely chores for the last few times, while the undemanding little boys play and talk to me so innocently unaware.

That wedding morning was a temperamental June day – wild clouds scudding across the brilliant blue sky and hot sun, a cool wind scattering rose petals which were gathered up for confetti. As in a dream, I put on the dress and veil, remembering something old and something new, something borrowed and something blue – blood red roses for a bouquet.

The little church in Symondsbury seemed full of glowing flowers and colour, as we slowly walked up the short aisle, my father and I. Supremely happy, I joined James and, as in a daze, I heard the dear old vicar announce one of the hymns

we had chosen as: 'Through the night of doubt and sorrow', by mistake, luckily giving the right number, so that apart from a slight guffaw from the two submariners in the congregation, his slip of the tongue went nearly unnoticed. Much, much later I always wondered whether he had second sight or some strange intuition, rather than the absent-mindedness presumed at the time.

All the faces at the reception were strange to me but what did it matter, for I was now Mrs Renton, proudly listening to James's short responding speech, mentioning the boat, which would enable him to have a wife in every port – 'his own!' My smile masked my misgivings; this day was mine, of divine and supreme joy, no doubts must mar it.

Finally, last hugs and kisses with our parents were exchanged, then we drove off gaily in 'William-and-Mary' bedecked with rattling tins and boots. Suddenly, I felt desperately shy until James said, 'It's funny, but I feel terribly shy, Mrs Renton – let's pull in to the next lane – just to remove all this paraphenalia of course.' How wonderfully understanding he was. The next minute his arms were round me and the long gentle kiss dispelled the unnatural emotions and tensions of the day. Then, his voice very low, he smiled and said: 'Now we'll try and remove the too obvious traces of our newly-wed state from the car!'

It was too early for dinner when we arrived at the guest house, charmingly misnamed, 'Monk's Rest'! so we went for a long walk, clambering along the rocky beach, while he told me of the submarine's movements, 'We have to go over to Londonderry next week and it *was* going to be for two months, but I think we will be back before the end of July, so we won't be separated for too long before our proper honeymoon begins, in *Pat*. Tomorrow you must drive the Austin 7 because I shall leave her with you to look after, at 'Jackmoor'. My parents want you to stay with them, in my old batchelor's room while I'm away – you can help in the garden and keep out of mischief!' I came to with a jolt realizing I had not even thought beyond these two lost and miraculously wonderful days, thankful that I had learnt to drive in the WRNS. It was a perfect evening, the clouds had disappeared, the sea was calm and in the distance Portland Bill stretched its long finger into the sea, through a sun-gold haze. That night James was so very gentle; we learnt to make love together, in sheer joy, with a sense of worship and wonder.

Next afternoon, the sun was deliciously hot sending us to sleep as we lay on the beach. I woke first, wondering for a

split second where I was, hardly able to believe in the luck of my proverbial wedded bliss. I sat, hugging my knees, feeling old and responsible; thoughts and impressions flickering through my mind like irresponsible butterflies, as I gazed out at the enigmatic sea. I felt his hand on my arm: 'Darling.' He grinned wickedly, 'Though I'd love to go straight back to bed, I think perhaps we should go for a rousing swim in what will undoubtedly be a freezing sea – come on!' Hand in hand, we raced over the sand and pebbles, splashing into the gently lapping sea – too cold to stay in for long, but loving swimming, we splashed, fought and kissed in the sea.

Over a bottle of wine at dinner, like an old married couple, we made plans, and he promised to write every day or telephone when possible. He entreated me to go and stay with Celia, 'She'll help you to clean up the boat and sort out what we need, so that we needn't waste time when I get back, but put to sea straight away.' Quietly, he added: 'You won't even have time to miss me!' I protested, 'How can you think such a thing. I shall be alone again every night, just when I've. . .' and I stopped, confused and blushing, not knowing how to phrase my meaning or my passion. 'I love you.' I whispered. He answered tenderly, 'I want you. Let's not have coffee. Come to bed now.'

CHAPTER TWO

A Rude Awakening

Never again would I know undiluted happiness. Were those years wasted? I had no appetite and curled up on the settee to live through the start of the sailing turbulence.

When I awoke just before the early June dawn, on the last day of our two-day wedding weekend, I cried quietly, thinking of him going away, for six long weeks, vowing that I would behave sensibly at the station. James woke too and made love to me again, kissing away the tears, whispering such ardent loving words I forgot my grief. The awe of actually driving 'William-and-Mary' all on my own helped me to control my feelings. I decided to go to Ramsgate after a few days, thinking I might even paint the galley in *Pat* as a wonderful surprise for James.

I felt quite proud of myself, bumbling along from Folkestone to my sister-in-law in Broadstairs, without getting lost and she greeted me warmly, 'How lovely to see you, and how beastly of my brother to make you drive all this way on your own. It'll be different when you're in *Pat*; then you'll go everywhere together – by sea – I do envy you both.' I wished I could agree.

Early next morning, Celia and I walked down to the harbour in Ramsgate. During the intervening months I had wilfully refused to remember the boat's dilapidated state, and indeed, in my mind's eye, had repainted her, making her quite habitable. It was therefore a dreadful shock to see *Pat* again, just as she had been, with filthy, peeling paint and decks black with coal dust. This time though, there was a big difference – *Pat* belonged to me! I felt a pang of remorse at my initial disappointment on seeing her again. (James had told me that boats and ships were all feminine!) Gingerly, we climbed down the wooden ladder set into the harbour wall,

and clambered across the two trawlers to where *Pat* lay. Her rubbing strake appeared more battered than ever, and I noticed there was only one old rope fender between *Pat* and the outside trawler. We found another lying among the untidy piles of rope littering the decks, and carefully inched it over the side, using the boathook to fend her off and make room for it.

Where to begin – and what to do first! There was no water on board, and no gas either. Celia said there must be some way of filling up the water tank with a hose; and a ship's chandler nearby, where we could buy Calor gas. She could see the despair in my face and felt sorry for me, 'There's not a lot we can do today, and you must be tired, so I suggest we make a list of essentials, and tomorrow we'll go shopping before coming on board again. We must be able to make ourselves a cup of coffee before we start cleaning up.' I was truly grateful to her for appreciating my inexperience, and thankful for her four years' seniority.

We went below. The tiny cabin was stiflingly hot in the June sun, with an overpowering smell of oil and bilge water; I pushed back the hatch and opened the skylight above the table. The paint below showed up in the strong light as grimy and peeling, of indeterminate colour. My ignorance about maintenance and upkeep meant I was unaware of the scraping needed before repainting. I felt near to panic, but pulling myself together, took a pencil and paper out of my bag and began a seemingly endless list. 'Soap, scrubbing brush, Vim, floor cloth, Brasso (for the dear little oil lamp and beautiful binnacle in the well-deck were black with age and disuse), paint, paint brushes, candles, matches, gas....' Celia called to me to come up on deck, which was a relief as once again the smell and movement of the boat was making me feel unwell. 'Let's tidy some of these ropes – make them into neat coils.' she suggested. Willingly, I agreed, 'Yes, it will make *Pat* feel someone cares for her again, no one can have been near her since before the War.' I went on, 'If only we had a bucket we could sluice down the decks.' And added bucket to my list. My WRNS training had taught me to scrub floors (or decks) splendidly! There was a bewildering amount of rigging, stays and shrouds; the main mast towered above us, and even the mizzen mast appeared quite tall.

Up for'ard a small square hatch caught my eye, which lifted easily, and proved to be the only ventilation, or light, for the galley. Close by lay the old-fashioned fisherman's anchor, with its cable stowed in the bows, sharing the galley! Slowly, I took it all in. Then I looked across the harbour,

towards the boats, then back towards the town. How totally different everything appeared, seen from one's own boat. The sun shone, and the sea, though not quite cerulean blue, glinted in a friendly manner. Some other yachts caught my eye, making me envious, for they gleamed with white paint and shining metal; their owners were obviously wealthy. Poor old *Pat*, I thought, 'One day, you will look nearly as smart as they are.'

We sat on either side of the well-deck. One could peer at the compass and hold the wheel, and imagine one was at sea – on a flat calm day! Celia remarked, 'In a way, it's a shame she hasn't got a tiller, rather than a wheel.' To me, it did not make much difference. She went on, 'Tomorrow, I'll come to the ship's chandler with you, and help carry all the stuff on board, but I won't be able to stay and help, as there will be no one to look after Maria.' On our way to the car I asked one of the fishermen how to get water. He pointed at the stand pipes, with various lengths of hose only needing to be hauled over to the boat.

Next day was a typical English summer's day – squally, with a brisk wind chasing the clouds, showers and sun alternating. Celia produced a couple of pillows for the double swing bunk, which meant we could make it up, with the two blankets and sheets still in the car. We drove to the chandler's, down by the harbour. It seemed like an Aladdin's cave to me, intrigued by the combined smell of new ropes, wax, tar, varnish and paint. There was a jumble of shackles, compasses, navigation lights, rigging wire, cleats, and bundles of heavy canvas. I felt rather shy and inadequate, hardly daring to ask for the humble items on my list.

A cheerful, plump old man came up to me and asked if he could help. I jumped at his offer, 'Oh! Yes, please. We've just bought a boat here, and my husband is away at sea at the moment, so I'm trying to clean it – her – up a bit before he comes back.' I stopped, aware of talking too much. 'Which boat have you bought?' he asked. '*Pat* the old RNLI lifeboat. . . .' I stopped as he interrupted, 'Oh! You've got a good, solid, unsinkable boat there Miss – I mean Madam. She may be old and dirty – but she's safe as houses.' This knowledge made me feel quite proud to be her owner – or part-owner. He continued, 'Let's go through the list together.' Soon a sizeable pile was building up on the wide counter. 'Paraffin,' he added, 'For your navigation lights.' I had indeed forgotten all about them, but now remembered two narrow L-shaped boards attached to the shrouds by the mast. 'Turps,' he added helpfully, 'to clean your hands and

brushes when you've finished painting.' Apart from soda and sandstone soap there was no easy way to dissolve grease and dirt from the paintwork. I mused aloud, 'I must have hot water; can you deliver a cylinder of Calor gas? I don't even know where it goes.' My mind whirled, 'I really need it today, to start cleaning her out – and, oh dear! I haven't got a kettle to heat the water in.' He encouraged me with a big understanding smile, 'There, there. You can't clean and paint all the time – you'll need a kettle for making tea too!' Suddenly I panicked, I'm not going to have enough money to pay for all this.' I remembered the new cheque book; James had organized a joint account, but so far I had not actually paid for any purchases with it: 'Will you take a cheque?' I asked hesitantly. He reassured me instantly, 'Of course. What about stores? We can fix you up with anything – and indeed if you're sailing a few miles offshore there are special rations, meat too.' I was amazed. The meat ration was so small it only amounted to the equivalent of a chop a week – and sailing was a hungry-making activity. I thanked him warmly, 'Well yes. But we're not sailing yet. My husband will come and see you when he joins me. He's a submariner.' I added shyly. It was so soon after the war that people were still grateful and full of admiration for the Services, and especially that particular branch of the Navy. 'Is he now? Just you come here for anything you need. I know there are shortages, but we can lay our hands on most things.'

Celia helped me to carry the booty out to the car. Down at the harbour we had a shock, for *Pat* was not lying where she had been the previous day. Obviously the trawlers had put to sea, and she had been moved. We soon spotted her, lying alongside, which was a relief with all the gear we had to ferry aboard. Thank goodness the tide was in and we only had a short distance to jump down on deck. Celia said, 'I must go home to Maria soon, but I'll help to fill the water tank first.' This turned out to be easier than we had anticipated, because of being alongside the jetty and not too far from the stand-pipe.

The one tap, in the little hand basin in the galley, sputtered, coughed and gurgled, finally disgorging a rush of rusty, filthy water. The inside of the tank must have lain empty and flaking for years, but it cleared after a while. A first achievement. However, we could not make tea, for we had forgotten the tea and the teapot – how inefficient! I realized I did not even possess a teapot! Celia left, saying she would catch a bus from the entrance to the harbour, and expect me back in time for supper.

I explored a bit, trying to find some cupboard space; there was storage space under the settee-bunks in the little cabin, and a locker in the galley – but this was full of sails! Then I discovered a minute hanging cupboard just for'ard of the hinged table and stove in the cabin. As I would be using most of the stuff I had bought straight away, I stowed some of it on shelves in the galley, wondering where any food might be placed. For the thousandth time I wished that James were there. I wished – Oh! how I wished it was a tiny cottage and immediately felt disloyal.

Tentatively, I filled the basin with water, stirred some caustic soda in, wrung out my cloth, which I rubbed with soap for good measure, and bending backwards, wiped a bit of the deck-head (ceiling) in the galley. It was impossible to stand up, except under the little square hatch, making it difficult to rub hard. My only reward was a stubborn, oily, streaky patch, causing the whole surface to look dirtier than ever. I hoped that hot water would improve the dreary chore. Soon, another list was under way, headed by brush and pan, for the tiny strip of carpet between table and bunks was quite respectable. A voice shouted, 'Anyone aboard?' I leapt up on deck to see a young man wheeling the gas cylinder I had orderd the day before, which he connected for me, ensuring that it worked.

At least I could now heat some water in one of the three· saucepans already stacked in the galley, and get on with the cleaning. By the end of the afternoon, I was ravenous, filthy, and very thirsty, as I had not dared to drink the rather rusty water until the tank had flushed through a few times, and with only a little patch of moderately clean paintwork to my credit. My hands stung from the caustic soda.

It was too early to go to Celia's, so I lay down on one of the bunks for a short rest. The cabin seemed bigger from this angle; lying with my head against the well-deck bulkhead, and my feet facing for'ard. Through the dirty skylight, silhouetted against the blue sky and scudding clouds, the mast stretched tall, appearing to sway. It was only an illusion, caused by the clouds, but coupled with the slight sensation of movement, I felt I was at sea and fell into a deep sleep, tired out by my exertions, gently rocked by *Pat*.

Over the next few days I did my best; like a squirrel hoarding nuts for the winter, I accumulated more vital possessions. Slowly, the deckhead (ceiling) in the saloon became lighter, despite the difficulty caused by a surface broken up every nine inches or so by strong beams athwartships. Beneath the small scuttles, some recesses stretched

above the bunks, where books might be stowed, then I noticed how dirty the bunk covers were so I removed them to be washed at Celia's; seemingly it had taken ages to achieve comparatively little.

Another fact became alarmingly apparent. I was very afraid I must already be pregnant! After all we had taken no precautions – totally ignorant of what they might be anyway! On the other hand my period might be late only because of all the excitement and upheaval. Perhaps the queasiness and undeniable feeling of seasickness could well be caused by just that. I put down my paintbrush, overcome by a mixture of awe, excitement, intense pride, and, yes, fear. What would James say? Poor James.

Hurriedly, in the last day or so before his return, I bought some tins; stewing beef, baked beans, peas, soups, whatever was available. It was too hot to buy anything perishable, like vegetables or cheese, as there was nowhere to keep it cool on board. It dawned on me that I had never peeled a potato! I just prayed it would all come instinctively – cooking, sailing . . . having babies!

During the long weeks of separation, James read up sailing manuals, memorized charts and brushed up his seamanship generally; he was already a brilliant seaman and navigator. He longed to sail *Pat* round to Weymouth from Ramsgate, for this would be an ideal mooring place as his submarine would be in Portland harbour, a short drive away.

On the day he was due to return I could not eat for excitement. Would he be pleased with everything I had done on board? Could I have done more? Finally, I set off to meet him in a state of apprehensive turmoil. I decided not to upset him by announcing my possible pregnancy straight away, nor did I want to complain about the seemingly impossible task of making *Pat* habitable; he would be tired and need to relax. On the platform I rehearsed careful, controlled greetings, such as Celia might give. Then his train drew in and he was leaning out of the window searching for me as his hand felt for the handle. I flew along to meet him; we embraced and clung to each other, his free hand stroking my hair. In the other he held a length of string attached to a truly Heinz-like mongrel. I gaped, 'Darling – where – how – did you get him/her?' His words tumbled out, 'She's a "she" – a total stray – wandering around the dockyard in Derry; she had puppies – they had to be drowned – I felt so sorry for her. . . I – I thought she could be our first crew!' I swallowed, trying to adjust, 'What's her name?' 'Paddy. She's *so* affectionate, you'll love her.'

The dog was like a mixture between a schnauzer and a collie, with a rough long-haired coat of indeterminate grey. The floppy ears pricked up at her name and trusting brown eyes peered anxiously up at him through the straggly fringe; then a long fluffy tail uncurled itself from between her legs and gave a tentative wag. Having always wanted a dog, I was completely seduced. 'How will she manage on board – how will we feed her?' I asked automatically, knowing we would manage somehow. I abandoned myself to utter relief at seeing him again, flooded with intense happiness and before I knew what I was saying the words tumbled out unbidden, 'Oh! James – I think I'm going to have a baby – and though I've tried so hard in the boat she's still filthy and there's so much to do and get and I. . . .' He kissed me and stopped the passionate flow. Torn by conflicting emotions, he had the strength of character, confidence and calmness to deal with any situation. 'Are you sure about the baby? If yes – well, I think it's awfully clever of us to have managed one so quickly. Actually, I'm thrilled – it'll take a while to adjust to the role of father – but we'll keep it a secret between ourselves for a bit.' I interrupted, 'You mean not even tell Celia?' 'No, not just yet, she might try and stop us going to sea – you still want to go don't you? Do you feel all right?' He asked anxiously. I had not got the heart to tell him how sick I felt. 'Of course I do, darling.' I lied. James went on, 'About *Pat* – you've been doing too much – I've got three weeks leave, that should be ample. We'll get her ready for sea in a week and given fair winds it shouldn't take longer than two weeks to sail to Weymouth.'

Fair winds – fair winds. Two magic words that were constantly repeated yet never materialized.

Celia accepted Paddy without a murmur, muttering vaguely about tripe and whalemeat, both unrationed and unheard of by me!

At the ship's chandler the next morning, James asked for the name of a good mechanic to overhaul the old engine and I remembered to buy two mugs, some coffee and a bottle of milk, so that for the very first time I could make James a cup of coffee. We surveyed the boat with pride, tinged with hidden misgivings. She needed a coat of paint as well as canvas and glue repairs to the torn rubbing strake. I need not have worried about Paddy; she was as nimble as a cat, jumping on and off the boats and sniffing round her new home contentedly, finally curling up on the settee and

pretending to go to sleep, whilst keeping an eye on us, lazily waving her plume of a tail when we talked to her.

I helped James to hoist the mainsail; it had a long and heavy gaff which had to be lifted onto a hook on the wooden ring round the mast. Protesting creaks and groans came from the ancient rigging. It looked huge to me; dirty grey but of stout canvas, it hung lazily flapping, decorated by rows of reefing points. James explained their use – for reducing the sail area in a gale. I protested, 'But I don't want to sail in a gale!' Jokingly, he replied: 'No one does – but occasionally they happen when one is already at sea.'

The mainsail was loose-footed, with an enormous shackle fastened to the clew. In theory this was, in turn, shackled onto a heavy ring bolt fastened to the reinforced deck at a certain point abaft the well-deck – one to port, the other to starboard. By this time a curious crowd had gathered on the jetty, idly watching; for there is a strange fascination about boats! A few unhelpful and derogatory remarks drifted down to us as we heaved and struggled with the sail; 'You won't get far – you're still tied up!' and, 'I wouldn't give you "nuffink" to go out in that – looks like it set sail with the Ark!' Paddy appeared on deck barking in obvious disapproval at the onlookers, and James remarked what a good guard dog she would be when I was on my own in harbour. The crowd soon got bored and left.

As I admitted my total ignorance, James taught me the little rhyme for port and starboard, 'When both side lights you see ahead – port your helm and show your red. Green to green or red to red, perfect safety – go ahead. Starboard is green,' he finished lamely.

Meanwhile, I had spilt the smelly paraffin on my hands whilst filling the navigation lights, 'Damn!' I said, surprised. James laughed, 'Don't worry – that's nothing – wait till we get to sea, I'm a different person. All skippers shout and swear dreadfully. We'll need to buy a dinghy. We shouldn't need one this trip, but sometimes one has to tie up to a buoy and row ashore.' I looked at him quizzically and remarked, quite caustically for me, 'It's a pity I wasn't boat crew in the WRNS instead of "signals" – I might have learnt to row.' Doubts gnawed at me, for a complete landlubber can be an awful handicap.

For a while we worked in silence, painting, until eventually the paint fumes seemed to suffocate me and I lay down, curling up by Paddy who gently licked my face as though in sympathy. James did not notice for he was busy with the mechanic discussing coils and batteries. After an

hour or so of drying out, priming and coaxing, they tried to turn the starter handle. This was long before the days of push-button, electric starters. It was hard work, with a lot of compression and a nasty kick to the handle.

I asked James about my paint problem, 'Why won't the paint in the galley go on properly? It's all streaky and looks worse than when I started.' He squeezed into the tiny space with me, not knowing how to put it. 'Well, it needed sandpapering and then a coat of undercoat before the gloss – that's what's happened, it's sort of slippery.' This was the last straw. Tears pricked at the back of my eyes. I felt a complete fool.

He put an arm round my shoulders, 'Don't cry. How could you possibly know? And you've done wonders. Far more than any girl like you, unused to 'messing about in boats'. Lie down for a bit while we fix the engine. Let's have supper on board – try out some of the tins.'

When I got back from the chandler's, the men had coaxed a few splutterings out of the engine and were nursing sore thumbs where the starter handle had caught them as it kicked back. I decided on soup then potatoes in a cheese sauce, with fruit for pudding. Resolving to get a basin for future pre-paring of vegetables, I peeled the potatoes in the hand basin in the galley, wondering what to do with the rubbish. Meanwhile, Paddy wolfed the tripe and dog biscuit, rushing up on deck to bark excitedly, when, with a throbbing roar, the engine started. They were so pleased with their efforts they decided to get some beer to celebrate and Paddy went with them for hygienic reasons and I wondered what on earth she would do when we were at sea.

Later, the evening had cleared; the scene was romantic and peaceful in the brilliant colours of the sunset and I sat in the well-deck to wait for James. We sat, hand in hand, our tense minds slowly calming. 'Why is it a well-deck and not a cockpit?' I asked. 'For the simple reason that it's a lifeboat with a self-draining well; look.' He lifted up some slatted boards fitted over a deep narrow 'well'. 'That's the sea down there. If a big wave comes over the side, it just drains away again. She's no common yacht or dinghy with a "cockpit". Let's call it the well, quicker than saying well-deck each time.'

While I was busy creating chaos in the galley, James filled and lit the gimballed paraffin lamp above the table, pulling the doll-like curtains across the scuttles, closing the hatch and transforming the cabin into a home. 'Perhaps tomorrow we could sleep on board,' suggested James. My heart sank;

there was no bath, only that little basin for all washing. 'Let's leave that for a day or two – we'll get so dirty painting and cleaning, we'll have to have baths,' I reasoned. The finality of never being able to have one had not yet fully hit me. To James it was a luxury, not having one in submarines.

We worked non-stop. August is a notoriously fickle month, proving the point again, with endless low pressure areas moving across the Atlantic and southwesterly winds of varying strength bringing rain. Little waves in the harbour lapped and gurgled around *Pat* and she danced joyously to their rhythm, coming alive, straining at her moorings. I felt sick. Paddy was our shadow, never straying from the boat except for urgent reasons. The after-cabin, which was to be our bedroom was bare, but too tiny to contain anything except the swinging double bunk and a tin trunk for our clothes. Among my many purchases I bought a bowl big enough for me to sit in, for use as a bath, small; but with knees drawn up I could sit in it and wrily I imagined it the correct size for bathing a baby. I had not been to the doctor; for one thing I did not know one in Ramsgate, for another I was now so certain there was no need to confirm it and I was perfectly fit anyway.

James was impatient to be off, but the weather held us prisoners with day after day of southwesterlies, until at last we had to leave, after a farewell supper for Celia and Martin, who brought a bottle of wine to drink to our trip and, kindest of all, a bowl of mixed leftovers for Paddy.

For that evening we forgot the frustrations and anxieties of preparation – worries about the trip itself – and enjoyed to the full the feeling of adventure and the unknown. After dark, the wind died down, enabling the four of us to sit on deck. James and Martin lit their pipes in the hushed stillness, the smoke curling straight up. The lamp in the cabin shone through the hatch and skylight, making an island of warmth in the dark night. *Pat* lay still, as though gathering her strength for what was to come, and my forebodings and dread receded as I sat, snuggled up to James, watching the lights of the town round the harbour. James looked at the leading lights into the harbour, and the distant flickering glow from the lighthouse, wondering if he would be able to negotiate the tricky channel leading out to sea. He mistrusted engines – noisy smelly things, only ever condescending to use it if there was no wind, or up a long winding creek or river.

Earlier that evening, a young man had turned up while I was preparing supper. He told James he had very little experience of sailing, but was at a loose end, and willing to

spare a couple of days to see us on our way. James was delighted, promising him the return train fare from the first port of call.

The mattress of the double bunk seemed damp, despite the summer warmth, and though James slept soundly, I lay awake, listening to the unfamiliar sound of the shrouds tapping against the mast, the slap of the wavelets on the hull, and towards dawn, just when I had finally dozed off, the screeching of seagulls, made restless by the rising wind. Once again, it was too rough to put to sea, and I was grateful for the respite. I had not yet bought the meat we were entitled to. As there were only two burners on the stove and no oven, a joint would be pointless; not only that, but I would not have known how to set about cooking it. I informed the chandler's meat store of our impending departure, which was, in fact, already known, and bought some chops, bacon, and – wonder of wonders – steak!

The young volunteer deckhand came on board that day, helping James to clip the foresail onto the forestay, sorting out the sheets, and freeing the anchor cable. James instructed me, 'Don't put any stores on top of the cable will you darling? We might have to anchor in a hurry.' Studiously he worked out which state of the tide would give us the maximum south-flowing tidal stream, to get us well past the Goodwin Sands, hopefully even round the South Foreland. The names meant nothing to me. Alan was not much help either, but cheerfully rolled himself up in a blanket and went to sleep on one of the settees.

James smoked a last pipe on deck, anxiously peering at the sky and the sea, hoping for a propitious sign. If we did not start soon, his leave would be up, which would be tragic, leaving me alone on board *Pat* in Ramsgate, while he and the submarine lay at Portland. The weather showed no signs of abating or improving, but at least it was not blowing a gale, and he reckoned that the best time to sail, taking full advantage of the tide would be about mid-morning. I waited anxiously for him; shivering in the swing bunk which was, in fact, quite comfortable, and excellent for backs, the mattress being laid directly onto hard boards. I prayed fervently that I would be worthy of my sailor husband, and not disgrace him by being too sick.

Neither of us slept much that night – James through excitement, and me from dread.

Alan slept like a child, having no responsibilities, and rather resented being woken up at dawn, being asked to rig up the hose to the fresh water point in order to leave with a

full tank. Water would have to be strictly rationed at sea: only being used for cooking and drinking: all cleaning of vegetables, and washing up could be done, apparently in sea water. I had bought a special liquid supposed to dissolve grease and produce suds. (It didn't!)

While the two men made final preparations, I gave the dog her last run ashore. I cooked their breakfast; the smell of frying bacon and coffee wafted up to them, and we all ate hungrily. Laughingly, and more truthfully than I could possibly foretell, I said, 'This may well be the last proper meal for days!' The wind was fitful, veering between South-West and South-South-West; no matter how hard we tried to ignore the barometer, which was on 'change', the needle kept on dropping – slowly. The sun shone cheerfully between the clouds however, and the gulls swooped merrily to pick up the contents of the gash bucket as I emptied it and cleaned it out, on the end of its stout bit of string. We were warmly dressed, as the day felt more like spring or autumn than early August. For the umpteenth time, I asked, 'We *will* be putting in somewhere tonight won't we, James?' Patiently he answered me, the same answer, 'Yes, if we reach Dover before dark, but there are wrecks in the entrances which haven't yet been cleared and, though our draught is shallow, I wouldn't like to risk sailing in at any time other than high water.'

I looked across Ramsgate harbour at the myriad boats and marker buoys, asking myself how could he avoid them as he sailed out? All was tidied up and secured below, so that nothing would fall off tables or shelves; the bunk was made and lashed to the bulk-head. I began to experience some of the excitement that James must be feeling.

On the jetty, Celia, Martin and little Maria had come to wave us 'Godspeed'. James wanted to sail out of the harbour – then changed his mind as the wind was so flukey, and started the engine instead. He called to his sister, 'Can you cast off for'ard when we're ready? And Alan, will you let go aft.' To me, he added, 'You get the fenders inboard, and stow the mooring ropes neatly, and you, Alan, stand by with the boathook to fend us off if we get too near anything.'

We were ready! The 'honeymoon' had begun. Utter confusion and chaos suddenly erupted as James shouted, 'Let go for'ard – let go aft!' putting the engine into gear, and *Pat* slowly staggered, like some drunken old woman, nosing her way round, finally pointing towards the entrance of the harbour. Clumsily, I clambered around, waved bravely to Celia, clung to the rigging and thought with embarassed horror that we were going to crash into a boat moored in the

middle of the harbour. *Pat* only had one screw and at that slow speed, with very little way on, was difficult to steer. By dint of careful handling and a few shoves with the boathook we avoided any serious mishaps.

Suddenly, all too quickly, we were at the end of the jetty, where I saw to my dismay, an angry choppy little sea awaiting us. 'Oh! James, it's so rough!' I cried. James spoke sharply, 'It's only because the tide's running against the wind. As soon as we're clear of the breakwater we'll hoist the sails and ride more easily.'

Pat plunged on, tossing and rolling. 'Come and take the wheel Toni while Alan and I get the mainsail up.' I obeyed, already feeling cold, frightened and queasy. How I envied the ease with which Paddy trotted up and down the catwalks, sure-footed and upright. She was excited and pleased, wagging her tail, coming to us for reassurance and attention, and my fear that she might accidentally slip and fall overboard diminished.

The men balanced on the heaving cabin top to lift the gaff into place. 'Take the clew – fasten it to the port shackle and bolt!' yelled James at Alan, as the wind tore his words away.This was no easy task, as the sail was flapping like a wild bird; James hoisting it as fast as he could. He tore back to the well, snatching the loose end of the sail out of Alan's inept hands, shouting at me to, 'Keep her steady as she goes!'

He soon had the shackle bolted and, taking the wheel, eased her round so that the sail filled majestically, thankfully. 'Now Toni, look at the compass and keep her on that bearing, while Alan and I get the mizzen and foresail up.' This was much easier; Alan brought the sheet (rope) back to the well and fastening it to a cleat on the side. The sudden panic of movement over, dear Paddy decided she could do no more to help and curled back up on the settee.

Due to the boat's rounded hull, we rolled atrociously; slowly the land receded. James wanted lots of sea room whilst I wanted to hug the coast. Innocently I asked, 'Why don't you turn right – I mean to starboard now? We're going the wrong way.' Having adjusted the mizzen James was back in the well, delighted and happy to be sailing again: 'Toni, darling – I've already explained – she won't sail close-hauled, we'll have to tack in long hauls. I'm starving – what about some lunch? How about you Alan?' The poor young man had been getting quieter and quieter and had now turned faintly green, like me. 'No. I don't want anything, I think I'm going to be sick.' he said and promptly was! Recalling old sayings, I wondered if I would feel all right

again once I *had* been sick. Was I seasick or pregnant-sick? Nobly, I went below with the intention of making James a cheese sandwich, but was utterly dismayed to find I could not even stand up. The boat pitched and rolled, wallowing like a drunken hippopotamus – I longed to join the dog on the settee.

Various objects had worked themselves loose, including some hurriedly stowed pots and pans from breakfast. There was an ominous swishing, slopping noise which puzzled me, as I clung to the basin in the galley, while I too was sick. The galley being in the bows, was the liveliest part of the boat with a motion resembling a hysterical corkscrew! In vain I tried to light the stove to put a kettle on, but had to hold on to avoid being thrown over. Never had I conceived such dizziness or discomfort; grabbing a packet of biscuits I struggled back to the well. 'Oh! James – I feel awful – and look! the land is still in the same place, we haven't moved!' I wailed.

The day was grey with a menacing sea to match, but James appeared impervious, calmly smoking his pipe, 'We'll need to go about soon,' he said, 'You'll soon get your sea legs, when we're on the other tack. Take the wheel and I'll open a tin. I'm so hungry. You ought to eat too you know, give you something to be sick on.' Alan was lying on the settee. James called him, but Alan answered, 'I can't do anything. I feel too ill. I want to go back!' However James was firm, shouting through the hatch at him, 'While you're on board and something needs to be done, you do it. You can be sick and lie down in between. But you will have to unshackle the sail as we go about. Tonia will take the wheel, while you change the foresail sheets, and the mizzen will look after itself as it's on a "horse" and should slide across.' Alan dutifully climbed up on deck, making me feel both angry with and sorry for James, lumbered with a sick wife and crew.

It would be the first time we would be going about and James wanted to do it in proper seamanlike fashion. He eased *Pat* round slightly to increase her snail-like progress, called out, 'Ready about!' quickly followed by 'Lee-o!' as he brought her head around. The great grey sail shook and tore at the shackle which assumed a life of its own. James roared, 'Unshackle it *now*.' Alan and I tried pathetically to hold the wilful sail and unscrew the pin from the shackle. The noise was deafening, as sheets snaked and slapped, the mizzen tore back and forth across the metal 'horse' while the boat lay in irons, and the careless wind plucked at the shrouds and halyards. 'Toni, quick, take the wheel!' James ordered, as he

tussled and fought the recalcitrant shackle. It fought back, cutting his fingers and hand, but he did not even notice, as he shouted to me what to do with the helm and brought the struggling sail across to the opposite side and shackled it up again. I was horrified to see his bleeding fingers and appalled at the thought of repeating the manoeuvre. We had no Elastoplast or bandages – how remiss of me. Tactlessly I asked, 'Will it be like that every time we go about? There's a funny sloshing noise below, what do you think it is?' James wound a dirty hanky, already used for cleaning sparking plugs, round his torn hand. 'No, of course not. We'll get much more practised at it. Alan, keep her on this course, keep the sail full. I'll go and investigate this sloshing noise.

He swung himself below, moving with such ease; not even being thrown about as I was and listened. 'That's the bilge water – the timbers above the water line are dry and this movement is working them a bit loose. I'll pump some out.' Alan yelled, 'I'm going to be sick again.' James had to dash back on deck, annoyed at the man. Why hadn't he warned James that he was liable to be as ill as this. As he himself was never sick it was hard for him to imagine what nausea the movement was inflicting on the two of us and he lacked sympathy.

Our progress was painfully slow. I took the wheel while James pumped away at the bilge pump. Despite my duffel coat, two jerseys and gumboots, I was shivering with cold, as the gusting wind blew straight through me, and the occasional spray from the bows hit an angry wave and scattered spray over us. I felt and looked awful. James looked at me pityingly, 'You go below and lie down, we'll be on this tack for some time now – and I'll stay on watch. Just bring me a tin and the opener. Oh! and a spoon. I'll eat it straight out of the tin – stew if you can find it.' The word 'stew' finished me and once again I dashed to the side. I just managed to retrieve the tin before collapsing onto the swing bunk. *Never* had I felt so ill.

We were in the two to three mile passage between the shore and the dreaded Goodwin Sands. These shifted to varying depths and were a menace to shipping, being marked by various buoys. Unaware of all this, I drifted into an uneasy fitful sleep; cold and miserable, wondering when we would reach Dover, wondering when the 'honeymoon' would begin. When I awoke, I was horrified to realize that the afternoon had vanished; I thought of James still on deck and struggling against my sickness, by wedging myself in the galley I succeeded in filling the kettle and lighting the gas

ring. I took him up a mug of steaming tea which he was longing for and, looking resigned, he explained, 'We're making very little progress what with head winds and the tide against us. I think we may have to turn back for Ramsgate at this rate. At least I know the entrance to that harbour. I wouldn't like to sail into Dover for the first time in the dark.' I sighed; 'How awful James, all that for nothing.' He contradicted me, 'Not at all. It's been an interesting practice run. We know how she handles and what to expect and I can't wait to put Alan ashore. I don't think we'll bother with another crew. You and I can manage.' He smiled warmly at me, 'Kiss me!' I was appalled by the idea and that he should think we could.

Paddy came up on deck, scanning the horizon for a sign of land, but seeing it was too far away, discreetly relieved herself at the far end of the catwalk, completely at home. She shook herself as the spray gave her a soaking, licked both of us and after finishing off what was left in the tin, jumped back up into bed. A quick dousing with the bucket cleaned it up.

We went about, therefore, defeated by the rising south-southwesterly wind, and made for Ramsgate. The mere thought of being in harbour, even Ramsgate, brought new life to me, despite the hair-raising operation of lowering the sails and starting up the sulky engine as we eventually neared the breakwater. It was humiliating to return and I knew that without such a hapless wife and crew he would have sailed on all night. Tomorrow the weather might improve, we would try again. Alan apologised for his uselessness as he helped to furl the sail and tidy the ship.

'Toni,' said James, 'We'll have supper ashore tonight – get up really early to buy things we've forgotten, and set off again with the tide.' Safely tied up alongside, I was ready for anything, feeling ravenous and determined to have one meal prepared in advance next day, which would only need heating up.

That night we lay in each other's arms, exhausted, falling asleep after one long kiss. The rain, drumming on the deck and sky-light woke us early. James groaned, 'When will this spell of bad weather change?' He vainly searched the sky for some sign of a break; but the wind remained perversely in the West, the cumulus clouds speeding along in the same direction.

Apart from milk and bread, I bought bandages, Kwells and Elastoplast, while the friendly man in the chandler's teasingly suggested we should sail on up the East Coast with the wind fixed so firmly in the West. After a good breakfast

of scrambled eggs, James prepared for sea, while I emptied the contents of a tin of stew and mixed vegetables into a saucepan, ready for a hot meal when the waves would allow, with enough too for Paddy, who had been delighted to renew her acquaintance with land again on a run ashore in familiar Ramsgate.

We repeated the previous day's undignified exit, with me dropping boathook and fenders, having taken a few Kwells; noticing the instructions warned one of drowsiness, a dry mouth and danger of exceeding the stated dose. In those days no mention was yet made of danger in pregnancy. As long as they delayed the dreaded seasickness I cared nothing for side-effects.

James decided to go to seaward of the Goodwins, taking a long reach out, in order to cut down the number of times we would have to complete the devastating exercise of going about. In those far-off days, shipping was minimal, with virtually no risk of being run down. For quite a while I staved off the nausea, taking the wheel for an hour or so, while James adjusted the rigging, making minor alterations, as well as pumping out the bilges. He also put the saucepan on to heat, which had to be held in place, despite the little rail, as *Pat* danced and bucketed her way through the choppy seas. I began to feel sleepy, due to the Kwells; the next thing I was aware of was an angrily flapping sail and the wheel spinning round in my hand! 'James!' I cried, 'Quick – I'm gybing or something.' He rushed up on deck in time to retrieve the situation, then down to the galley to collect the stew, which he brought up on deck with two spoons, wolfing it down hungrily. I managed one or two spoonfuls.

We were sailing on a beam reach, and our progress was faster than it had been the day before, but to my dismay I could no longer see land: only what appeared to be a world made up of clouds, sky and sea. A menacing sea – not angry yet, but holding back its might and fury, waiting for the right moment to unleash itself. James wanted to go about on the other tack before dark, in view of the difficulties, and sail south on a long reach down to the South Foreland headland.

We sat together in the well, each of us deep in our own thoughts. Though he was completely confident in the seaworthiness of the lifeboat, and in his own competence, he was worried about me and the seasickness which caused him real concern – something he had not anticipated to this extent. Celia, his sister had never been – nor were his brother officers in submarines. Unaware of his thoughts, I told him I was going to take another Kwell, and risk putting

a kettle on for tea. Grabbing the doorway and hatch I struggled for'ard to the galley. It seemed much worse below, as the hull crashed into the short steep seas. Gritting my teeth, feeling nausea and dizziness overcome me, I nevertheless lit the burner, holding the kettle over the flame. Even filling the kettle required a major effort. In my eagerness to get back up on deck, I grabbed both mugs, and made a dash for the companionway. A 'seventh'· wave (superstition has it that the seventh wave is always the biggest) threw me off my feet, spilling the precious hot tea, and knocking me over onto the port bunk. Some of it scalded me slightly and I screamed out in anger, fear and disappointment; bringing James down in a rush, leaving *Pat* to her own devices. He was beside himself with remorse and pity, comforting me with a big hug, 'Go up on deck darling and take the wheel. She's nearly sailing herself on this tack. I'll make some more tea and bring it up.'

Afterwards, feeling stronger, and warmed by the tea I said, 'I'll keep watch for a bit while you have a sleep, you must be so stiff and cold, and tired after all those hours up here.' He was very touched, 'Yes – you're right – we'll go about, then I'll do just that – you're marvellous.'

For some reason, possibly to do with the steepness of the seas, *Pat* refused to go about. Finally, I had to go up for'ard and back the foresail; it was terrifying, and I got soaked with the spray coming over the bows. Slowly she responded and I dashed back to the well to help James unshackle the flailing mainsail. Once again his fingers were torn, and the superhuman effort to control so much lively canvas so often tired him out. The movement of the boat was even more uncomfortable now, as we headed closer into the South-West wind, Force 6, nearing gale force, making the most dismal howling and shrieking in the rigging. I sat wrapped in an old army sleeping bag peering at the compass, gripping the wheel and praying that we would reach port – any port – before dark. It was more a nightmare than a honeymoon. Perhaps I would wake up and find it had all been the most horrible science-fiction film. Occasionally Paddy crept into the well to comfort me and lick my face before sensibly going back to a dreamless sleep on the settee opposite James.

Most of the waves now had white tops to them; whole rows and armies of white horses. I remembered how romantic it had looked from the shore, the memory contrasting devastatingly with the present fear I tried unsuccessfully to master. Dusk was slowly falling. After only one hour I had to wake poor James, 'Look at those seas.

Where are we? What are we going to do? And I must go to the loo.' He had slept soundly, as only sailors off watch know how, and felt much less tired, 'Darling, it's rougher because we're outside the shelter of the Goodwin Sands. I think we'd better take in a reef, and light the navigation lights.' Sitting up and stretching, he asked, 'Can you sail her for just a bit longer while I climb up on the cabin top and take in a reef?'

He lowered the sail a fraction in order to tie the reef points, balancing dangerously on the slippery surface; there were lots of them and it took ages, but he was pleased with the result. After I had scrambled aft to the loo in the stern, I perilously retrieved the lights which we had filled in the peace and quiet of Ramsgate harbour. James replaced them in their brackets, content to know that any passing shipping would be aware of our presence and give us a wide berth – or so he hoped.

Secretly, he was a bit worried, as the barometer was falling quite rapidly, at the same time as the wind increased. He made his decision, 'Toni. I think we'll run back to the shelter we had from the Goodwins. We're perfectly safe – plenty of searoom – and tomorrow we'll try again. If it blows any harder, we'll just lower the mainsail and amble along under the mizzen.' I was horrified, and though not actually sick, the effort of keeping upright had exhausted me, plus the strange dryness in my mouth, a pounding heart, and the drowsiness induced from the Kwells. It all seemed unreal. I thought of my parents, and how furious they would be if they knew where James and I were at this moment!

Supper could only be some soup and a tin of spam. Even this took hours, because of doing it all single-handed, holding on tight with the other. Everything was a shambles below deck, a bottle of milk having shaken itself loose from its niche, rolling drunkenly among the tea leaves and spilt milk on the deck in the galley. Wet clothes lay piled on the bunks in the cabin. The noise and smell gave me a headache. I gave up and lay down, wedging myself in, feeling useless and miserable. The tune of the beautiful hymn, 'For those in peril on the sea,' sang in my brain, alternating with Mozart's *Eine kleine Nachtmusik*! I must have dozed off, as James's voice calling down woke me abruptly, 'Sorry darling, but can you come up on deck. I'm going to lower the mainsail, and I want you to take the wheel.'

The Force 7 gale tore at my clothes roughly and rudely, as I sleepily crawled up the steps, to sit huddled on the seat by the wheel, like a sleepwalker. I implored him, 'Oh! darling, do be careful, I love you so much, and you know we haven't

even got a lifebelt on board!' 'Don't worry darling,' he shouted, as he went along the catwalk, 'I've got prehensile toes and fingers!' I could hardly see him in the darkness, nor could anything be heard but the howling wind and roaring sea, like a living hell.

The only light was the candle in the compass. As James began to lower the sail, it bellied out dangerously, threatening to drag itself into the sea, pulling *Pat* right over. 'Toni!' he yelled, 'Can you gather it in – in folds – while I lower? Hold on tight!' I would never have thought myself capable of such a feat, and at times the sail seemed to engulf me, wishing to pull me overboard too. I grabbed great armfuls, throwing myself on billowing lumps of sail to squeeze the wind out of them, acquiring an unknown strength, while wordless, unformulated prayers seethed in my tormented mind.

Pat was relieved not to be carrying so much sail and eventually we did reach the lee of the Goodwins where the seas were smaller. It seemed disheartening to have spent a day and a half sailing hard, only to find ourselves geographically further back from where we started. James experimented with the wheel, lashing it but allowing it some play. As we were only drifting he reckoned we could both get a little sleep before dawn. Possibly the wind might veer round to West-nor-West overnight, (possibly pigs might fly) though he prayed that it would not back to the South-East as that would mean we would be on a lee shore.

Huddled together for warmth, we lay on the settee in the cabin, wet and exhausted, trying to stop ourselves being thrown onto the floor. We drifted off into a jumbled nightmare – terrified and shattered by the piercing blast of a foghorn. Imagining our last moment had come and that we were about to be mown down by a cargo ship, we leapt up on deck, followed by Paddy in desperate need to use the catwalk. Dense fog surrounded us. Out of the wall of fog – frighteningly close – loomed a ship. My heart was in my mouth, as James flashed the torch on the mizzen. The ship gave no sign of having seen us and passed by, unhurried, merely yards away, leaving us weak-kneed and trembling, collapsed in the well, quickly joined by Paddy who thought the whole exercise had been for her benefit. James recovered rapidly, checked that the navigation lights were still alight and went below to put the kettle on. By now we were weak from lack of proper food. He made some coffee and used up the remains of the bread, spreading butter and marmalade thickly, to give us energy.

Meanwhile, I sat in the well, eyes straining in the dark, positive I could hear another, fainter foghorn, which he identified as a bell buoy, with a deep, doom-laden tolling note, marking a channel for shipping. As the grey, uninspiring dawn crept up, the fog lifted, but the wind was still in the same quarter – worse, it was strengthening – even Paddy had lost her appetite.

Revived by our snack, we refilled the navigation lights and hoisted the mainsail, leaving the reefs in. Thank goodness we did, for the weather deteriorated still further, squally showers soaked us. Only James had an oilskin – his naval one. Even with clothing coupons they would have been unobtainable. I crouched by James's feet on the deck of the well for comfort and protection. Visibility was very poor and occasionally we worked *Pat's* foghorn, which consisted of a simple non-mechanical device – in short, a plunger in a metal tube that one pulled up and pushed down hard. The noise was deafening – a mixture between an angry bull and a hysterical donkey!

Apart from the foghorn, the bilge pump needed regular attention; everything below was wet and smelt mouldy. We both longed for a hot bath and dry clothes. Certainly *Pat* lived up to her reputation of being an unsinkable vessel, as she never heeled over too far, the bulging rubbing strake proving incredibly buoyant. I wondered if this nightmare sail would ever end, doomed to sail the Channel till the end of time, while my imperturbable husband tried to fill his pipe with spray constantly splashing over him at the wheel.

No land was in sight, so it was impossible to tell if we were making any progress on each of the long tacks. Going about in these seas was really hazardous, for if the foresail had to be backed, I got drenched through standing on the bows, where whole seas now broke over the wildly plunging boat. At about noon, soaked and very cold, James decided a tot of rum would warm us up – an excellent idea except for making us so sleepy. I took the wheel for a short spell, but found myself nodding off, sitting bolt upright. As we were in mid-Channel, it was impossible to leave the wheel because of shipping. James opened a tin of spam, which he ate with a ship's biscuit. He offered some to Paddy, but though she tried to wag her tail, only sniffed obligingly at it, before curling up in an even tighter circle, determinedly going to sleep till all this would end.

Inwardly, James cursed the filthy August weather, but outwardly he remained calm, reliable and utterly in control. I admired him with all my heart; more than that I hero-

worshipped him, admitting that no one could handle a boat like him, adding inwardly that I definitely did not like boats. Finally, as the afternoon wore on and the gale rose once again to Force 7, we were forced to run for the lee of the Goodwins. In fact, he was getting extremely tired, almost to the point of hallucinations and knew he must get some sleep before taking drastic action of some kind, 'Toni, do you think you could sit by the wheel, if I lash it, while I curl up in a blanket on the deck beside you?' His fingers and hands were covered in filthy, wet bandages where they had been ripped by the murderous shackles.He fell asleep straight away and I envied him his supreme confidence in the boat. The wind moaned and shrieked as *Pat* lumbered her way through the white-capped seas and the underlying swell resulting from bigger seas meant that at times we appeared to be on top of a mountain with endless vistas of identical waves, then next moment deep in a threatening engulfing valley. I felt numb with cold and fear. This was all wrong – not a honeymoon – a sickening nightmare.

In the galley all was confusion and chaos. A broken mug had joined the spilt milk, which was now adding its own vile smell to the oily bilge water; the little basin was blocked with tealeaves. I wanted to cry. How far removed from the idyllic dreams.

As usual James woke refreshed, but disappointed at the fury of the gale, 'It's just not possible for it to go on day after day like this. *Look* at the barometer, I've never seen it so low in the summer.' I sniffed back my tears, but my face was so salty and wet they would not even be noticed. He went on, 'I'm afraid we'll have to lower the mainsail – it's not safe to carry so much canvas – it's an old sail and it might tear.' I pointed *Pat* into the wind, while he lowered the furiously billowing sail. Next, exerting all my remaining strength, I struggled with him to enfold and tie it up, after he had lifted the heavy gaff from its hoop around the mast.

Having lost her steadying influence, the boat pitched and tossed and we clung to what we could, to avoid being swept off the slippery cabin top. This mammoth effort tired James out, forcing him to sit in the well to get his breath back. He knew it was unlikely that he would have the energy to lift the gaff and wet sail up again for some time, but as the elements showed no sign of abating it did not matter.

I was retching with nothing inside me now, and curiously, began to worry about the effect on the baby. Another superhuman effort enabled me to put a kettle on for a mug of cocoa with lots of sugar, using condensed milk, which James

carried to the well, 'Goes well with spam, doesn't it?' he joked, feebly. I kissed him.

We were now the wind's plaything as the mizzen and foresail could only steady us without actually making any headway. Yet another unbelievable, similar day went by. Suddenly, we could see land! I was relieved but shaken by the fact that it was France! Only a short year ago I would have been thrilled at the prospect of seeing France again – but now it was all wrong. I wanted Weymouth – near Portland. James came to a decision; 'Toni, it can only be Calais, if my rough calculations are right. We'll have to put in there if we can. It won't be easy – I'm not sure of the entry into the harbour, which is still damaged.' The thought of dry land inspired me and I felt ready to attempt anything. He went on, 'We'll *have* to hoist the mainsail again. I've been trying the engine while you were dozing, and there's no sign of life – must be waterlogged. Blasted engines – always go wrong when you need them.' Weak and stiff as we were, visions of hot food and dry clothes gave us wings. Tantalizingly the coast seemed to remain at the same distance. 'The tides are against us, and we're being swept past Calais. Damn. We'll have to go about again.'

Darkness fell as we strove to get nearer. The lighthouse off Cap Gris Nez flashed away, but James possessed no charts, at that time, of the coast of France, so was ignorant of a safe channel or the existence of any sandbanks near the entry. The seas became progressively steeper, denoting shallower or shoal water. For the first time James was anxious and afraid, being in unfamiliar waters, and dreading the thought of grounding his boat – his home – outside the entrance to a foreign port.

The coast was in total darkness for, in 1946, war conditions still prevailed over the devastated coastal areas of France where only two years previously the landings had taken place. He felt sure it *was* Calais nevertheless, straining his eyes to see any leading lights, 'Stay right here, beside me, Toni – just in case anything should happen,' he pleaded. It was calmer in the shoal waters near the entrance and I felt less sick, even quite light-headed with relief at discovering the safety of a harbour, though unaware of his tenseness as I stood quietly beside him.

The tide was with us now. Suddenly, above us to starboard, loomed a blacker shape against the black sky. James whispered in his excitement, 'That must be the mole or jetty sticking out from the harbour – and – *yes* I can see a small red light – and a white one – further back. We've made it

darling.' No time for celebrations. The next minute *Pat* bumped against the tall harbour wall, which we could now see was in ruins. Great gaps and holes appeared where the sea surged in and out. We would have to claw and sail our way in as best we could. All appeared deserted. The wall was taller than our mast, and James gave a gasp as he saw the first of the overhanging crumpled derricks, threatening to become entangled with our mast and rigging.

'Quick, Toni. Back the foresail while I fend us off with the boathook.' We hardly dared to breathe as the swirling tide bore us inexorably up the long entrance. The broken derricks were impossible to see until we were right underneath them. Torn and splintered planks and vast logs stuck out too, trying to grab us. The silent stillness of sheltered waters after two days and nights of buffeting gales and growling seas was miraculous. Suddenly we were at the entrance proper, where most of the damage had been repaired. *Pat* slid round the bend in the jetty, and there we were in a calm haven. She gently nudged against a trawler moored alongside and James ran for'ard to lower the foresail, then jumped on board the trawler with a mooring rope to secure us, while I put out some fenders.

Drunk with exhaustion, we fell down the steps into the cabin to reassure Paddy – but the settee was empty. Where was she? This was a culminating horror; even as we called her name with lips frozen and wet we knew what must have happened. Our eyes met and the naked truth flashed out of them. We dropped our gaze and knew. During the last desperate few hours, when we had been too occupied to think about her, she must have come up on deck to relieve herself. She was so clean in her habits she would never have thought of dirtying the cabin, so trusting she would never have perceived the danger with both of us on deck. Oh dear God. The fate I had dreaded for her had happened. I felt we had murdered her – pictured in my mind the wave washing her overboard, her frantic attempts to swim, in that cruel vicious sea – and sobbed aloud at our wicked carelessness; 'James, oh James! We have drowned her and she loved and trusted us completely.' I was hysterical, with no control, in my exhausted state. James took me in his arms – too devastated to talk.

Too tired mentally and physically to remove our wet clothes we fell into our bunk – not into a dreamless sleep, but tossed and torn by nightmare hurricanes, waking with a start from time to time. At dawn a babble of astonished voices woke us, as French fishermen and harbour officials hailed us from the trawler. Sleepily we emerged to a disbelieving chorus – no fishing boats had put to sea for days; how had we got there?

By a strange and bitter quirk of fate, the dawn was beautiful, heralding a perfect summer's day, already hot. Luckily, I still spoke French like a native and explained to them our horrible adventures. They were full of admiration for James's seamanship. To have entered the harbour, without an engine, in a gale and in the dark was nothing short of miraculous. We agreed. The men offered us coffee; the hot drink was like nectar. But the memory of Paddy was constantly with us. I was haunted by what must have been the utter horror of her last moments. But we could not sit and brood, there was so much and *so* much to do. The vividness of it all still makes me feel unutterably guilty and sad.

Our first priority was to sort out and tidy the jumble of sails, sheets and general clutter on deck. James busied himself with this while I went below, steeling myself for the inevitable chaos; where should I start? Systematically I swept up the broken crockery and tea leaves, ditching everything over the side. Next, I asked James if he could fix up some sort of clothes line round the rigging, in order to dry the sopping wet clothes, blankets and towels. He protested, 'It's not going to look very seamanlike, but of course I will.' Being so tired and sleepy made each effort agony, but we persisted. Boiling up two kettles of our precious water, I wiped down the filthy work surfaces and deck in the galley.

The harbour officials, completely at a loss as regards any action concerning our unauthorized presence in Calais, had asked us to report to the Gendarmerie as soon as possible. Having washed our face and hands and combed our salt-sticky hair, we set off in the least wet and dirty clothes we could find. The distance from the port to the town was a mile or more and as we started our walk I had the impression the land was moving; coming up to hit me. James explained that this often happened after a long spell at sea, 'You can call yourself a sailor now.'

The walk seemed endless in dusty August heat as we dragged ourselves along, asleep on our feet. James mumbled, 'We must find a mechanic for the engine too – but we've got no francs, so that's no good.' At last, we reached the Prefecture. As yet, no British people had crossed the Channel *on holiday* so we presented a problem! Once again I explained the position, and after much gesticulation, shouting and excitement, our passports were marked with an official stamp, across which was written, 'Propriétaires d'un yacht en difficulté!' (Owners of a boat in trouble.) Having solved this unorthodox problem, the officials relaxed and became helpful and friendly, advising us which bank to go to

where we might obtain a repayable loan, on the strength of an English cheque. After more hilarious discussions this too was accomplished, by which time we were incapable of anything but sleep. There was no question of returning to *Pat*, as with no transport I knew my feet and legs were incapable of carrying me further. Accordingly, we went into a little café for a meal, to find out if we might have a room for the night. Hungry as we were, halfway through the meal, I looked at James, to see his eyes closed, his head nodding. All assumed an unreal, dreamlike quality.

The patron of the bistro was sympathetic and voluble, insisting on telling us about the occupation, the excitement of the Allied landings, and especially how he, personally, had *never* collaborated! I pinched myself to keep awake, choosing a tactful moment to ask if we might have a bed for the night as everything, including our bunk on board our boat was soaked through. Immediately, he offered us a room for practically nothing. I shook the sleeping James, 'Darling, he's got a room – we'll have to sleep for a couple of hours now, then go back to *Pat* to collect our washing things before tonight.'

The walk to and from the harbour was purgatory – blazing hot sun, combined with blisters on our feet contributing to the general discomfort. However, by now, most of the wet gear was dry, so we were able to stow it below, as well as lashing up the mainsail. I could not bring myself to look at the corner of the settee. Putting our sponge bags in a shopping basket we trudged wearily back, too tired to talk. That night, simultaneously, we had the same nightmare. The bed faced a wide window. As we awoke, clutching each other in fear, the centre of the window appeared as a mast, with the pale reflection of the glass on either side resembling a sail. 'We're grounding!' James shouted, before realizing it was a dream. Our minds and bodies ached with tension and strain, when they should have been replete and relaxed with lovemaking.

By next morning, with yet another beautiful day and a southeasterly wind, James felt we should set sail as time was running out. With this wind, we should be in Dover in a few hours, where someone would be able to mend the sodden engine. 'There's too much walking in Calais!' he complained.

How different it all looked in sunshine I thought, as I climbed on board our home again. I had bought fresh fruit, bread and cheese in Calais; milk and meat were unobtainable. Our small stock of tins was dwindling fast, but we would soon be back in England.

Even with a fair wind, negotiating the long entrance past the dilapidated mole was no easy matter, and James heaved a sigh of relief as we cleared it and he was able to hoist the mainsail. 'We'll make Dover on one tack with any luck.' He exclaimed.

The seas had abated after the storms, transforming the whole world. Very soon the English coast appeared on the horizon; the sun shone and *Pat* was in her element, sailing her fastest, on a broad reach. If we could have waited a few more days, Paddy would have been enjoying it all with us. I saw her everywhere.

James explained the procedure once we reached Dover, for with no engine it would be difficult, 'We must sail in the southern entrance at high tide, because of the wrecks, so I won't lower the mainsail till I'm sure I've got plenty of way on, then I can steer to a suitable berth.' The coast loomed up at an astonishing speed while I took the wheel and he 'tidied ship'. At first I could not distinguish the entrance among the massive grey harbour walls and breakwaters. How would we be able to stop in time, skimming over the waves so fast. Unbelieving, I cried, 'James – it's crazy – it took us nearly three days to get to Calais from Ramsgate, and here we are back in Dover in only six hours!'

This time, sailing in past the breakwater, I felt as triumphant as if I had discovered a new continent. The harbour master indicated where he wished *Pat* to lie, then James lowered the mainsail and she stopped behaving as though she were a battering ram intent on running down all before her, and meekly slid, under James's masterly handling, to a berth alongside an immensely tall jetty. Huge cranes rumbled along their tramlines above, and a thick layer of coal dust from freighters and coaling ships soon settled on deck. The customs officers in their launch drew up neatly beside us, 'Anything to declare?' they asked as they clambered aboard uninvited. I wondered how they could have known of our unscheduled stay in Calais. James replied, 'Unfortunately, no. We were blown in there by the gales – with no money!' We found a phone booth and I spoke to my mother, who reacted with the classical mixture of relief and anger, having been worried stiff.

James had more or less the same reaction from his own mother, though as she hero-worshipped her son, believing him to be the supremely confident seaman that he in fact was, she did not ask any questions. We walked on, along the endless jetties, full of ruts and holes, discussing what should be done next. James said, 'The first priority is a mechanic to

get the engine going – then we must stock up with fresh food and set sail immediately. Do you realize I've only got a couple more days before I'm due back off leave?'

My heart shrank. I was aware of the fleeting days, knowing we could never get to Weymouth during this leave, and spoke hesitantly: 'I know Folkestone isn't a very good harbour, as it's so exposed, and has such a surge and send, but we *could* tie up alongside the long jetty, and perhaps I could stay with my parents – until there's a weekend or something,' I finished lamely. James thought it a good plan.

A mechanic finally started the engine, which had been flooded with salt water. We did not get much sleep that night, for Dover was a noisy port with floodlit ships coaling all through the night, the noise of engines and the soughing of a rising wind flitting through the rigging. Early next morning we filled the water tank, and bought provisions.

At low tide we could see the masts and spars from sunken wrecks protruding through the broken water at the entrance. We had been fortunate to enter unscathed, but decided to sail out of the western entrance when we left. Catching the maximum west-flowing tide we duly started the engine and motored round the tortuous channel to the entrance before hoisting the mainsail: James swore under his breath, 'I don't believe it, the wind has gone round to South-West again. At least it's not blowing a gale – we'll have to do a dog-leg. Sail out on the starboard tack and then run back in on a long reach to Folkestone. We won't get any further today.'

Poor James, his hands were still raw from the sores of previous tacking manoeuvres. During the morning he was very quiet, smoking his pipe, contemplating the mainsail and mizzen. Finally he said triumphantly, 'I think I've got it! Why shouldn't the mainsail be on a travelling "horse", like the mizzen, then it would go over of its own accord when we went about.' I was very impressed by his inventive genius, but once again was feeling sick and cold in the short choppy seas, due to the tide and wind opposing each other. I asked him, 'Where could you fix it darling?' With the stem of his pipe he pointed at the water tank abaft the wheel, describing an arc over the engine hatch, 'It would have to be quite high up, so as not to get in the way of the engine or wheel, which means losing a bit of sail area, but that's no bad thing – we wouldn't have to take a reef in whenever it blew a bit hard.' He continued, 'Yes, we'll see if someone can do that while we're in Folkestone – it'll make such a difference to sailing westward, make going about a joy.'

I wished I could feel more excitement and enthusiasm, but

I felt drowsy from the Kwells, with a dry mouth and thumping heart. When I went below, attacks of giddiness overcame me, forcing me to lie down for a short while. Utterly useless! Self-pity caused tears to overflow from my unwilling eyelids. 'Ready about!' James called from the well, rousing me. 'Better back the foresail. I'll manage the shackle and wheel while she's in stays,' he explained. Then, 'Lee-o!' he shouted, and I held the foresail back. Shuddering, straining and lurching, the manoevre followed its clumsy course. James could see the strain on my face. 'We'll be in Folkestone before dark, darling, and you can have a spell ashore and recover from the gales of the last few days.' I sat beside him, tears flowing unashamedly, 'But you won't be there – I'll be all on my own, it'll be awful without you or Paddy.' He tried to comfort me, 'I'll be back for a long weekend as soon as I can, then we'll sail on down.'

We were not making such fast progress as the sail from Calais to Dover, but the cliffs between Dover and Folkestone were becoming more distinct, and eventually the long arm of the mole – or jetty – at Folkestone stretched out clearly. James warned me, 'There's no proper harbour inside. I'll lower the sails, and go in slowly on the engine. We may have to be prepared to go alongside very quickly.'

Once inside he nudged up to a fishing trawler, throwing a line across to a fisherman on board, He made it fast, but explained they were putting to sea at 4 a.m. the next morning! We promised to be up and about before then, and set about folding and securing the sails, tidying the boat ready for inspection by my parents; making ourselves as respectable as possible before going ashore.

Though extremely relieved and pleased to see us, there was nevertheless a slightly strained atmosphere. I had my long-anticipated bath, so did James, as a result of which we felt really refreshed. Over dinner, we discussed the immediate future. My father asked, 'Where will you stay, Antonia, while James is in Portland? You can't live in the boat all on your own.' Secretly, I hoped my parents would ask me to stay with them in the little hotel. This however would prove too expensive, so James told them he had intended looking for a bed and breakfast or a boarding house the very next day, before rejoining his submarine.

We were both so sleepy, conversation lagged. We soon made our way down to the harbour, collapsing into the folding bunk, falling into a deep dreamless sleep before our lips touched – our first unbroken sleep in days. James woke first, sitting up with a start, bumping his head: 'Damn! I told

the fishermen we'd be up by 4 a.m. to untie our warps!' We dressed hastily, noticing guiltily that it was after 7 a.m., and dashing up on deck, realized the trawler had indeed gone out, having resecured *Pat* to another trawler inboard. It was such a kind gesture, to have let *Pat* drop astern before tying her up again, without waking us; our fatigue must have been all too apparent.

'Now,' James said, 'I must organize you and *Pat* before going back to the sub. First of all, we must get a safer permanent berth alongside.' There were not many boats in those days, and autumn was approaching, so it was easy to secure a berth up at the far end of the jetty where it turned at right angles towards the shore. An old fisherman stood watching us, sucking an empty pipe. He had bright blue eyes, no teeth, and little gold earrings. I recognized him from our first visit. 'That's a grand old lady of the sea you've got there.' He remarked in a broad Kentish accent, 'It's lucky she has such a stout rubbing strake – you get a great swell and send along this jetty. Best to have a lot of slack in your mooring ropes or they'll snap like straw!' James was touched and grateful that he should take such an interest, inviting the fisherman on board for a mug of tea. His name was Jim, and his eyes took in the little cabin with approval, while noisily drinking his tea. I was intrigued by the earrings, for in those days it was an unusual sight, and asked him whether he had pierced ears. 'But of course,' he answered, 'It keeps your eyesight keen. I'm very old – don't know quite how old but I still don't need glasses.'

It was hard to understand everything he said because of the smacking, sucking noises of the hard old toothless gums. James had a sudden idea, 'Jim. Do you still go out fishing?' He shook his head sadly, 'No. They say I'm more trouble than help now. I just stand about, smoking my pipe and securing the odd warp.' James looked across at me, and I nodded encouragingly; half guessing what he was going to ask this heaven-sent philosophizing old fisherman. 'Jim – would you be prepared to keep an eye on *Pat* for us? I'm in the Navy, my leave is up and I've got to go back to my submarine tomorrow . . . .' Jim interrupted, 'Submarines – that takes some guts.' James went on, 'My wife will be down most days, but I don't want her to sleep on board on her own, so she'll stay in a guest house. We'll be happy to leave it to you to tot up how much time you've spent on board – just let us know.' Jim's clear blue eyes wrinkled at the corners in an infectious grin; 'I'd be happy to have some responsibility again. It's lonely since my wife died. I'll look after yours for

you – and I won't ruin you neither – my needs are few – tobacco mostly.' We could not believe our luck.

Secretly James had been extremely worried at leaving *Pat* in such an exposed harbour: a southeaster would be most uncomfortable. He shook Jim's hand, simply saying; 'I am most grateful to you.'

Then started a whirlwind day – first of all finding a boarding house. Most were too expensive for us. Though harbour dues were slight, repairs were quite costly, and Jim would have to be paid too. At last we found an attic room – cold and bleak, with linoleum on the floor, reminding me of the WRNS!

Next, a visit to a ship's chandler where James asked for someone who could do metal work, but on a boat. The man we needed to see was down in the harbour fixing some stanchions for one of the trawlers. When he had finished his welding, he came on board, where James outlined what was needed. He saw the point immediately, and was amazed to hear that between us we had shackled and unshackled the clew of the mainsail each time *Pat* had gone about. He told us; 'In the old sailing lifeboat days, I've heard they usually had six men on board, mainly so that three could hold the sail, while the other three unshackled it!' James held up his swollen, torn fingers, 'I can quite believe it,' he said quietly, 'I wouldn't like to do it again.' The engineer promised us a solid 'horse'.

James thought that old Jim would probably know of someone who could make us a boom for the mainsail. 'It'll have to wait till I can come over for a weekend,' he said miserably. It was a sad, unforeseen end to our honeymoon, that we should still be parted. Nearing the jetty, we saw Jim waiting, leaning against the harbour wall smoking his pipe, a few mackerel strung on a line. Laconically he greeted us, 'Thought these might come in handy. I don't eat a lot myself – pity to waste them – can't be bothered with the bones anyway.' I could have hugged him, and James took the fish gratefully, remarking, 'I'll be back on board tomorrow, so perhaps you could use some duty-free pipe tobacco. Come back to the boat with us, then we can talk about reducing the mainsail and fitting a boom.'

I had shopped for essentials, so after watching Jim gut the mackerel, which I had never seen done before, I went below to the little galley to peel potatoes and fry the fish. It would be our last supper together for ages, and after Jim had left we both felt depressed. Vainly, I tried to overcome my misery, 'I shall buy some white paint and transform this cabin while

you're away. Oh! it's so unfair that the weather should be calm and sunny now, when it doesn't matter any longer.' James tried, manfully, 'Darling – it won't be for long. There will be weekends. I'll go back by train tomorrow, but if you can manage to collect the car from Celia's before I come back, it'll save a lot of time. Yes. It would be lovely to have this cabin painted, to match the galley – but don't overdo it.' He added, shyly, 'Because of the baby!'

Certainly, I was missing out on the joy and special care meted out to expectant mothers! 'Let's go to bed early,' I pleaded, wishing to forget the lonely weeks ahead of me. Boiling up a kettle to wash with, I thought enviously of the luxury, previously taken for granted, of hot water streaming out of a tap, into a bath. That night *Pat* lay very still, not even the halyards rattled or shook; no wavelets slapped the hull, as we slid into our double bunk. James murmured sleepily, 'Darling. I want you so much – are you sure it won't hurt the baby?' I could not imagine why it would upset the tiny being safely curled up inside; 'Of course it won't. I want you too. I love you so – and I wish I wasn't seasick.' I would have cried, had not the wonder of our lovemaking swept and whirled me into another world.

Next day I went with him to the station, tears streaming down my face as we clung and kissed goodbye. He showed no distress, but I hoped that inwardly he too hated this parting, after such disasters. Part of him was already on board his submarine, his wife of secondary importance, and he never talked about Paddy again.

It was a stange interlude, that spell at Folkestone living in limbo. My present heartache and agony of mind is soothed by the memory of Michael's birth – my future comfort and joy – until he too would go into the world, but by then I would be so resigned and old, I wouldn't need solace.

CHAPTER THREE

Baby on Board

Sad and forlorn, I decided to go and see my mother before tidying up the boat. I wanted to share the intense pride and happiness I felt about the baby, but her reaction hit me like a physical blow, 'Oh! No! Tonia, so soon. And where are you going to keep it, in the boat? You'll have to sell the boat.' In my heart of hearts I knew she was right, but at this early stage I could not have suggested anything so shattering to James, who lived for his sailing home. She did not like babies and was too busy with her bridge and golf even to come down to the harbour to see dear *Pat*, so I did not see much of her.

Thus started a succession of dreary, similar days, heightened only by Jim's unfailing cheerfulness and calm philosophy. He helped me to sandpaper the cross beams of the deckhead and the bulkheads of the cabin and, on fine days, we would drink our mug of tea or coffee in the well, while he told me horrifying tales of his fishing days, mixing fact with fantasy, 'Yes, one day I was hauling in the net, when I saw this vision and heard this sad voice. I swear it was a mermaid caught up with the silvery fish. I had to let her go. Most of the fish got out too. The skipper couldn't understand why the catch was so small that night.' He told me of storms and rocky headlands off Brittany; of seals, sharks,and ghostly voices blown on the wind. I do not know what I would have done without him. If anyone suggested moving *Pat* to another berth he refused flatly, muttering maledictory curses in a menacing low voice. Everyone knew and respected Jim, even holding him in some awe, like a mascot.

Because of his anchor earrings, I decided to get my own ears pierced, wandering round the steep back streets of Folkestone, looking for a little shop. Eventually I saw a

scruffy notice advertising, 'Ears pierced 10s.' and went in. A gypsy-like woman dabbed my ears with spirit, put a cork behind the lobe, and before I had time to scream, stabbed through the lobe with her sharp needle. No disinfectant was used. She then sold me a pair of 'sleepers', 'They must be gold dearie – twist them round each day, to stop the hole healing over.' By the next day my lobes were swollen, red and suppurating, as well as being painful. Jim reassured me, 'Just put a dab of vaseline on. They'll calm down in a few months!'

James wrote every day – passionate loving letters, but bringing the sad news that the submarine was going to carry out an exercise off the coast of Ireland, so he would not be back for the next two weekends. I was heartbroken. How I missed the companionship of dear Paddy.

From time to time, I went up to the hotel to see my mother, but usually she was out playing golf, or busy writing letters. I wrote too. Endless letters to James, describing in detail my life and *Pat's*. I told him the boom was nearly finished and that the sailmaker wished to know if he should alter the sail in order to lash it on. When his reply came telling them to go ahead, Jim was overjoyed. He would be in charge.

Hoisting the sail in harbour was easy. Suddenly *Pat* seemed full of men, shipwrights and sailmakers, all measuring and drawing plans, while I made endless pots of tea, and Jim supervised, sucking his pipe. Having sand-papered and cleaned the paintwork below, I wanted to start painting, but once again, as in Ramsgate harbour, the smell of paint in the confined cabin space overcame me and I was violently sick. Jim sympathized, 'I'm not much good with a paint brush myself, Missus, but I'll find a lad who wants to earn a few bob – a *few* bob – don't worry.' Sure enough, a young lad appeared the next day, inexperienced but willing, and the result was a vast improvement on the old dingy yellow.

Jim looked at me quizzically one day, remarking, 'You're going to have a babby, aren't you?' I blushed, nodding, and asked, 'But how do you know?' His eyes grew gentle and wise as he spoke, 'It's the second sight – one knows these things.' I thought it was probably because I had been sick, but was impressed nevertheless.

About a week later I went to pick up the car from Ramsgate. Celia was delighted to see me again. She sympathized with me over the continued seasickness, adding subtly, 'Are you sure it isn't caused by anything else Toni?' So, I told her about the baby, and when she had explained that one was always sick for the first few weeks, felt this

sorry state might be purely temporary. 'I don't think it would be a good idea to attempt the long sail round to Weymouth just at the moment though.' Celia paused, 'I would so love to do it with James. Would you mind terribly? I'm sure Martin would look after Maria.' I struggled with conflicting feelings, knowing Celia was right. I also knew that Celia was never seasick and would be a much better sailing companion than I was at the moment. At the same time I hesitated, purely because of an irrational jealousy I could not entirely suppress. Finally I said; 'That would solve everything – if you could manage to get away. James will be so pleased. Thank you Celia.'

We arranged that when James had a free weekend, he should telephone Martin Farrant, his brother-in-law, to organize it. As I drove back to Folkestone, I knew it was the right decision, but it did give me an even bigger inferiority complex. Added to my inability to play chess or do the crossword, was now the humiliation of being a hopeless sailor. My love for James was all-consuming, overpowering; what could I do to hold his esteem?

He arrived back on Friday evening in September and the deep joy we shared in seeing one another again, helped to heal the pain of separation, especially as he was delighted with the new boom and 'horse'. 'It does make the mainsail look a bit small,' he sighed, 'But it will be safer, and my fingers won't get chewed up any more!' The weather was right, for the first time, nearly a 'soldier's wind', (blowing offshore) with a hint of West in it. We met Celia at the station, and went straight back to the boat in order to prepare her for the following day. Next morning I stood sadly on the jetty to let go for'ard, while Jim let go aft. Together we watched as James hoisted the newly designed mainsail, admittedly reduced in size, but seemingly efficient: *Pat* responding to the calmer seas, her three sails bellying out as she ploughed through the waves. She soon became a speck, on a long leg out to sea.

When I went down to the harbour to say goodbye to Jim and give him some of his favourite tobacco, it hurt me not to see *Pat* swaying in her usual place. After all, it was my home, uncomfy though it was, containing our precious possessions, and I wanted to be back on board. For a moment I resented the baby – but no, that was blasphemy, I wanted James's child more than anything in the world.

God answered my prayers for a fair wind, and only three days later the anxiously awaited telephone call came. The long drive westward in 'William-and-Mary' seemed never-

ending; I longed to hear all about the trip. Leaving the car as near to Weymouth harbour as possible, I walked along the harbour wall, looking for *Pat*. There she lay, among a jumble of boats, between a yacht and a motor cruiser, looking clean and tidy. I climbed on board, relieved and happy to be home. James held me tight, 'Oh! darling, it's wonderful to have you back. This is a perfect mooring – it's such a long entrance you'll never feel any movement at all – safe as houses!' We laughed. Avidly I asked, 'What was it like, how did she sail?' James took me below, 'I'll tell you in a moment. Let me kiss you properly first.' The tension and worry melted away.

By late October it began to be cold, and we lit the little round black stove which gave off a wonderful heat. The coal had to be kept in a bin, on shore, which was perfectly safe in those days, but meant that I had to carry the heavy hod each day over the boat lying between us and the jetty. James left early every morning, just after 7 a.m., returning at about 6.30 p.m. There seemed to be an endless amount of chores, most of them taking quite a lot of time. Firstly, the water tank had to be filled each day, necessitating lugging the hose pipe across the deck of the inboard boat, and fixing it to the stand-pipe, then all the washing had to be done in the tiny basin in the galley, and hung to dry on a line which James reluctantly fixed to the rigging, grumbling, 'It looks most unseamanlike!' Milk had to be fetched each day, and the paraffin lamps filled and cleaned. Because of the small amount of space, everything below had to be kept neat and tidy, and I began to find the low passageway through to the after cabin, necessitating bending double for a few feet, a painful exercise.

Tiny flutterings inside me, as though a moth or butterfly were beating its wings, surprised and astonished me. I marvelled at the first awareness of the baby's physical presence. Sometimes though, when I was out shopping, a sharp pain would cause me to gasp and bend over. As James had the car in order to drive to Portland every day, I walked long distances, which was occasionally a bit tiring, but I dismissed any doubts or fears and reasoned that probably all expectant women experienced these symptoms.

I was determined to learn to cook properly, despite the lack of oven, and bought a simple war-time cookery book, attempting the easier recipes – sometimes a success. After supper, sitting snugly in the warm cabin, we were supremely content, as I knitted for the infant, and James read and smoked his pipe. Soon however, the pains got much worse,

lasting longer, and leaving me weak and trembling, forced to bend over double when out shopping. They frightened me and when a high temperature prevented me getting up, James too was desperately worried.

His parents told us to drive over and stay with them until I was better. It was heartbreaking having once more to leave *Pat*, and poor James, but my concern for the unborn baby was paramount.

The Renton's doctor diagnosed an acute cystitis, which had been left far too long untended, necessitating a stay in hospital to combat the infection. Reluctantly we had to agree with his parents and the doctor, abandoning, for the time being, any hope of living in a boat with the strenuous exercise involved. I wept at this further setback, but James refused to let me be upset, 'Toni – the most important thing in my life is for you to be well and comfy – then comes the baby. Until he's . . .' I interrupted him, 'How do you know it'll be a boy?' James looked surprised, 'It never entered my head he would be a girl!' He continued, 'When he can walk, and you are fit and strong again – we'll go back on board. In the meantime, we'll rent a little cottage, near my parents.' I pleaded, 'But I'll only see you at weekends, its too far to come every evening from Portland.' He did his best to comfort me, 'I'll go on living on board, and look after *Pat* – there's a lot to do. For one thing, I shall have to fit a bunk beside the engine, for the boy – there's just room underneath the catwalk.' Personally the idea of the baby sharing the engine room did not appeal to me, but it was literally the only available space.

We found a dear little cottage, which had the luxury of a bath in the kitchen; the hot water was heated in an old-fashioned copper, and ladled out with a large saucepan, but this was such an improvement on the boat, it nearly reconciled me to the fresh separation.

James wrote amusing letters during the week, telling me of his 'antiseagull device' and other improvements. The gulls in Weymouth *would* perch on the flat round top of the mainmast, decorating the deck and cabin top with unseemly droppings. He therefore hoisted a prickly twig up on the RNSA (Royal Naval Sailing Association) burgee halyard, making it painfully impossible for them to perch there!

Each weekend we went for walks and prepared the little boxroom off our bedroom for the baby. I was huge and knew perfectly well that it would now have been quite impossible to negotiate the treacherously low passageway. Sometimes we played chess, but though he taught me the

moves, I could never think more than a move or two ahead, which meant I could not even give him a decent game. Being on my own a lot, with no telephone, James gave me a wireless for Christmas, which opened up another world, beyond that of books and knitting. It was sheer joy to listen to concerts, talks and plays.

Once the infection had cleared up, my robust health reasserted itself, in common with most pregnant women, a calm egotistical frame of mind blotted out what was happening in the world. I became introverted, conscious only of the baby, unable to go anywhere because James had the car, but relishing the enforced idleness. The doctor had no need to see me again, for this was long before intensive prenatal care and clinics. No one enlightened me as to the role I was expected to play when the time came to have the baby; as in so many aspects of my life, I relied on intuition. The only person I knew who had had a baby recently was Celia, and she lived at the other end of England. To ask her would be admitting yet another discrepancy!

The spring of 1947 was bitterly cold for several months, which was blamed for the lateness of the infant's arrival. Sheep and cows were both slow in giving birth: the tiny beings reluctant to exchange the warmth of the womb for the freezing conditions outside. March turned into April, when at last, a month late, the baby decided to arrive. I felt shattered at having to work so hard, but immensely proud to produce a ten pound boy – James was right! He got compassionate leave, arriving the day after the baby was born, unable to believe he was a father. We christened him Michael.

During that winter my mother had become seriously ill, but was reluctant to burden me with the knowledge, in view of the imminent birth. She came to Dorset once to see young Michael, but this was the only time she saw him for, shortly afterwards, she became bedridden. The lonely long months passed in a monotonous yet fascinating world learning to look after a new baby. Never having held one in my arms, I was extremely grateful for the fact that he was so big he would come to no harm should I accidentally do something wrong.

James returned at weekends, bringing a spaniel puppy home when Michael was a few months old, saying it was good to have a child and a dog brought up together. The puppy, christened Jake, was admittedly adorable, but meant a lot of house-training and exercise. He made up for the extra work by the enchanting picture both of them made

rolling about on the floor together, with Michael chortling, pulling the long silky ears, while Jake padded at him with huge soft paws. It helped to ease the painful memory of Paddy.

Hopes of moving back into *Pat* receded when James's appointment in submarines changed, obliging him to join a frigate based at Portsmouth.

A traumatic few months followed, as my mother's health slowly deteriorated. She had a serious operation, and I managed to find a young eighteen-year-old to look after Michael, now eight months old, in order to go and see her, if only for a few days. A second operation could not save her, and getting the girl in to cope in the cottage, I only just managed to reach the hospital in York where she lay, the day before she died. She was so young, only just over fifty; my poor father was distraught and grief-stricken, making my own distress seem selfish.

Later the following spring, we drove down to see *Pat* and spend a day on board. Michael, at a year, was still not walking, which soon proved how impossible it would be to live afloat and sail with him; as yet his little bunk had no sides, so that he could easily fall or scramble out. I remembered Paddy's ghastly death, yet with that inherent, ebullient enthusiasm of youth, was willing to make our life a success at sea again.

We both longed to go on a trial sail, just to get the feel of the new rigging, modified so that two could sail her easily.

Michael's godmother, Mary, my old friend from the Wrens, now married with a child of her own, offered to have him to stay, enabling us to embark on a small spring cruise during the Easter leave. We had no ambitious plans: just to potter about in the shelter of Portland Bill. *Pat* felt different somehow, familiar yet strange. Of course, it was not *Pat*, but I who was altered.

The winds were gentle, with an early hot April sunshine making one believe that it was summer. Despite the alluring calm, I nevertheless took the seasickness pills, and we sailed across to Lulworth Cove, taking advantage of that halcyon breeze. The entrance stays hidden until the last possible moment, when an astonishing view is revealed, and one is surrounded by a tiny, perfectly circular bay, with a background of towering cliffs plunging down to the sea. All was quiet and golden, broken only by the metallic clatter and racket of the anchor chain finding a firm hold. Cows with the foothold of goats walked along the very edge of those precipitous cliffs, causing one to gasp lest they should slip and crash into the sea! I believe it hardly ever happens!

The canvas folding dinghy which we had been towing enabled us to row ashore with our picnic lunch. *Pat* looked noble and serene, lying at anchor in the middle of that spetacular setting, contrasting strangely with our previous sailing trips. Her hull was now black and shining, instead of dirty pale blue. It was a perfect day. We spent the night in Lulworth Cove, watching the sun set, and the tiny far-away cows like a cut-out frieze against the evening sky. No whisper of wind blew, the cove might have been a pond, and I felt reconciled to a permanent life on board. The next day was an unusually lazy one, spoiling us with blue sky, hot sun and the lightest of breezes. I wanted to stay in the sheltered haven of Lulworth all day, rowing back to the little beach under the towering cliffs for another picnic – followed perhaps by an afternoon's gentle lovemaking... James had other plans. He wanted to try out *Pat*'s manoeuvrability in these calm waters and light airs, to show off her paces to HM ships, including his own, anchored in Portland harbour. So we sailed across the bay, a pleasurably slow and calm sail. The breakwater, or mole, around the harbour in 1948 was still in some disarray, consisting in the main of great chunks of broken-up concrete piled on top of natural rock, strewn higgledy-piggledy in a long, massive line either side of the wide opening which faced East. In order to sail in we would need to tack as we were now heading into the light wind.

Naturally I presumed we would start the engine and motor in, but James wished to test his and *Pat*'s tacking skills. The tide must have started to ebb for we hardly gained more than a foot each time he laboriously put her about, which involved a mad dash by me up to the bows to back the staysail and catch the flukey breeze. Occasionally this did not work and our bows came dangerously near to the jagged rocks, whereupon James would yell, 'The boathook – grab the boathook – fend us off!' Finally I lost patience and yelled back, 'Oh! start the engine damn you – this is too silly – we're getting nowhere' as I stood panting with my exertions, my hands scratched and torn, my arms aching. He calmly and maddeningly retorted, '*I* want to sail her in – I'm the skipper and, while we're sailing, you do as I say.' I was beside myself with rage. What a waste of a beautiful day.

Next time he shouted, 'Ready about!' acting on impulse, as the bows once more scraped the jumble of concrete and rock, I jumped ashore, shouting back, 'Do it yourself! I hate you and I hate the boat – I'm leaving.' I could not see his face as I precariously found a foothold and started to leap from boulder to boulder along the breakwater. Rude words

and shouts followed me as I distanced myself from him, wondering already where on earth I could go for I was on the southern arm of the breakwater, heading out to sea! Vaguely, I wondered if the officers on watch on board various ships were following our antics through binoculars – probably vastly amused. I did not care. Beside myself with impotent fury, I soon tired of the rough going, which forced me to sit dejectedly, hunched up, chin in hands, wondering what James would do. Glancing sideways, I could see that he had made it through the entrance, which was infuriating. He then started the engine for it was flat calm inside the harbour, and nudged *Pat* very gently along the breakwater till she was just below me. In a cold voice he urged me to get back on board at once, to stop behaving like a small child and making us a laughing stock. This stung me into an angry tirade, 'How dare you talk to me like that – I don't care what anyone thinks – and it's typical of you to mind what others might say – you don't care a damn about how *I* feel.' Finally, we both had to admit how absurd we must look; our remarks became less heated, and when I eventually scrambled back on board in an undignified fashion, having to be hauled up by James we collapsed laughing in the well. It was my first rebellion. The presence of the boys prevented any future actual 'mutiny'.

The next two days we spent in Weymouth, working hard, scraping down and varnishing the masts and boom. There would have to be guard rails fitted to prevent Michael slipping overboard.

Before the end of the ten-day leave period, we took her out to sea again for a day's sailing. The reduced sail area meant she was slower, but the resulting comparative ease with which she now went about more than made up for it. We resolved to try and sail again during the summer leave provided someone could look after Michael. This would be our long overdue *real* honeymoon cruise, as the storm-tossed, gale-ridden fortnight in August 1946 was more like a living hell, even in restrospect.

The sweet young girl, Dorothy, who had cared for Michael when my mother had been ill, happily agreed to look after him during the summer for ten days. I had not seen James for two months, because of naval exercises, but in our daily letters we had agreed to explore further west if the weather seemed willing.

It would be *Pat's* first time round Portland Bill – that notorious tide rip where the waves toss crazily in all directions. As James checked the rigging, he remarked, 'If

the wind is at all strong tomorrow we'll take a long leg out, on the starboard tack, till we're well outside the race – might be five miles or more.' With our usual luck the weather appeared to sulk, staying overcast, with the inevitable southwesterly moaning ominously round the rigging, reminding me too vividly of 1946.

Next morning, though, the barometer was steady, and the sun shone. With a favourable wind and butterflies in my tummy, we slowly eased our way out, under power. I now knew more or less what was expected of me and tried to carry out any orders quickly and efficiently. Once the sails were hoisted and we were out of the shelter of Portland Bay, we could see the angry jumble of broken foaming water denoting the distant race: one could even hear it roar. The wind stiffened, heeling her over slightly, as she assumed her distinctive, clumsy, yet joyful gait, making me feel ill when I went below. Was I never going to overcome this weakness?

For a long time we kept on this tack, until James reckoned we were well clear of the race, miles out of sight of land. When we went about it seemed doubtful whether we would make Dartmouth before nightfall. The tide was now against us, and we hardly seemed to be moving. The wind dropped with the sunset, and slack water, leaving us rolling about among the phosphorescence of the waves. Berry Head light shone comfortingly at us, while night fell, and we remained stationary. It would have been foolhardy to try and sail in to the river entrance in the dark, so James tried to start the engine before lowering the sails. Maddeningly, it coughed and spluttered while he sweated over the treacherously back-firing starting handle. How dreadful if we had to turn and run before the southwesterly while waiting for dawn! Silently, I prayed and willed it to start, which eventually it did.

Cautiously we nosed our way past the castles which in earlier days had guarded the entrance to the river. The phut-phutting of the engine seemed incredibly noisy in the dark stillness of the sheltered river, but the rattle and clanking of the anchor cable must have woken the entire surrounding country side as we finally came to rest, well after midnight.

High up in the trees on the hilly banks of the Dart, the wind blew and shrilled, while down on the river all was calm. The dinghy, towed astern, had hardly shipped any water, and was waiting for us next morning to row ashore with our milk can. We walked quite a long way before finding a farm, finally coming across a hidden farmyard where the milking had just been finished, with the creamy

frothing milk from the South Devon cows filling the pails to the brim. We even met a bread van doing an early morning round on our way back to the shore. How delicious the bread tasted later on, back on board, as we were ravenous from the dawn walk and the previous day's sailing. Later we drove on up the beautiful Dart to Stoke Gabriel, anchoring a short distance from the pub, where the local cider was deceptively strong and excellent, inducing us to sleep and kiss and sleep the afternoon away. I was loath to leave this haven of quiet warmth, where one could row ashore for picnics in secluded coves, bathing in the clear tidal waters of the Dart.

James, however, was restless, and before turning back for Weymouth, wanted to slip round Start Point to Salcombe. The weather was ideal, with a light southeasterly wind, and it seemed a shame not to, even for a landlubber like myself. So, we hoisted the sails as we neared the castles at the mouth of the Dart and literally ambled round to Salcombe. In fact, the wind died on us, and we had to use the engine for the last few miles, when we entered another river paradise.

Darkness had fallen by the time we anchored, and we were rudely awoken in the morning by the ferry – we had anchored right in their path! They seemed to think we had done this on purpose and it took quite a lot of persuading to convince them otherwise.

By now, a week had gone by, so that we started to worry about getting back to Weymouth before James's leave expired. Endless pleas of southeasterly gales, like cries of 'wolf', would be no excuse in the eyes of the Navy. Accordingly, after a day exploring one of the many alluringly lovely wooded creeks, we set sail for home. *Pat* liked a following sea, wallowing in sunlit waves, even attracting an entrancing dolphin, or porpoise, to accompany us for part of the way; we were too slow for it though, and after a short spell of spectacular leaps, it dived and disappeared. I tried to keep watch that night, but, as usual, kept falling asleep, only being woken by a contemptuous, flapping mainsail. Luckily this did not wake James, who slept a boy's deep sleep.

We stood well out to sea, giving Portland Bill Race the respectful wide berth it deserves, beating up into Weymouth harbour once we were clear. As we tidied up after the usual shambles, we knew that the next trip would consist of the three of us, plus Jake, as a not entirely able-bodied member of the crew.

An unexpected posting came for James, back to

submarines for a few months up in Campbeltown on the west coast of Scotland. There was no reason why Michael and I should not follow him, as he was now tottering and staggering along in a fair imitation of a walk. James found two big rooms for us in a lovely big Scottish manse, run by a very kind landlady, situated right on the shore, a long way out of the town, opposite the island of Davarr. It was not quite an island, as at low tide a causeway joined it to the mainland.

The three winter months spent up in Scotland were very happy, if bitterly cold. The manse naturally boasted no heating, apart from an open fire in the high-ceilinged room that was our living room. We went beach-combing every day on the shores near the house, piling the sackfuls of wood high in the little pushchair I had taken up with us. The bedroom was freezing, but none of us caught colds, merely chilblains. One red letter day towards the end of our stay, we braved the walk across to Davarr island keeping a careful eye on the tide. We had been told that in one of the myriad caves round the island, was a life-size painting, on a rock, of the Crucifixion. Dragging the pushchair over the bumpy pebbles, we ventured into them all, beginning to doubt its existence, and whether we were going to miss the tide without seeing it, when we were at last rewarded. At first we did not see it, then our eyes became accustomed to the gloom; suddenly it towered above us, impressive and eerie in such surroundings.

Meanwhile, *Pat* was being fitted with the essential guardrails, waiting patiently for us, and Jake the spaniel had spent the months we were away with farmer friends near Bridport. There was not long to wait now.

In March, when an early blustery spring made one long for adventure, Michael and I returned to Dorset with only a month to go before the momentous Easter leave period. As yet, we had no idea where we would have to sail, as James had not received any inkling of a posting. It would be a truly naval 'pierhead jump', but we hoped against hope it might at least be along the South Coast somewhere.

During that short month I feverishly packed all the belongings I thought would fit into the boat, into cardboard boxes. Michael's clothes would have to stay in a small tin trunk, whilst ours could fit into a larger one in the sleeping cabin aft. With infinite relief I realized that at last the little boy – no longer a baby – was out of nappies. How could I have coped with them on board?

The blow fell with a letter from James to say the ship he

was going to was based at Sheerness. This was quite near to where we had bought *Pat* in the first place, at Ramsgate. He was exploring the possibilities of various creeks in the Medway, or possibly the Medway itself, right up the river. Luckily, he had an extended Easter leave, as his appointment to the cruiser did not take effect straight away. Our first cruise with little Michael was going to be a very long one. James was also trying to find a young lad to take along with us, as I would be too occupied stopping Michael falling overboard to help with the sailing.

Events moved fast, and through friends we heard of a delightful young man, waiting to join the Royal Marines, with a month or so to spare. Paul Dickson was not quite eighteen, and throughout the perils and hardships, excitements and near disaster, his unfailing cheerfulness and good humour never faltered. He told us with great pride that he was never seasick! That clinched it, and he was signed on as official 'crew' for the entire voyage. James arranged to meet him at Weymouth: from there they would sail *Pat* round to West Bay one weekend before we were due to embark.

I had many mixed feelings, of apprehension and excitement, as Michael and I celebrated his second birthday on 25 April 1949, waiting down at West Bay near Bridport for our 'home' to sail in. I held the reins attached to his harness as we walked to the end of the jetty. He showed an alarming tendency to stagger along the edge, unperturbed and unaware of any danger, arousing certain forebodings in me over life on board.

Slowly *Pat* rounded the last headland, the light breeze barely filling her sails, but with James's unwillingness to use the engine, I knew he would sail her up to the last minute, even ghosting up the narrow entrance between the jetties at West Bay if he had enough way on her. He and Paul waved cheerfully, as they coaxed her into the little harbour and alongside, while Michael varied his astonished cries of 'See boat', with 'See Daddy!' Their trip had been uneventful, proving that sailing can be fun, and even safe some of the time.

Paul would sleep on board for the next few days while we loaded our minimal worldly possessions on board, the bulkiest item being the folding pushchair. The rented cottage had been fully furnished, so that only clothes, toys, kitchen equipment and food needed to be moved. It was hazardous working on board, with Michael on the cabin top, attached by his reins, while we tried to stow reluctant pots and pans into non-existent spaces. Paul kept an eye on him, playing with toys, when I was for'ard in the galley which seemed to

have shrunk since the last time I had been on board.

The length of the journey was a daunting thought, but at least the prevailing southwesterly wind would be on our side for once. Below decks, Michael was in his element, as he could walk along, standing upright, under the catwalks between the cabins, and he had his rest in the bunk specially constructed for him, sharing the engine room! It was dark in there, unless the hatch was open, but as he would only be in it at night or for his rest, it did not matter. James had slotted a plank into grooves to make a side, which would prevent him rolling out at sea. Underneath the bunk was a locker for a few clothes and toys, and Jake the spaniel shared the full-length bunk with Michael. Sensibly, Jake appreciated the quietness and seclusion of the minute cabin, contrasting with the hustle and bustle of the rest of the boat, occupied by three adults tripping over each other as we vainly tried to stow the stores, spare sails, clothes and personal belongings. He loved Michael dearly, trotting beside him, occasionally picking up a brick, but always bringing it back and jumping onto the bunk to lie at his feet, obviously relieved to have him to himself, in peace.

At last *Pat* was as ready as she could be. The water tank was filled, the petrol tank too; a new Calor gas cylinder was fitted, and the folding canvas dinghy lashed down on the cabin top. Suddenly, unbelievably, the momentous day of departure dawned. It seemed too good to be true, a perfect, cloudless, still day, with the barometer high and steady. We were up long before dawn, on that 30 April 1949, frantically packing last-minute things into the car: enough bread and milk for two days in case we did not make our first harbour that night. We would have breakfast on board with Paul that morning, so as to be ready to slip our moorings as soon as the tide turned to flow east, and carry us past Portland Bill. Paul was really very excited at his adventure, for though he had done a lot of sailing, this was his first long cruise.

CHAPTER FOUR

The First Long Sail

The blissful drug of eternal optimism, youth and enthusiasm – tenderness and anger alternate. . . .

James had hoped to sail out of West Bay, but there was not a breath of wind; the sea as calm as the proverbial mill pond, so, reluctantly, he started the engine for us to chug out until we picked up a sea breeze. A fisherman cast off our lines and we slid majestically out into Lyme Bay – deserted except for *Pat*. We might have been the only boat in the whole Channel that early April morning, venturing into a vast expanse of hazy pearl-grey seascape which turned into pink and then blue as a warming sun pierced the dawn mist, a truly auspicious start. Jake was puzzled. He had never been on board at sea before and he trotted up and down the catwalk, while I watched him anxiously, with Michael on my lap, ready to grab him if he showed signs of jumping overboard – memories of Paddy casting shadows and doubts in my mind.

Very soon, catspaws of wind ruffled the sea as we left the Bay and the men got ready to hoist the sails while I kept her on course. The breeze increased as the sun rose; a kind and helpful northwesterly, filled our sails, heeling us over gently. As the weather was so unusually idyllic, James decided to sail right through the tide race. No sooner had this been decided than we were in it. A quite extraordinary experience. We were making no headway as the winds were so light, therefore James decided to start the engine again. I held Michael on my lap in the well as we all watched mesmerized, fascinated by the leaping boiling waves, resembling a witch's cauldron. Despite the favourable, calm conditions, the waves were quite high, at least three to four feet, colliding with each other and *Pat* in a tumultuous

dance, spray splashing over us. It was quite awe-inspiring, even frightening, but Michael just found it funny, trying to catch the spray with outstretched hands while I clung on to him. The noise was deafening – sails and sheets flapping furiously as the boat rolled and pitched uncontrollably. The seething tidal race appeared to stretch endlessly – but ended as suddenly as it had begun.

Once again we were in calm blue seas sailing peacefully along; greatly relieved to be safely through. Jake seemed as sure-footed as a cat, exploring the boat as though he had been born at sea, and after inspecting one of the stanchions, decided it was his, and duly christened it, thus solving one of the problems that had been worrying me!

James reckoned that we would reach Swanage before dark, which had a sheltered bay and a long jetty which he hoped might provide shelter. Soon we were dancing through the comparatively tame tide race off St Alban's Head and, after rounding Anvil Point, we started up the engine, lowered the sails and gently eased our way into a spare berth along the jetty. Our first leg of the journey had been a kind and gentle initiation, and we all felt a happy sense of achievement. James and I so appreciated the great character of our crew, who did anything he was asked with happy willingness, whether it was taking Jake for a walk, doing the shopping, or feeding Michael!

The tide was low when we moored, so there was no question of disentangling the pushchair from its bed of ropes and sails in order to take Michael for a walk. The men heaved Jake up the ladder let into the stone wall, promising to find a stand-pipe for water on their way to a 'small pint' in a pub. By this time the usual crowd had gathered on the jetty to stand and stare, whilst making inane comments, which they obviously thought one could not hear from on deck.

Boats with people living on board were comparatively rare in those days, eliciting genuine sympathy from some on-lookers, downright contempt from others. Mostly they liked being asked to do something, like securing a mooring line, or handing down a basket. As Jake barked with excitement at being on land once more, rushing round greeting people with puppyish enthusiasm, comments flew, 'Cor – what do you do if he falls overboard? Can he swim?' followed by even more horrified remarks as Michael appeared in the well and stared solemnly back at them, 'Poor little mite,' and, 'It isn't right you know. Shouldn't be allowed,' and so on. To begin with I felt indignant at being treated as a peep show, but found out quite early on that when nothing exciting

happened – such as a drowning I presume – they soon got bored and would drift away.

It was Michael's bathtime. By heating a kettle and a saucepan of water, which when mixed with some cold, nicely filled the bowl, I was able to bathe him in a fairly civilized manner. He could sit down in it and splash happily; the drips trickled down into the bilge. But emptying the bowl was an awkward business, involving ladling the water out with the saucepan, into the basin. Soon, his biscuit and milk were devoured, teeth brushed, and duly pyjamaed, he was tucked up in his bunk with the hatch propped open half-way, so that if it rained in the night he would not get soaked. He accepted his new home and surroundings without question.

Next morning dawned another beautiful day with a following wind – but I forgot to take my Kwells. By this time we had edged out past the jetty, and were gently rolling along, like a waddling duck, which made me feel decidedly sick. I belatedly took the pills, lying down for a while, hoping they would take effect. The movement of the boat that day was decidedly uncomfortable, with not enough wind to steady her, and more West than North in it resulting in a disagreeable swell. Even Michael felt sorry for himself, not wanting to play, but lying down on the floor of the saloon with his thumb in his mouth, sensibly going to sleep.

Lymington was to be our haven that evening, and when the Needles, off the Isle of Wight, came into view I began to recover rapidly. The tide was now against us, so that though we appeared to be moving rapidly through the water, owing to the light wind, *Pat* was making practically no headway at all. We sat in the well and stared at the Needles for a long time; boats from the Solent sailed around us, fast dinghies mocking our slow progress. They were racing yachts of beautiful proportions making us seem a truly ugly duckling in comparison, as we plodded painfully along. It was fun to wave at them, and took our minds off the danger of the swiftly flowing tide which became apparent as we sailed past one of the many buoys rather too close. The wind became flukey, and without enough way on, we were in danger of too close an encounter with the Needles themselves, so the engine had to be started, enabling us to steer through the comparatively narrow channel into the Solent.

Suddenly, there were boats everywhere, or so it seemed, making navigation quite a hazard. Skirting Hurst Castle we went into Lymington, drawing alongside a rather smart yacht. Paul had lowered the mainsail and now jumped on board to tie us up while I busied myself with the fenders. We

were proud of such a masterly navigational feat, until the irate owner came up on deck and asked us 'what the deuce' we thought we were doing? Unfortunately, Michael, who had been tied to the compass in the well during this manoevre, was getting bored, deciding to tell everyone, rather loudly, and Jake, delighted at smells and visions of dry land, jumped aboard the immaculate yacht and up onto the jetty, lifting his leg on the way. This was too much for the yachtsman in his blazer and cap, who probably spent half of his time in clubs in Cowes. Admittedly we looked dirty and untidy, but at least Paul had a yachting cap tucked away below, which he went and put on, thus impressing our reluctant neighbour, who relented when we explained our journey and purpose, nodding his head approvingly at our RNSA burgee. We promised to find a berth alongside the jetty anyway, as we wished to fill our water tank and he told us where to find the stand-pipe as well as the various shops.

We slept soundly, knowing there would be no great hurry the following morning. Michael had not been ashore for a couple of days, so after breakfast we carefully carried the pushchair across the gleaming decks of the toy yacht, and I set off with Jake on the lead, to replenish our larder. There was no room to store large quantities, so it was essential to stock up frequently. Despite it being a time of austerity the ship's chandler knew where I could go for some meat and eggs without ration books, as we were a sea-going boat. I always mentioned the Medway, *without* explaining that we would probably be putting into harbour every evening! Michael was most useful. The shopkeepers took pity on him, producing eggs and even butter, whilst the greengrocer delved into the back of his shop and handed me a bag with two oranges and a banana in it! We had not seen either of these for *years*. Jake lived on whalemeat, tripe and scraps generally; nothing left over for the seagulls! The smell of the whalemeat cooking was extremely pungent – only to be contemplated in harbour.

Sailing through the Solent was a joy, in sheltered calm waters, with so much to look at, from tiny sailing dinghies to smart schooners, and even the excitement of a large liner serenely making her way to Southampton. We all got heartily tired of Michael's 'See boat!' Having land on both sides made it seem safe, and I had never seen the Isle of Wight before. As we sailed past Cowes, we saw the *crème de la crème* of the yachting fraternity snugly at anchor in rows. The wind was light and we dawdled, taking advantage of the fine weather, deliberately ignoring the long way still to go.

James had decided to tie up in Old Portsmouth harbour that evening. Once again we had a berth alongside another boat, but this was a very different type of port. Huge cranes rumbled alongside, coaling ships on the opposite side, while a goods train shunted and clattered. Michael was overjoyed – adding train and crane to his one sentence, which came out as 'See t'ane, see c'ane'. The letter 'R' eluded him.

The next day, we lollopped along in a gusting south-westerly, rolling like some extinct sea-cow, helped by the tide. By now I knew we would hardly hold our own, once the tide turned, in this choppy sea. Jake had started out in his nest in the lifebelt on deck, but decided to join the sleeping boy in the warmth of the cabin, making it impossible to walk to and fro, except by stepping over them. I lay down on one of the settees, cuddling into Paul's sleeping bag, dozing fitfully, hoping the Kwells would take effect. How I envied the ease with which the men were able to relieve themselves over the side, whereas Michael still had to use a potty of course, and I had to struggle aft, hardly able to keep upright, only to find I had not yet made the double bunk, having to lash it back before I could squeeze through into the sail locker and loo. Each minor movement involved a vast physical effort.

By now we were a long way from land, in a tossing grey world. I dipped my bucket on its line over the side for water to peel the potatoes, which Paul immediately volunteered to do for me, and I took a turn at the wheel, wondering when we would go about. James sat smoking his pipe, content-ment oozing from every pore, as he gazed at the bellying mainsail, pulling us reluctantly through the hostile Channel, 'The wind's decreasing. Damn!' he informed us. I could not share his displeasure, but felt better, and asked where we might be putting in that night. 'Let's look at the chart again. We may have to change our plans with this wind.'

Down in the cabin, tripping over the sleeping pair, we sat at the table, with a flap up, working out positions with the slide rule, resulting in a decision to try and reach Littlehampton. Not many harbours along the Sussex coast are easy to sail into, and we might have a long haul over the next few days. His voice and eyes were tender as he warned me, 'Darling – it will be hard for you, but after tonight we may have to sail for two or three days without putting in anywhere – but we're making such good progress, and it's so wonderful to be in our own home.' He put his arm round my shoulders, holding me close, instilling such confidence, warmth and love that I would gladly have circumnavigated the globe – at that stage.

Soon the tide turned, and though we went about, our progress became sluggish. I hoped and prayed we would reach the haven of Littlehampton before dark, though the navigation lights were filled and ready in case we should need them. Living on board and at sea is a total commitment, mentally and physically, leaving no room for philosophizing or time for reading. One is literally submerged by the will of the waves, sky and clouds; forming one's whole world. Thoughts come in snatches, unreal, like a mistily remembered dream. Parts of books that I had read about the sea and sailing, from Captain Slocum to Smith and Violet's *The Wind calls the Tune*, as well as *Isabel and the Sea* by my all-time favourite author, George Millar, were unrelated to my own experience. Their accounts breathed adventure, romance, exhilarating and exciting experiences, whereas my day-to-day drudgery of seasickness, appalling cooking and washing facilities, coupled with dingy, cramped conditions were hardly inspiring. Whenever I was frightened I prayed, then felt guilty at doing so purely to ask for protection. At the time, nothing as coherent even as these random sentences formed itself in my mind.

Being with the person I loved and admired past any description or definition sufficed: the wish to be part of the life he loved helped to deaden the concern growing in me, that I was inadequate in not being able to share his wholehearted enjoyment of it. At that stage, all these feelings were subconscious. All one was aware of was a sense of foreboding if the sky was grey, or the clouds and wind tore menacingly at the sails and rigging.

That evening though, all was calm, too calm: the sails were lowered, the engine started and, as a treat, Michael was allowed to sit on the cabin top, while I held his reins, as we motored into Littlehampton.

Later that evening, James called me into the cabin after studying the Medway in detail, above Rochester, where it wound its sluggish way through the country, 'Look – there's a perfect spot, just near the village of Aylesford – we couldn't go any further anyway, as there seems to be a bridge, and I don't think the mast will unstep.'

I was delighted, already imagining a settled home life, 'Darling, it sounds fine, but won't it mean an awfully long drive for you to get to Sheerness each day?' It would entail at least an hour's drive, with a very early start, but to be together every evening was reward enough.

Next morning I slipped ashore early to buy two day's supply of milk and bread, plus some home-made pies the

baker had just made for his 'regular customers'. It was a lovely morning; James told me on my return that the weather
forecast had been good, and the barometer was steady. The
old battery wireless, held in place on a shelf by curtain
stretch wire, was not very loud or clear, but we only turned
it on for the 6 a.m. and 6 p.m. forecasts.

By now I longed to wash my hair, some clothes and the
sheets on the bunk needed changing. 'Housework' had been
badly neglected. I never felt well enough to do it at sea, but
there was no time in harbour, so it all looked untidy – even
smelling unpleasant, due no doubt to spillages in the galley
adding to the distinctive whiff of bilge, which hardly ever
needed pumping out.

We took a long leg out, and while it was warm, sat on
deck, lazily talking, even singing the odd sea shanty – such
as, *Farewell and adieu to you fair Spanish ladies*, and *In the
hills of West Virginia*, which Paul had never heard before.
Pat tossed, splashed and gurgled her way through the not
unfriendly waves and ever-present Channel swell. Up on
deck I felt fine. Below I felt sick.

HILLS OF WEST VIRGINIA

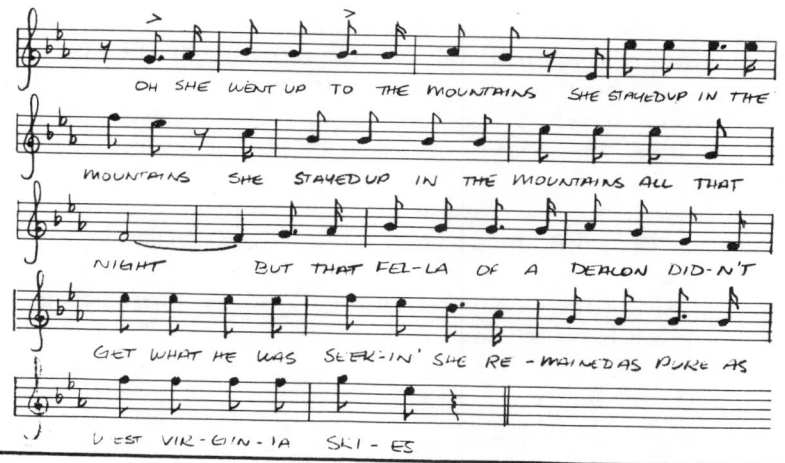

OH SHE WENT UP TO THE MOUNTAINS SHE STAYED UP IN THE MOUNTAINS SHE STAYED UP IN THE MOUNTAINS ALL THAT NIGHT BUT THAT FEL-LA OF A DEACON DID-N'T GET WHAT HE WAS SEEK-IN' SHE RE-MAINED AS PURE AS WEST VIR-GIN-IA SKI-ES

Then there came a rovin' cowboy full of laughter and of song,
He took her to the mountains, but she still knew right from wrong.
And she came down from the mountains,
She came down mighty wise,
Yes she came down from the mountains mighty wise,
She remained as I have stated, uncontaminated,
She remained as pure as West Virginia skies.

Then along came Bill the Trapper with his accents sweet and low,
He took her to the mountains, but she still knew yes from no.
And she came down from the mountains,
Yes she came down from the mountains mighty wise,
But despite the trapper's urgin'
She remained a local virgin,
She remained as pure as West Virginia skies.

But there came a city slicker with his roll of dollar bills,
He put her in his Packard and they drove up to those hills.
And she stayed up in the mountains,
Yes she stayed up in the mountains,
She stayed up in the mountains all that night.
Came down in the morning early
More a woman than a girlie
And her mother kicked the hussy out of sight.

Now she's wining and she's dining and she's on a couch reclining
And those West Virginia hills can go to hell.

But there came a big depression hit that slicker in the pants,
He lost his brand new Packard and he lost his little Nance.
And she went back to the mountains,
Yes she went back to the mountains,
She went back to the mountains as of yore,
And that fella' of a Deacon, now can get what he was seekin'
For she's nothing but a West Virginia whore.

We stood well out, dimly able to recognize Beachy Head,
then sailing quite close to the Royal Sovereign Light Vessel,
whose crew gave us a cheery wave. The tide turned,
resulting in the familiar sensation of sailing backwards.
There is nothing more frustrating than watching the

coastline appear to advance, while though ploughing through the water, one is inexorably borne backwards on the tide. The Seven Sisters mocked us for hours.

As dusk started to fall, out of sight of land, an eerie feeling crept over me. The noises which in the daytime were cheerful, familiar sounds, became menacing, even threatening. The wind seemed to increase, whistling, crying through the rigging; the sea appeared vast, all encompassing, as though the land had been swallowed up. *Pat* was lonely and vulnerable. Then the strange phenomenon of phosphorescence changed the mood. As the waves hit the hull, and the bows plunged, the foam of the crests shone and glowed in an unearthly ethereal fashion – quite beautiful.

The men took two-hour spells at the wheel, lying down, when off watch, on the bunk nearest to the entrance to the well in case of emergency. The Kwells made me sleepy, overriding my sense of guilt at not doing my share. Getting up at dawn at sea is usually a nasty experience, however Paul brought me a mug of tea as an encouragement, suggesting that I drink it up on deck, taking the 6 a.m. to 8 a.m. watch as all was quiet.

The world was entirely grey – no sight or sign that England had ever existed. I was horrified and asked, 'Where are we?' James looked so sleepy and I felt such an aching and tender love for his endless careful seamanship, 'Oh darling – I didn't mean to sound grumpy – sorry to do nothing but sleep and be sick. I think I feel better today though.' He smiled, 'You're getting another pair of sea-legs!' It struck me as so unfair that hardly *any* dogs or cats are sea-sick, yet the vast majority of human beings are.

We hoped to reach Dover that evening, but the wind was all over the place, making our progress slow and wallowing. We took a tack in towards the shore, on order to take a compass bearing and find out exactly where we were, and by midday we rounded Dungeness; then the tide turned, leaving us rolling horribly, without enough breeze to fill the sails and steady us. The mainsail block crashed to and fro on the steel horse, the sails flapped and cracked taut again, the rigging banged against the mast. Moving about was a major effort, and Michael had to stay in his bunk, content to suck his thumb and doze. Jake sniffed the salt air, managing to convey a hunching of shoulders and rolling of eyes heavenwards.

Dover was out of the question for that night. *But*, I hardly felt sick at all, proving fairly conclusively that if I stayed continuously at sea I could conquer it. Eventually, the wind veered and increased, compelling us to go about and stand out to sea,

allowing us searoom in the dark, whilst we waited, safely, for the welcome dawn heralding another turn of the tide.

It was strange to see a familiar port, recognizing the vast stone walls like arms stretching into the sea. The wrecks in the entrance had still not been cleared away entirely, but our draught being so shallow, we sailed in over them, seemingly flying over the water, close-hauled on the port tack. Thanks to our honeymoon visit, James knew where to go, carefully choosing a berth near stone steps, making it easier for some of us to go ashore. Jake was beside himself, jumping all over the deck, barking joyfully, while Michael pointed out the boons of civilization, 'See c'ane. See t'ane. See boats.'

The Goodwin Sands lay ahead, which had given us so much trouble in 1946, but James decided we could risk sailing between them and the land, providing no unexpected gale blew. Michael enjoyed his bath enormously after two days without one, and I read to him for a long time, to make up for the sea-going bedtimes. How I longed for a bath myself, having to make do with a sketchy affair in the little tub, while the men stayed on deck, as there was no door between the galley and the cabin.

Next morning the sun shone, and with no need to sail at the crack of dawn, all below was shipshape before casting off and the water tank had been duly replenished. Ramsgate was our next port, so we had not got far to go, and the fearsome waters of the Goodwin Channel seemed very different from our previous experience of it. I thought we would make it in record speed, but for some hours, as usual, we merely held our own.

We looked forward to sailing *Pat* back into Ramsgate where we had first seen her, and proving to ourselves that occasionally a dream can come true. Paul listened patiently while we explained for the umpteenth time what a state she had been in then, how difficult to sail, how abandoned. A slight southwesterly breeze blew fitfully, pushing us along in uncomfortable jerks, slowly creeping ever closer, finally sailing triumphantly into the harbour.

It would have been nice to spend some time in the familiar and friendly port, but our fortnight was nearly up and naval leave does not allow one to be overdue, so the shopping trips to restock were done in a hurry.

A mere breath of wind next morning helped us to ghost our way out using a limp mainsail and the boathook, until we caught a light, fine-weather southerly, once we had cleared the harbour entrance. It was still dark and the North Foreland Lighthouse winked and beamed its blinding light,

as with both following wind and tide we rushed past at 'the rate of knots'. Once round Foreness Point we were on the home stretch of our journey and virtually on the outskirts or the mouth of the Thames. We sailed close-hauled, near enough to see the coast clearly, while the sun rose on our beam, warming and beautiful.

The entrancing sight of a Thames barge majestically overtaking us was a true excitement. The traditional 'man and boy' waved in response to our enthusiastic greeting, though their dog and Jake maintained a dignified silence. They were low in the water, weighted down by their cargo of grain, or coal, seeming to slip along effortlessly without rolling or pitching due to their heavy stabilizing load.

Paul helped me to clean out the little cabins, bringing the sleeping bags up on deck to air, then trimming and filling the lamps. James disapproved of the boat being turned into an airing cupboard or clothes horse, but we promised to clear it all away before reaching Whitstable. I longed, with all the normal instincts of a housewife, to put down roots, even if only temporary, at some mooring near a village where I would be within walking distance of shops, a telephone, a doctor, daily water for the tank, milk, bread and all the other commonplace essentials one takes for granted, until deprived of them. How lucky we had been over the fortnight's sailing not to have needed a doctor urgently. We must all have been daydreaming, when James's clear and steady voice called out, 'Ready about, lee-o!' Whitstable was only a stone's throw away, at the end of our shortest day's sailing time. Hastily we threw the aired and sweeter-smelling sleeping bags down the hatch, waking up a disgruntled two-year-old and a delighted dog.

Whitstable is a beautiful and excellent harbour, which appeared to be full of Thames barges, so we decided to anchor. Surrounding us lay the picturesque old part of the town, while colourful fishing boats lay alongside the barges with their huge tanned sails, black sides and long fluttering burgees, transforming the scene into a Dutch seascape.

Jake looked puzzled, as up till now he had been able to clamber ashore somehow. Michael held on to him as we furled the sails, tidied up and unlashed the canvas dinghy. James rowed Michael, Jake and me ashore, leaving Paul to make sure all was secure and that we were not drifting or dragging anchor, before returning for him. This was real civilization, being able to shop before closing time, though with Jake on the lead pulling in one direction and Michael dawdling in true and maddening toddler fashion, I found a

third arm sadly lacking for a basket. When we returned, with fresh fish for supper, plus essentials, and a highly-prized little wooden boat for Michael, the dinghy was waiting, tied up, with no sign of the men – busy dealing with water and the ship's chandler. We sat on the jetty admiring our dumpy tub. *Pat* looked just like a duck among swans.

When Michael had seen the toy boat in a shop window, he had pointed at it firmly saying, 'I want boat – like Daddy,' or words to that effect. He had been so good on the trip, playing contentedly all day, sleeping soundly all night and hardly ever crying, I could not resist buying it for him. I fished round in my pockets for some string to tie to the bows of the tiny squat open boat with its diminutive sail, cautiously climbing down the steps to be nearer the water lapping against the stone. The expression on his face was utter happiness as I held his reins and he clutched the string tightly, tightly in an agony of fear that he might lose it. I let go of Jake's lead; he soon got bored with sitting still and gingerly went down the steps into the water. He had never been swimming properly, but the sight of the little yellow boat bobbing on the end of the string was too much of a temptation for his latent retrieving instincts, and the next minute he was dog- paddling round in circles frantically. I was worried that the tide might pull him away, but it must have been slack water. Michael shouted in fury as Jake made a lunge at his precious boat, and I yelled 'Din-Dins' at the top of my voice in order to get him back out of the water. By this time we had attracted quite a crowd, who duly admired the dog and the boat,but we were joined by an embarrassed captain and crew who briskly rowed us back on board. Sailing the yellow tub in the basin was not so much fun. The boat and Michael took it in turns; a lot more water was added to the bilge that evening.

Despite the excitement of reaching our destination, it was mixed with the sadness of an end-of-leave feeling. We would probably never see Paul again, and James would resume his 7 a.m. start in the morning, returning late in the evening, interspersed with frequent duty nights when he would have to stay on board his ship. His new ship was HMS *Berryhead*, off Sheerness on the northernmost top of the Isle of Sheppey.

A grey and sunless dawn next day, with a hint of East in the southerly wind that had been kindly pushing us along, was perfect for the final burst. We had to time our arrival at Aylesford, up the Medway, absolutely accurately, to coincide with high tide, otherwise, despite our shallow

three-foot draught, we would not be able to sit on the blocks by the bank. By sitting on these, at low tide, we could scrape and paint the bottom.

Pat sailed past the Isle of Sheppey on a long leg out from Whitstable, passing quite close to *Berryhead*, and though we waved and shouted we were too far away for anyone to hear us. It had been cold in the morning with no sun, and navigation was tricky with so many boats about, consisting of fishing smacks, barges, ferries and cargo boats, all part of the busy traffic at the mouth of the Thames. The passage between Sheerness and the Isle of Grain was about a mile and a half across, with flukey tides and winds, necessitating constant tacking; but the estuary was beautiful for a few miles, dotted with various islands and, of course, peacefully calm! Cooking lunch was easy by comparison with the previous fortnight.

On the southern bank of the Medway, the densely populated towns of Gillingham and Chatham hove into view, with factories, wharves and smoking chimneys. Michael was entranced at all the excitement of a constant stream of things to watch, in stark contrast to James who missed the peace and safety of the open sea. The channel was now too narrow to allow us to go about, so we had to lower the mainsail. After a few nerve-wracking moments, the engine spluttered into life, enabling us to motor up the twisting, winding river. The busy city of Rochester would soon appear, and though James knew the height of the clearance under the bridge, he could not remember at what state of the tide it was measured. Our mainmast was roughly thirty-five feet; it seemed reasonably safe to assume all would be well.

We were going upstream on a rising tide, and suddenly, round one of the sweeping turns of the river, Rochester bridge appeared. There are in fact, two bridges – road and railway. Ships and barges lay moored alongside wharves and jetties, the river narrowed, the tide quickened and we stared aghast at the inexorability of our route. Surely, we would never scrape through under them – they looked so low, so wide! We could not stop, so with our hearts in our mouths, we steered *Pat* towards the very centre of the first bridge. To have come so far and find we could not navigate past it was unthinkable, but it seemed to get lower as we approached. The mast soared upward and skyward, tall and proud. Quickly I put Michael and Jake in the cabin, in case the mast came crashing down, devastating them and the boat. Next moment, we were under it, and surely there could only have been inches to spare! The road bridge,

which came second, seemed even lower. The tension was unbearable and we hardly dared to breathe, despite the endless moments. As we crept out on the other side, I looked at James and Paul. Like me, they were crouched on the deck of the well, as if by so doing we were reducing the height of the mast! It took a second or two to recover from our fright at what had been a very close thing; then we grinned shamefacedly at each other as we stood up, finally bursting out laughing.

After the bridges the river narrowed considerably, becoming muddy-coloured, sluggishly flowing upstream with the rising tide, between grey banks which varied in height, but prevented us from seeing much of the countryside. This was a new experience after the hills and varied landscape of Dorset, resulting in a strangely claustrophobic feeling, tinged with unease. Had we come all this long way merely to find the eagerly awaited river and its banks hostile? Obviously one conjures up a mental picture of what one hopes to see; I had envisaged a clear, flowing river where grass and trees came down to the edge, their branches dipping into the water.

Aylesford was only a few miles up river – two or three at the most. Then *Pat* would not be able to go any further as a very low bridge crossed it at that point. Our excitement of the morning evaporated, we fell silent, unable to put into words our depression. James was worried about the state of the tide, it being nearly slack water. Another bend in the ever-narrowing river showed us Aylesford bridge, only just clearing the water. One building on the left was all that indicated the village. James knew the underwater blocks lay on the right-hand side and gently nudged the bows over to starboard, whilst Paul, up for'ard sounded the depth with the boathook. His face was ashen as he touched the first block, calling out, 'James, there's only three feet over this block!' At the same moment our bows gently grounded on it halting us abruptly. Shocked, we stared in dismay at the bank so tantalizingly near. James reacted instantly – ordering us all aft in order to reduce the weight in the bows. Meanwhile, he unlashed the dinghy with phenomenal speed, leaped into it, taking a line and rowing with all his strength towards the middle of the stream, vainly trying to pull us off, whilst Paul jumped over the bows onto the blocks, with the boathook, pushing and shoving with all his might to try and free us. I did not want Michael to be frightened, and tried to make light of our plight, while Jake tore up and down, barking with excitement, seeing how close to land we were!

We were stuck fast, pinioned by one small spot a foot or so below the water line on our starboard bow. Imperceptibly, the period of slack water ended, and inexorably the tide started to ebb. Within an hour the boat, held fast by the bows, would inevitably start to heel over and eventually, at dead low water, might break her back. We could no longer stay on board. Exhausted by his vain efforts to pull us off in the dinghy, James nevertheless rowed swiftly back to the boat in order to row Michael and me ashore, only a few feet away. He was utterly heartbroken as he held my hands for an instant, tightly, murmuring; 'My darling – what have I done to you both – our home. . . .' Then, recovering his usual composure, 'It's much safer at sea – never did like the land!' I had grabbed an eiderdown from Michael's bunk, as it was now late afternoon, nearly his bedtime, and the evenings were still chilly. Jake came with us, to reassure Michael that we were merely giving him a walk, making the landing on the bank a splashing and muddy affair, as the sides were steep. Tears were not far away, making me blink and swallow hard. James and Paul quickly lashed down what they could on deck to prevent things floating away, before joining us on the bank, where we sat huddled close together, shaken to the depths of our being, unable to speak. Jake tore off on his own ploys, returning often to nudge us with his cold nose, and give us a comforting lick.

Pat was not just a boat, she was our home, our world, and had brought us safely all those hundreds of miles, which made us feel akin to murderers, as she lay there like a stranded whale. I visualized the huge gap torn in the bows at the point which would bear all the weight of the boat as the tide fell, then the grey, slimy, muddy water rushing in through the hole as the tide rose again in the early morning. Everything would be ruined. Despair and misery overwhelmed me, and I sobbed quietly, too tired to try and restrain myself. James put his arm round my shoulder, 'Darling, don't cry – please – she's a stout old tub, and we'll save her somehow.' Mesmerized, we stared at her, as in some slow-motion film, she started to list to port. Not knowing how deep the channel was, we could not tell whether she would turn right over before the ebb ceased. James muttered, 'Perhaps it is too long after the spring tides, which would explain why there wasn't the depth of water over the blocks I had expected.'

Just then, the first of the crashes on board could be heard loud and clear as those objects below, not very securely lashed, became dislodged and fell. As the masts listed over in

a painfully slow arc we wondered whether the shrouds and stays could possibly bear their weight, or whether they might both snap off, flush with the deck. We dare not voice these gloomy thoughts aloud. We listened in a tense agonising silence, as saucepans, plates, tins and anchor cable hurtled to the deck in a sad death knell. The awful realization that there was nothing more we could do for her appalled us.

Dusk fell, heralding a dark, moonless night, hiding *Pat* in her undignified and humiliating situation. Still we waited close by, unwilling to abandon her in such a sorry state, for to us she was a living creature. Michael had snuggled up in the eiderdown and was fast asleep, Jake having joined him. Finally, an hour or so later, when darkness was total and we could not even see her, James said, 'She must be over as far as she's going now, can you bear it, I'm going to shine the torch?' From where we sat the masts were hidden; only the keel or bottom faced us, as she hung drunkenly from the bows. Still the shrouds held firm. Now we could clearly see the widely spaced, massive blocks. He went on, 'Paul, you stay here with them while I see if that house can put us up for the night.' Paul was as appalled and shaken as James, but tried to comfort me, promising to stay and do what he could next day. This reminded me that James's leave was up and he was due to report back to HMS *Berryhead* the following morning. Soon James was back with the reassuring news that the house was in fact an inn, where we could stay, and our bedraggled little convoy stumbled over the bridge, James carrying the sleeping boy.

Before falling on the bed fully clad, James shone his torch across the river; we were now opposite the 'disaster area', revealing the entire cabin top and deck, with the masts pointing towards us. He was near to tears, and it was my turn to try and comfort him. My brain was not functioning very well but I did my best, 'Darling. It was no one's fault. Paul will stay, and we'll ring up a boatyard tomorrow – because your leave is up isn't it?' He answered ruefully, 'I think the Navy will understand that going aground might be accepted as a reason for an extra day's leave.'

The kind owners of the inn, feeling so sorry for us, made us hot drinks, and found some scraps for Jake, after which we went to bed fully clad, thankful not to be sitting on the bank. We slept fitfully, haunted by the living nightmare of the previous evening. I awoke at the first grey gleam of dawn to see James standing at the window, rubbing his eyes disbelievingly. 'Toni,' he whispered; so as not to wake the boy,

'Look – it's a miracle. *Pat* is still afloat! She's rising with the tide. But goodness knows what will happen when the water reaches the hole in the bows – which must surely be at the point where its caught on the blocks.' He paused, thinking rapidly, 'I must go over there now, take up the floor boards and try and plug the hole somehow, till we can get to a boatyard.' He went next door to wake Paul; he too was staring out of the window with the same look of amazement. Together they tore across the bridge, scrambling down the bank onto the blocks which were still exposed, in order to examine the damage. Incredible as it may seem, the bows were not even stove in – merely dented. The hull being of double teak, criss-crossing timbers, was immensely strong and had withstood the entire weight of the lifeboat, only splintering slightly at the precise point of contact. The tide continued to rise, but not a drop of water entered the hull! Back came the two men, overjoyed as they had been dejected the previous evening.

After the initial relief, came my next thought – what sort of a mess would we find below? The innkeeper collected a friend to help shove us off, as we all hoped that this tide might be a few inches higher. As we left, his wife gave me a loaf, some eggs, and a bottle of milk, surmising quite rightly that what had been left on board would probably be swilling about in the bilges by now.

Once more, James took a rope out in the dinghy and heaved with all his might, whilst Paul and two local men rolled up their trousers, gingerly making their way along the offending blocks, ready to shove really hard. *Pat* was lighter of course, without the four of us aboard, and casually slipped off the block which had held her prisoner. One of the men held a mooring rope to steady her, as we climbed into the dinghy and quickly transferred to the boat.

Paul came down below with me to give me moral support while we surveyed the damage. It was in the galley that the mess was at its worst. After all, in a boat, everything is pretty well lashed down, ready for rough weather. Vegetables had tipped out of their boxes and were mixed up with the anchor chain, which was spilled out of its coil right up in the bows. Mugs and plates, of the unbreakable variety, lay jumbled up with tea, saucepans and sugar in a tangled mêlée. Depressing, yes; but one small and astonishing fact took our minds momentarily off the chaos. One bottle of milk had transferred itself from a shelf over the galley door, to another shelf above the basin on the port side, without breaking – and with its top still on! We were ravenous, reeling under enough emotions to fill a lifetime, let alone twenty-four hours.

The tide would soon turn and we were to be on our way with the ebb back down the Medway to Rochester where we would get the splintered timbers expertly scarved and mended at a boatyard. Holding our breath we watched while James swung the crank handle to start the engine. Another small miracle – it started. As we left, the innkeeper called out the name of the best yard he knew, lying above the bridges.

Michael and the dog took it all in their stride – but I knew that without Paul I would have been in tears. My respect and fondness for him grew and were very deep. I think he felt the same.

CHAPTER FIVE
Return to France

We found the boatyard downstream without difficulty and the foreman examined the boat, amazed at our lucky escape, and agreed to put us on their blocks straight away in order to look at and assess the damage. It was still early in the morning. James telephoned his ship, assuring them that he would be there later that day. Paul, our 'hero', firmly stated he would stay and look after Michael and me until such time as we were whole, mended and ready to seek another berth. I hugged him in deep gratitude. Living on board would be difficult while *Pat* was in dry dock, as obviously no water could be used; however, the workmen in the boatyard offered us their washroom.

James was enormously relieved. He kissed Michael and me goodbye promising to find *Pat* a safer resting place the following weekend.

The next few days were chaotic and disorganised with three of us living on board whilst *Pat* rested on the blocks of the dry dock. It took the boatyard a little time to procure the seasoned teak for such a job, but they took an immense amount of care and trouble over it, being full of admiration for the 'old lady' as they called her. They were a friendly crowd, allowing Michael to play with bits of wood and shavings while I kept an eye on him, popping up on deck every few minutes, while at the same time sorting out the jumble of tins and clothing in lockers under the settees. Paul did the shopping and often took Michael, pushing him in the pushchair, not in the least embarassed by this which was unusual for his age, and I was deeply touched, becoming extremely fond of him.

James telephoned the boatyard office after a few days with the wonderful news that he had heard of a creek called Otterham, much nearer to Sheerness; he was going to inspect

it that weekend, after he had been down to Bridport to see his parents and collect the little Austin 7.

As soon as the job was completed and the new timbers treated and painted, the yard slid us back down into the water where we lay alongside a pontoon. It had been dark in the vast shed, and it was a real joy to be out in the open and afloat again. Now we concentrated on renewing any worn bits of gear on deck, greasing rigging screws, and checking the wire luffs of the foresail. The weather was warm with the sweet scent of May, slowly freshening and drying out our damp, musty-smelling cabins. Another message reached us from the office to say that James would be back at the weekend just before the end of the month to sail us to our new berth. The joy at the thought of seeing him again after nearly three weeks wiped out the muddle and discomfort of our time in the boatyard. *Pat* was whole again, stronger than ever, longing to be at sea, even if I was *not*!

This time, we waited for dead low water before slipping away under the dreaded bridges. We had not far to sail, and as we did not wish to reach Otterham Creek until high water, we hoisted the mainsail and sailed the long way round, north of the little island of Bishop's Marsh. James told us about *Pat's* new berth, where the creek was fairly narrow, therefore sheltered, just past Rainham Quay, where, at high tide Thames barges loaded up the bricks from the kilns nearby. She would lie on the mud for about half the time, as the creek, and indeed most of the Medway estuary, dries out except for a narrow channel.

This was all lovely open countryside, flat but green and unspoilt, so very different from the tortuous river. We were soon at the entrance to the creek, passing Thames barges slowly and majestically waiting for the tide, like us. Cautiously, we motored up it, having lowered the mainsail, and were carried by the flood tide until we reached a perfect spot by the bank right at the head of the creek, where there was, in fact, a tiny boatyard. At high tide we lay level with the bank and tied up to a few old mooring posts stuck in the ground along the edge. Our journey was over – we had reached our haven.

Over on the other side of the creek lay a motor torpedo boat (MTB) converted into a houseboat with a young couple living on board who came round to help us tie up. Anxiously we waited for the tide to ebb in order to see how comfortably we would sit on our mud bed. Being May, they were neap tides with no very great rise and fall, so that for at least four

hours twice a day we would sit thus, and it was important to sit as flat and upright as possible. As we drank our mugs of tea, I suddenly realized how still it was, with no gentle rocking; dashing up on deck I saw the vast expanses of mud which a fast receding tide left beind. Quietly and gently as a duck or hen sitting on a clutch of eggs, *Pat* nestled into her mud berth. This was perfection beyond our ·wildest hopes after the disaster of a month ago. We adjusted our mooring ropes fore and aft ensuring that we would always settle into that self-same spot, which also entailed a line across the creek to prevent us being blown too close into the bank if a north or northeasterly gale blew.

Next morning they went off together very early, James to his ship, and Paul to catch a train. As I kissed Paul goodbye, and tried to thank him again for all he had done for us, I felt tears in my eyes; I had not appreciated how fond of him I had grown. He too was moved, having become one of the family, but an exciting life lay ahead of him and no doubt we would soon be forgotten.

There was so much to see to, the most important being a gangplank, as neither Michael nor I could get ashore except at high tide, so, on his way to the station, James visited the little boatyard, a mere hundred yards from us, to ask if they could rig one up. I was busily brushing the cabin when Michael called importantly, 'Man Coming,' heralding the arrival of a splendid gangplank, with little slats of wood across it at intervals to prevent us slipping. The men also provided us with a hose long enough to reach the tap in the yard, which meant I could fill the tank every day, an undreamt of luxury.

The initial crossing on the gangplank was a nerve-wracking experience on my own, as neither Michael nor Jake trusted it, nor did I feel very confident as I had no head for heights. One of the urgent summer evening jobs was for James to fix stanchions at each end with a length of rope stretched between, giving the illusion of safety, though fatal if leant on! The land beside us was flat, common land, with bracken and brambles, and a footpath meandering on down towards the end of the creek, making it ideally safe for dogs or taking Michael for walks in the afternoon. Up past the head of the creek was a minor road where a solitary shop provided all we needed in the way of groceries. I registered our ration books with them; the total sum for a week's rations for three being 10 shillings (50p)! This included sugar, butter, tea and bacon; as far as I can recall, all still rationed.

Such small amounts were measured in ounces.

Being at sea for so long with special concessions in the ship's chandlers I had forgotten how restricted the diet was, with only one egg per person a week. Milk also was rationed, but a child was allowed a whole pint a day and the milkman actually called at the boat, leaving it on the shore.

About once a week I would retrieve the pushchair from the stern, put Jake on the lead and walk the mile or so to catch the Rainham bus on the main road. Michael loved the bus, not having been on one before, but it was a hazardous performance, folding recalcitrant pushchairs, disentangling an enthusiastic dog who wrapped his lead round everything, and usually ending up with me dropping a brimming basket. It was much easier to go in on a Saturday morning with James in the Austin 7, unless he had too much work to do on board, or alternatively, weather permitting, we would sail out into the estuary.

To me this peaceful interlude was the zenith of contentment, an unhoped-for happiness, where at long last, problems, separations, illnesses were over and I had James to myself. We knew no one in that area, nor did I particularly wish to; his ship was too far away for us to go to any official guest night when wives might be invited, in any case there was no one to leave Michael with. Entertaining anyone on board, except for sailing, was out of the question, as with only two gas rings on the cooker, and a biscuit tin for an oven, which perched on top of the flames, 'cunning cookery' remained a culinary dream! James did not talk much about his fellow officers, apparently content to tend *Pat*, renewing gear where needed, painting the cabin top, caulking the deck, or smoking his pipe in the well, trying to ignore Jake's frenzied demands for yet another walk. It was amazing how quickly he forgot his twice daily walks with Michael and me! Meanwhile Michael played with his cars on the cabin top, whose sloping area provided just the right angle for them to run down. He also built Emmett-like barges with his bricks below. Supremely selfish, I assumed James to be as happy as I was, living in a spiritual paradise; having forgotten my inadequacies during the long and tiring journey when seasickness made me useless.

He was quiet, and any conversation centred on the boat – the next sailing weekend, or speculation as to where we might go next. No political or serious discussions developed between us, which I presumed was because we shared the same views on anything of importance, and we never – or

hardly ever – talked about our respective wars. I was not perceptive enough to realize how boring it must have been for him that I *had* no conversation; remaining unaware of this, so absorbed was I in my overwhelming adoration, my possessive and jealous love of him, living each day for the dear familiar sound of the little Austin 7, and Michael's call of 'Daddy's car!' He, too, was happy to be back on board; we would kiss, we were very much in love, and our lovemaking in the double bunk was sweet and rapturous.

The boat was so small we knew there was no room for another child, and though I took fairly amateur precautions, I soon realized that I was pregnant again. The proud joy of having another baby vied with the dismay of having nowhere, but nowhere to keep it. I went into Rainham to see a doctor who confirmed the fact.

Secretly, I was exultant and, at the back of my mind, barely admitted to myself, crept the idea that here was the excuse – the reason – for moving into a cottage. I prayed it might be so – with just a dinghy for weekend sailing. I decided not to mention living ashore yet to James – the news of the baby would be enough of a shock to assimilate at first. 'I'm going to have another baby – I'm sorry – I know it's not practical, but it can sleep in a carricot on the tin trunk in our cabin to begin with – I'll feed it and Michael will so love to have a . . . .' James stopped the awkward flow, holding me tenderly and hiding any apprehensions he might have over the impossibility of *Pat* with four on board. 'Of course, darling – somehow we'll manage.' He joked, 'We'll get a bigger boat!' I did not take him seriously.

Meanwhile, we continued with our plans for his summer leave. My cousin and godmother wanted us to go and stay with them in Lamorlaye, near Paris, and James intended to sail to Calais, leave *Pat* there for a week or so, then sail home. It sounded perfect and I longed to return to my beloved France, possibly showing James some of Paris.

Once or twice a week James was on duty at night or even for whole weekends, when the little boat seemed very vulnerable despite the fierce guard dog, Jake. Should an emergency arise, in lieu of a telephone, there was the old foghorn with the call of an hysterical donkey, easily waking the couple in the MTB on the other side of the creek. Their craft was moored permanently, therefore wired up for both electricity and the telephone, arousing our contempt, though secretly I envied the ease and speed this would bring to daily chores. Admittedly, we had a little gas light over the basin in

the galley, but the paraffin lamp needed filling every day, not to mention lighting the stove for ironing – a primitive method: the heavy flat-irons being heated on it, then slid into a 'slipper'. I suppressed these thoughts for they seemed disloyal and, anyway, I enjoyed keeping *Pat* neat and trim, polishing the brass binnacle and bell – keeping the cabin immaculate.

All too soon July slipped into August with the usual unsettled weather, making the forecast compulsive listening as we would need to sail on the first day of James's summer leave in order to have the maximum time in France. Poor Jake would have to go to kennels, because of the quarantine laws.

It was around this time that we became increasingly aware of the 'smell', attributing it initially to the bilges, in the heat. Quite soon though, distinct gnawings and scuttling of tiny feet could be heard, quickly identified as mice, for which a mousetrap seemed ineffective as they never put in an appearance. Eventually, from between two boards directly underneath the catwalks, a tiny naked pink body protruded, accompanied by shredded material, denoting a hidden nest. A nest meant chewed up material or paper, sending me frantically searching under the settees where I found to my sorrow that indeed the horrid mice had lined their nest with bits of my one pretty 'trousseau' dress, a strawberry-coloured one, covered in wild fruit and flowers. They had chewed up other things too, but the dress was a great sorrow. Unable to get at them, we resolved to get a cat, for Jake was not interested in mice and his presence did not deter them! I told the sad tale to the kind greengrocer in Rainham, who immediately offered me one of her young cats, a tabby streaked with ginger, 'a great mouser', and we collected her that same Saturday. Tactfully, Jake was introduced to her on neutral ground, that is to say, ashore, where he eagerly sniffed at her and tried to play, but receiving a hard cuff from her paw, was convinced she meant business. We named her Tilly, and she decided the boat was a cat's paradise with unlimited mice. She worked hard, sitting quietly for hours in a corner of the catwalk – suddenly so aptly named.

She was gentle, soft and loving, with a purr like an engine, choosing Michael's bunk as her private sleeping quarters. Jake moved into the saloon. Cat and dog got on extremely well, often curling up together on the settee, but once ashore Jake would exercise his doggy prerogative, chasing her excitedly until she would sit down calmly and start to clean her hindquarters with one leg sticking high up in the air, stating

clearly that she was bored with the game and chase. The greengrocer promised to look after her for the fortnight we would be away, also recommending a kennels for Jake.

Despite my pathetic eagerness to prove that I was a capable and keen sailor and crew, conflicting emotions over the safety of the coming voyage with young Michael caused me to become irritable and argumentative over the merest trifles. James would have infinitely preferred to spend his entire leave afloat, exploring the unknown harbours on the South Coast, so that he was being extremely noble in agreeing to a drastically curtailed sailing spell, followed by a week in Lamorlaye. Somehow the real problem or issue was never put into words, merely causing disharmony that I wilfully pretended did not exist.

Finally, when all preparations were made, we chose our tide, leaving our berth one afternoon with a light east-north-east breeze. Helped by the ebb, we sailed peacefully down the Medway, James only needing me to help with going about. The forecast had been good, but I never trusted it completely, always imagining the wind to be increasing, despite our sedate passage down the river, hardly heeling over at all. It was a different story when we reached Sheerness, where the ebb flow and wind were in conflict causing a nasty cross swell. We had to go about in a hurry; *Pat* heeled over as the sails filled again, resulting in Michael falling down with a bump, and howling his displeasure. I rushed to pick him up and comfort him, with James yelling orders at me, in the time-honoured fashion of all skippers, either to check the mainsheet or let go the jib sheet, neither of which had been done. I yelled back.

It was not an auspicious start, added to which I was already feeling sick, made worse by going below with Michael to settle him on the cabin floor, surrounded with toys and cushions. James dashed from the wheel to do my jobs, and when all was under control again, called me to him, full of remorse for the rare show of temper. He asked, 'Is Michael all right? Darling I'm so sorry – it all happened rather suddenly.' I reassured him, full of so much inexpressible love for him, 'Yes, he's fine – but I feel *awful*!' and suited the words by the action. Anxiously he asked, 'Are you sure this won't harm the baby darling?' The spell of nausea being over for the moment I smiled, 'It's no worse than morning sickness really, except that it goes on all the time. I'll take some Kwells and lie down for a short while to let them take effect.' Why could I never remember to take

them in time! He agreed, 'Yes, you do that. I'll call you if I need you. I'm afraid we'll have to tack fairly frequently till we reach Foreness and the Goodwins.'

I consumed quantities of Kwells during the trip, but the danger had not been assessed in those days. By 10 p.m. my eyes were closing, but I could see the North Foreland light inside the Goodwin Sands, familiar of yore, which meant we could now go about and sail down the coast. As usual, James's naval training enabled him to keep awake all night until at dawn he called to me to take over, his eyes red with tiredness.

The dawn was beautiful, with only a playful, endless sea whispering and gurgling around us encouraging *Pat* to indulge in her elephantine wallowing. Before James went below he had told me with great pride that we were making excellent progress now with the wind on our beam, sailing close-hauled; we would be in Calais some time that same day. How vividly I recalled our gale-ridden, groping, clawing entry into that harbour three years ago, and Paddy drowning.

Soon I could see land – France – my beloved France. Tears of affectionate nostalgia pricked my eyes, immediately making me feel disloyal for loving it so much more than my own country. Slowly we entered the inner harbour and were allocated a quiet corner where we could lie undisturbed for the ten days we would be away. We packed two zipper bags, having dealt with customs and passport officials who had boarded us as soon as we tied up. The harbour had more boats in it now, and was teeming with life, luckily for us, as we were given a lift to the station in one of the customs officer's cars, largely due to Michael, for most people on the Continent feel tender and protective towards small children. Despite feeling tired and dirty, the happiness of hearing French spoken all around me, in the urgent, excited tones denoting instant drama, accompanied by that indefinable smell of Gauloises, scent, heat and garlic, transformed me. Obviously James could not feel the same, nor could he speak French, but Michael, though puzzled, was torn between excitement and fear of the great steam engines that roared and puffed into the station.

I rang my cousin, Diana, to tell her what time we would reach Paris and was moved to hear her voice after five long years, saying that she would meet us. Our meeting was an emotional one, each of us remembering the five long war-shattered years, that subsequently we had both striven to

forget. She had not changed at all. Warmly and affectionately she shook hands with James, swiftly bending down
to kiss Michael on both cheeks. 'You must be exhausted –
and hungry. We'll drive out to Lamorlaye as quickly as
possible – then you can have a bath before supper.' I sat in
the front with her, while the two tired men dozed in the
back, lulled to sleep by our hushed conversation. There was
so much to catch up on for we had written very few letters
over the past years. Her French husband had been killed near
the end of the war, and she was now married to an American,
older than herself, whom she had known for many years. She
said how adorable young Michael was, which delighted me
naturally and I confided that I was expecting another baby in
March. Though pleased for me, her concern was touching, 'But
Toni, how *can* you manage in a boat with two children –
think of all the washing, not to mention the worry about them
falling overboard.' I nodded agreement, 'I know, and I daren't
tell my father and step-mother. They think it crazy enough,
living in a boat – but James so loves sailing – and I so adore
James. . . .' The sentence needed no ending. I went on, 'I want
to forget all that for this one glorious week with you – please
– don't tell anyone.' She understood so well.

Their house in Lamorlaye was only an hour's drive from
Paris, in among the pine trees, along a straight wide avenue,
standing well back in a beautiful garden, glowing with
zinnias and dahlias. Like so many French women, Diana was
lucky to have a *bonne* who lived with them, doing all the
cooking and cleaning in the house, which to me seemed the
epitome of luxury. No one who has been without a proper
bath for months, can appreciate the sheer undiluted pleasure
of sinking into hot water, scented with bath-salts. I lay there,
totally at peace and relaxed, eventually falling asleep.
Meanwhile, Thérése, the *bonne*, and Michael, though unable
to communicate with one another, began a firm friendship
needing no words. He would 'help' her in the kitchen,
something he could never do in the boat, making pastry, or
playing with Diana's dog. Ted, Diana's husband was kind
and gentle, a quiet American who walked round the large
garden holding Michael by the hand, and talking in his
soothing accents.

That first night we could not keep awake, slipping
ecstatically between the cool clean sheets, in a bed with a
proper mattress, falling asleep before our lips had parted in
a goodnight kiss. James did not show how much he missed
his boat, but subconsciously I felt it, trying to make up for it

by loving him deeply. Each day, as the sun, food and wine soaked into our tired bodies and minds, I would live for the night-time when I would lie in his arms, responding with my whole being to his tender lovemaking.

Diana volunteered to look after Michael for us if we wanted to spend a day or two in Paris, which thrilled me as I was longing to show James those places I especially loved. We caught an early train from nearby Chantilly and spent an enchanted day, walking down the Champs-Elysées, and along the Rue de Rivoli. He too was overwhelmed by the beauty of Paris, dusty though she was, and crowded with tourists as it was August. At the Place de la Concorde we crossed over the bridge by the Chambre des Députés and I showed him the bullet scars in the walls, still there in 1949, from the shots fired at Pierre, my fiancé, in 1944, as he raced away from the Germans who had lined him up against a wall to be shot. It all seemed to have happened to another person, in another age, another lifetime.* After lunch in a bistro, we took a metro to Notre Dame, and walked along the cobbled quayside down by the river, as lovers do. He sensed my emotion, unable to share it fully. I was asking, expecting too much – that because he was my husband he should feel and experience all my bitter-sweet joy.

He gazed thoughtfully at the boats and barges moored on the Seine, 'We could have brought *Pat* up the Seine – if we lowered the mast.' Mentally I cringed from the thought of the suffocating, claustrophobic cabin awaiting us. Loving him so completely it did not occur to me how utterly apart and strange to each other we were. Selfishly, there was still one thing I desperately wanted him to do with me. I longed to introduce him to the Demoiselles Duponts in Neuilly – the three spinster sisters where I had lived for a year, from 1941 to 1942. Patiently and sweetly he agreed; once again we dived down into the metro to reach the Porte Maillot. The walk to the Boulevard Jean Mermoz was long, but the beautiful chestnut trees I remembered so well, shaded us, as we limped along, tired and footsore after so much sightseeing.

The three old ladies, Thérèse, Gabrielle and Marie were beside themselves with joy at meeting me again. Their eyes lit up softly, tears gathering, as they kissed me warmly, voices trembling with emotion. After all, I had never even said goodbye to them when I escaped from Paris with false papers in 1942, leaving a pretended elopement note in my bedroom. They clustered around James, shaking his hand,

* Years retold in *Little Resistance*.

congratulating me on having married such a handsome and kind young man. All this in French so as not to embarrass him. 'Vous faites un beau couple!' We sat on the edge of the formal, uncomfy chairs in the *salon*, drinking tiny cups of tea without milk, all talking at once. How wonderful to be able to laugh at those grisly days; to discover that even the pompous fat businessman had in fact been working for the resistance. There in a corner stood the same wireless that I had stealthily listened to, trying to get the BBC, incurring their wrath, because of the penalties if caught. Gabrielle took my hand: 'Viens, je vais te montrer ta chambre.' It was all exactly the same, with the little balcony overlooking the shady garden. She told me they had always thought of it as my room, and had been so worried about me after my clandestine departure, having guessed that my elopement had been fictitious. I kissed them goodbye, aware that I would never see them again, they were so old. The knowledge made me very unhappy. In silence we caught the metro and train back to Chantilly. A spell had been exorcized, but with unforeseen resulting emotions. And now their house has been pulled down. Blocks of flats line the Boulevard Jean Mermoz.

Too soon, the halcyon holiday was over and we had to return to *Pat*. I knew too that it would be many years before Diana and I would meet, so our *adieux* were sad and loving. Indeed, nearly twenty years elapsed before I had a home big enough to ask them to come and stay.

Dear *Pat* lay where we had left her, sedately bobbing on the swell in the harbour, looking pathetically small. James gripped my arm, 'I'm going on board to open up all the hatches and try to get rid of the smell before you come down.' We could smell the rank, dank stink from the quayside. He tried to enourage me, 'Once we get to sea with a good wind blowing it'll blow away.'

James sat on deck smoking his pipe and later I joined him. My heart ached twice over – with the physical pain of my love for him – and with the dread of the boat; also I hated leaving France. I kissed him, unable to express myself. He drew me close, his blue and piercing eyes seeing something of what I thought and felt – tenderly returning my kisses. Then the urgency of the return became important, 'The forecast isn't very good, but we must make a start with the tide – I daren't be late back from leave again this time!' I hardly dared to ask, 'You mean we must sail tonight?' He nodded, 'Don't worry, darling – I'm so beautifully rested

after our lazy holiday – except for when you kept me awake. . . . What I mean is I shall be able to stay on watch all night until the early dawn when I shall wake you – unless I absolutely have to do so sooner.'

He was determined to sail out without the engine, so having let go one of the warps, he hoisted the mainsail which flapped furiously till it filled; a fisherman let go for'ard and slowly *Pat* responded. James called to me, 'Hoist the jib and stand by.' I rushed up for'ard, all fingers and thumbs, unable for a moment to remember which halyard to pull. There was no time to look lingeringly at the quayside, for the brisk breeze, mainly offshore, quickly filled the sails, and I sheeted down the foresail on the tack which would take us out of the harbour and clear.

Once we were on the tack taking us past the Goodwins I went below, feeling as sick as a dog, angry with myself for forgetting, yet again, to take the Kwells. I now knew the hopeless weakness would never be overcome.

On the following morning, pleased with our progress James predicted that we would just make it to Otterham creek, unless the tide turned. As usual, it did, before we could get near enough to the Medway, so we put into Whitstable for the night. From there it was a short and easy sail next day, timing the tide just right, sails lowered, under power. Tired and triumphant we tied up; home again.

There remained one day of James's leave, so we all piled into the Austin 7 to collect Jake, the spaniel, and Tilly. Jake was ecstatic, licking our faces, climbing over the seats, beside himself with excitement; but Tilly remained rather quiet and aloof in her cat box. She looked fatter, much fatter, and it became obvious she was going to have kittens. Despairingly I wondered where she could give birth. I put a little blanket in a cardboard box at the foot of one of the settees in the cabin, but she never settled in it; always on the lookout for mice which had disappeared thanks to her, though still in plentiful supply ashore. Finally, she gave birth simply and comfortably at the foot of Michael's bunk while he was having his afternoon rest, watching with wide-eyed awe and keeping very still. Poor James had to drown all the kittens except one ginger Tom, which was Michael's, whom we called Lt Pinkerton, Pinky for short. We had Tilly spayed and Pinky neutered; however, he was a naughty cat, never becoming fully 'boat-trained'.

As the equinox approached, the spring tides got higher and higher, especially if there was any East in the wind

pushing it up the creek. This was quite fun when the weather was calm and sunny for Michael could paddle on the bank, sailing his boat safely while I watched *our* boat, making sure she did not ride up onto the bank herself, causing a repetition of the Aylesford disaster. When James was on duty and away at night, I would like awake, listening fearfully to the halyards and rigging slapping against the masts as the equinoxial gales got into their stride. At this time, with high tides around midday and midnight, which seemed to be the case at springs, if the wind was from East-North-East *Pat* would jerk against her mooring ropes, as though she were trying to escape, sometimes bumping against the bank, and I would rush up on deck in my nightie, grabbing the torch in order to check the lines fore and aft; the long warp straining across to the other side of the creek, praying that it would not snap. If it did, nothing could prevent us from riding up onto the flooded bank. In the black, wet and howling night, the feeble light of the torch just showed an endless expanse of water, like being at sea. It was frightening and I would hold the boathook ready to shove us off until the tide turned.

Occasionally, we would be blown slightly out of our comfy berth, sitting with a slight list until the next tide. It was funny to watch the small boy, dog and cats all trying to walk and stand upright, but I found it extremely tiring, as I was now more than a little fat and uncomfortable myself. By the time James came home; another tide would have risen and ebbed leaving us upright once more, making the story hard to believe. With the colder weather, we lit the stove, which stayed alight all night, shut down, making it ideal for cooking porridge in a double boiler. We found an old bunker lying rusting away in a dump, brought it back to Otterham and kept out coal in it ashore. *Pat* was snug and cosy in the evening, warmed by the stove, with the soft glow of the paraffin lamp disguising her cramped quarters.

My pregnancy seemed trouble-free this time, and I never went to the doctor; after all I was getting all the exercise I needed, bending double under the catwalk! We decided that Chatham was near enough and duly booked me in to a hospital for the tenth of March. One small problem remained. As James was away all day, and some nights too, someone had to be found who could spend the day on board, and if necessary take Michael home on the nights when his father could not be there. It seemed ridiculous to be fussing about this so many months ahead, but those same months

103

appeared to kaleidoscope into each other at an alarming rate.

Shortly before Christmas, HMS *Berryhead* held a children's party, followed by a drinks party for the mothers who had brought them. This was a tremendous excitement, alarming too for the weather was atrocious, and *Berryhead* had to be approached by the liberty boat. Heavily pregnant as I was, I nearly missed the ladder steps over the side as I jumped across! Michael was speechless with a combination of shyness and joyous bewilderment. He had not seen many children in his short span of two-and-a-half years, not to mention balloons, crackers and the glorious panoply of a naval children's party. For days afterwards, his conversation consisted of something that sounded like; 'Biew biewoons,' which we finally translated as 'Blue balloons'. His idea of complete happiness.

In answer to advertisements in the local paper, a surprised young girl of eighteen, came to see us; under the impression that *Pat* was the not unlikely name of a house. Patricia was a sweet girl, totally unruffled by our strange, unusual home, promising to take Michael and Jake for a walk in the afternoons; willing also to look after them during my short stay in hospital.

James and I discussed the future in the evenings whilst listening to the old wind-up gramophone, playing our few but favourite records, inspiring me as I knitted small shapeless garments, of a pinkish nature. I did want a girl. James said firmly, 'We really must have a bigger boat. I'll start advertising, or answering advertisements.' My own words died unspoken. Secretly, I had hoped that with two children, we might possibly move into a house, keeping a small dinghy for weekend sailing. My supreme hope and wish was that James should go on loving me and be happy. If the only solution to that was a bigger boat – so be it! Would it have made any difference to the eventual outcome! I doubt it.

The winter months began to be stormy, rain-lashed and tempestuous, each evening rent with a cacophony of sounds. James left in the dark at 7 a.m. each morning, returning well after dark too, with no weekend sailing to look forward to. The little old Austin 7, dating from 1937, a brave and valiant car, finally coughed and gasped her last splutter, compelling James to find another second-hand car. He acquired a slightly younger, and much larger one, a Vauxhall, nicknamed the 'Merry Widow', which seemed smooth and luxurious in comparison; though we never got

over the feeling of guilt at having parted with 'William-and-Mary'. It would not surprise me if she was still trundling around, lovingly cared for as a valuable vintage car.

An unprecedented treat was organized by James – a visit to the cinema, while Patricia looked after Michael. Two or three years had passed since either of us had been to a film, and this was a very special one indeed, *The Third Man*. Unfortunately, a northeasterly gale chose to blow on that January day – of all days – making even the snug little cabin cold; Michael and I huddled below, cats on our laps, pretending we were on a raft. Gradually I became aware that *Pat* seemed more lively than usual, and glancing out of the scuttle, saw the bank slipping past. Buffeted by wind and rain, we emerged into the well, to see our boat straining at the leash as she travelled up and down to the limit of the two mooring ropes fore and aft. Quickly I looked for the restraining warp across the creek. It had vanished, snapped in two. One useless end hung over the side; there was nothing I could do, fat and useless as I was, to renew or repair the warp. It was anybody's guess as to where we might eventually sit, for as we charged up and down the bank with nothing to restrain us, *Pat* was blown right up against the side, finally coming to rest, as the tide receded, on the extreme inner edge of her lovely nest – heeling over until her side snuggled into our hollow – at about a 45 degree angle. Jake and the cats merely moved to the opposite settee, but I could barely stagger with the steep angle and shamefully sat down and cried. When James came back there was no question of the long-awaited trip to the cinema, for no one could be expected to stay in the boat under such conditions.

He was genuinely heart-broken, and in fact for the last time, at the discomfort for me. Tears were in his eyes as he comforted me, 'My darling – only an hour or two now, before we are afloat, then I'll get another warp across. . . .' I interrupted, 'But how can you – in the dark?' 'Easy, you can shine the torch this end, and Tom and Jane in the MTB can light me from that side – they'll give me a hand too.'

The enterprise was fraught with difficulties. Rowing the flimsy dinghy in the dark gale-filled night, he managed to retrieve the broken end of the rope, which was drifting on the rising tide, brought it back on board, then set off again to pick up the other end. He untied that half from the post, bringing it on board where he fastened the two lengths together with a sheet bend. Once again, he rowed across

securing it with a bowline round the far post, so that despite the gale we sat upright once more. We did get to see the famous film later that week, with its evocative zither music.

By February, I was hugely pregnant, and this was no daughter, impatiently, thoughtlessly, heaving and kicking around. It had to be another enormous boy. Every chore was an effort and I could only get from one cabin to the other by putting my feet wide apart, then bending from the hips and staggering headlong though the low passageway. I became obsessed with the weather forecast, afraid of a repeat performance, and sitting at an angle on the mud. Starting at 7 a.m. I would leave the wireless on, through *Workers Playtime*, or *Music while you work*, on the alert for any fresh gale warning. These were frequent, but provided they were not from the quarter which had caused the previous damage, I could relax. Soon, though, I was so huge that it became impossible to squat down on the galley floor to give Michael his bath in the tub. All I could do was to fill it with the kettles of hot water, cooled down by jugs of cold, soap his little body and then he would sit down importantly by himself to rinse off, watched by his fat mum, standing in the doorway. Once, and once only, he looked at me and said, 'Mummy fat like Tilly' followed by a hopeful, 'Baby Tillies?' I took the coward's way out, not bothering to explain, following my lazy, naive philosophy that all would become clear in due course. His own games, the stories we read together, filled his mind and imagination. Patricia was ready to help for a fortnight in mid-March, and I hoped fervently that this child would not be a month late like Michael had been, if so, surely one day I might actually stick fast in the beastly passageway.

Early March brought a false spring. Though sailing *Pat* was out of the question, we rigged the dinghy and took her down the creek in the hope of hastening the birth; I even tried my hand at rowing which we felt must be a nice loosening-up exercise. All I really achieved, being unwieldy and ungainly, was a near capsize, provoking ribald comments from James; the baby meanwhile stayed put; warm and snug, presumably loathe to start a sailing career so young.

The Navy had granted some compassionate leave to James over the date of arrival, so that he need not be on duty at night during my time in hospital. Neither of our parents could help. In any case, poor Michael, who did not know any of his grandparents would have been miserable all on his own. There were no tears from him as James drove me off

to Chatham. He kissed me goodbye, promising to be back to see 'us' the following evening. The infant proceeded with undignified haste, arriving in time for lunch on the same day. Certainly the bending exercises must have helped for he was no lightweight at ten pounds. For two seconds I regretted deeply not having a daughter; this was followed by unreasonable pride at producing a second son, how useful too, to be able to use Michael's grown-out-of clothes! I think James was intensely pleased at a second son, and we decided to call him Peter.

I lived for his few visits; sadly he could not get away for long and Patricia went home at 6 p.m. so I saw little of him. Because of living in the boat and the size of the baby I was extremely tired so the hospital kept us there till we were fit and strong. On our last evening, James arrived in a state of quietly controlled excitement and told me, 'We've got the perfect boat – our new home – it's been in the air for the last two weeks, but I didn't want to say anything in case of disappointing you.' I could hardly believe it, 'Darling – what? where? when? Tell me everything, from the beginning.' Just then a proud nurse came in, weighed down by a hungry, vociferous baby, asking if James would like to hold him. How could the poor man refuse, but handing him to me he commented: 'He feels solid enough – what a good thing you can feed him – it'll save a lot of trouble on board. No messy bottles.' He was a hungry businesslike child, soon contentedly sucking, peace and quiet restored.

James told me about the boat, 'She was advertised in *Yachting Monthly*. A Dutch barge, a Boeier....' I interrupted, 'What on earth is that? How big?' 'I'm *telling* you. She's fifty feet long, nice and broad, with leeboards.' 'What's that?' 'They're massive great boards, like folded wings – on each side – that you lower when you're on whichever tack you're sailing on – instead of a keel really. She has a huge mainsail, bent onto a curved gaff – 1,500 square ft of sail – imagine. A jib and a foresail and a dirty great bowsprit.' I asked 'What's her name?' James laughed, 'How typically feminine to want to know her name! It's Elsa'. It sounded a good name. 'Where is she?' James looked pensive, 'That's one of the snags – she's up the river Dart, at St Germain's Quay. I think I shall have to go and look at her this coming weekend. Can you manage without me? I'm sure Patricia will sleep on board for those two nights.' I nodded, and asked, 'I expect she's very expensive though.' He agreed, 'Well yes. £2,500 – which is over £1,000 more

than we gave for *Pat*, but you see, very few people want a boat as big as that, so there won't be many wanting to buy her. Perhaps I can beat them down a bit'. We sat making plans and daydreaming, while Peter having eaten his fill slept peacefully. James kissed us both, proud and happy to have organized a more spacious home, 'Tomorrow I shall bring the carricot and the shawl. I can't wait to have you back on board. Michael and I miss you so much.' How I treasured his rare tender remarks, vowing to myself that I would try very hard not to let this precious new child interfere with any sailing plans.

On the way back to *Pat* I steeled myself to face the discomfort, lack of facilities and the cramped quarters; all forgotten when I saw Michael on deck, holding his teddy bear, waving excitedly to greet us. I ran on board to hug him, but he was never very demonstrative, and wriggling free, he shyly peered into the carricot James had carried on board, shoved the teddy bear in beside his sleeping brother and self-consciously ran off. I was so touched, reminding myself to let him have it back without hurting his feelings. Surely this was a sign that they would get on well together. Having been an only child, actual jealousy between them had never even entered my head. The only jealousy I could visualize was that which I would experience if James ever fell in love with someone else. The mere thought of this nightmarish possibility made me feel sick with dread.

James placed Peter's carricot on the tin trunk in the after-cabin. Jake had nearly knocked me over with his welcome, peering into the carricot with a puzzled look, tail held stiff, which after a few prolonged sniffs started to wag excitedly with approval. The cats came back from hunting ashore, for it was near to their feeding time. Tilly came to me, putting her paws on my lap like a dog, but with her whiskers twitching and ears constantly moving, aware of some strange presence. A small sound came from the cabin aft; she turned, dropping to the floor in a crouching position while she decided what to do next. It needed investigating, so she stalked through in a dignified manner followed by Pinky. Worried lest they might scratch the baby, I went through the low passageway in time to see them circling the carricot, before jumping up on the tin trunk to have a good look. Relieved at seeing something holding no threat to them, they immediately sat down and began a complicated washing operation, hind legs in the air.

I wanted to talk to James, to hear more about *Elsa*, and

when we would be able to get her. Eventually Michael had his supper, then his bath in the tub, said goodnight to sleeping brother, and having fed the animals, I called to James who was busy on deck, renewing some worn out rigging, smoking his pipe. He could see that tears were not far away, and drew me close in a wonderfully comforting embrace, 'Sit beside me – unwind and rest before getting supper. We'll have bacon and eggs – Pat has done the shopping.' I burst into a flood of tears, 'Oh! darling . There's so much to do, and there'll have to be a washing line both sides between the shrouds – all those nappies. . . .' He kissed me, holding me tight, 'My love – I know, I do understand. Look, that's what I've been doing. My tears stopped. I had been dreading his reaction to the clutter of daily nappies flapping round the boat. 'But that's perfect!' I cried, 'All we need is a good dry spring with a stiff breeze.' He smiled, 'Spoken like a true yachtsman – woman!' I knew he was longing to put to sea again, and I refused even to think of all it would entail. 'Sufficient unto the day. . . .'

On returning from the stores one afternoon with Michael and Jake, I could see, from a distance, some young hooligans swinging on our mooring ropes. I ran, as fast as I could with Michael, calling to them not to do this, but they were gone before I reached *Pat* . It could have resulted in the boat not sitting in her hole again, which would be disastrous with small Peter; I worried dreadfully, wondering what on earth to do, as I dared not leave the boat at all until I found a solution. Suddenly an idea struck me. In a muddled way, I reasoned that once a sense of responsibility or a purpose is given to any young person; something to *do* in other words, rather than idly kicking around looking for amusement, it might have the desired effect.

Accordingly, one afternoon, after the children were back from school, I waited below deliberately until I heard the boisterous shouts and laughter as the boys ran along the path; then heaving the heavy carricot up on deck I called to them. Three or four of them clustered round on the bank while I placed Peter on the catwalk, then with a beating heart I asked, as casually as I could, 'Do you think you could keep an eye on the boat for me while Michael and I go to the shop? The tide is going out, and I'm frightened that the boat might heel over if the ropes are pulled on.' The ring-leader, with red hair looked at *Pat* in amazement and asked; 'Do you *live* here? With the baby?' I answered simply, 'Yes – it isn't easy when it blows.' He agreed to keep an eye on the

'nipper', but asked me not to be too long. It was hard, to walk away from the boat, leaving the sleeping Peter to their dubious care, even though they were not actually going to be out of sight, except while I was in the shop. I made it a brief shopping spree and walked back, as nonchalantly as possible, holding Michael's hand, while Jake gambolled round us. The three boys sitting on the bank were idly chucking stones into the fast receding waters and one of them said, 'Bleedin' nipper nearly started to cry just now – we would have come for you if he had – 'e's all right now though.' I thanked him for their help, and to my amazement they said they would be happy to look out for him any time, 'We've got baby brothers,' they said in disgust. I promised to ask them again if it blew, or the tide was ebbing – and never had any more trouble from them at all.

CHAPTER SIX

Farewell to *Pat*, and *Elsa's* Dutch Cruise

Yes, Elsa *will always be remembered with deep affection, gratitude and pride. She should never have been submitted to some of the seas and situations – yet somehow she nursed us through them. The wrench of parting from her would be much more painful than leaving a house – a more inanimate dwelling.* Elsa *was alive.*

James returned jubilant from his weekend in Devon, having succeeded in reducing the asking price of the Dutch barge to £2,000. He tried to describe her to me, 'The saloon is really roomy, stretching the whole width of the boat, and you can stand up everywhere – not only under the skylight. There's even a little sit-down blue bath in the galley. I can't wait for you to see her. We must advertise *Pat* straight away.' I asked when he would bring her round. He paused a moment before his hesitant reply, 'Well – I have already thought of that. I'm afraid it will have to be during the Easter leave, which could be cold and stormy.' He was quiet as he worked out how to tell me his plan, 'I rang Celia while I was down there to see if she could get away for a fortnight. . . .' I felt my unreasonable jealousy, coupled with a feeling of impotent rage at my uselessness, but tried to conceal it. James lit his pipe, looking at me with his steely, mesmeric eyes, knowing my resentment and went on as understandingly as he could, 'She says a girlfriend can look after Maria and yes, she'd love to come. She knows you can't possibly sail with Peter being so small. He sounds in good voice – is he hungry?' This last remark was made as a loud wail came from the after cabin. Feeling hurt, I answered coldly, 'No. You must realize that babies sometimes just cry for nothing.' Michael went through to try and comfort his baby brother and for a moment there was peace. James continued 'With any luck

and a prevailing southwesterly, we should do it in less than a fortnight, so that I'll still be on leave to help move in from *Pat*. We'll need another man as crew, unlike *Pat*. One of the men in *Berryhead* can crew for us.' There was nothing to say. I should have been grateful to Celia for being able to cook and sail with them, but in my heart could only feel resentment, increasing my inferiority complex.

James suggested that we might ask Patricia if she would live on board when we were installed in *Elsa*, 'There's a comfy, big after-cabin, abaft the well. It even has a double bunk.' She agreed to this and I was relieved for I knew what a difference it would make, as regards the safety of the children.

That spring of 1950 was gentle, warm and balmy, making up for the fearsome gales, frost and hail of the long winter. It was a long time since we had put to sea and James longed to take *Pat* to sea one last time before she was sold. Peter was only one month old when we gently motored down the creek to the Medway proper, his carricot nestling on the catwalk. Patricia came with us to see if she would enjoy the sailing side. The sun shone, and the Force 2 to 3 breeze barely filled the sails, which James hoisted once we were off Sheerness. Whitstable was our destination which was not too ambitious and we had a happy, uneventful weekend. We felt sad to be abandoning *Pat* after all our adventures. I wonder if she is still afloat?

A week later James began his Easter leave and joined his sister in Devon. Spring reverted to winter, making their trip hazardous but exhilarating, with a northerly gale forcing them to shelter in Dover for two days. I felt isolated and left out, but made a big effort to shake off the tenseness and gloom – all part of post-natal depression, neither under-stood nor acknowledged in those far off days. I bought a birthday cake for Michael and went into Rainham while Patricia stayed with the boys, in order to buy him a wooden train set, more boats and bricks as well as some blue balloons! He loved his day, feeling important, unaware of my anxiety, sharing his cake with an appreciative Jake. At each day-time high tide, he and I would walk along the path towards the end of the creek, scanning the horizon for a sign of the Dutch barge. At long last, with leaping heart, I saw in the distance what appeared to be a graceful, smaller version of a Thames barge.

We jumped up and down with excitement, waving and shouting hoping they had seen us, before running back at full speed to the boat, to be ready for the complicated berthing

operation. *Elsa* looked truly magnificent as she ghosted up the creek, sails lowered. Her great tall mast swayed high above us, making *Pat* look very squat. James cupped his hands, calling instructions for me to let go our mooring ropes to the bank in order to allow *Elsa* to lie alongside in our old hollow, with *Pat* on the outside.

James was so tired after the strain of the long hours on watch, that he fell asleep as soon as he returned. Both boats sat upright as we settled on the soft mud; *Elsa* sank gratefully into our old hollow and *Pat* was far enough out into the middle of the creek to make a new dent. Michael was so excited at our new home, it was difficult to stop him clambering over, but I promised we would all explore her together the next day. Meanwhile, the cats had already started prowling around on deck, cautious as Red Indians, waiting perhaps for some resident cat to jump out at them. The decks seemed vast and the 70-foot mast tapered above us, impressive, even awesome. Jake scampered across her to the bank, unlike the cats, not in the least bit interested.

There were two days of leave left, so next morning, I was eager to see our new home. James was already on board, lashing up the massive mainsail, tidying up on deck, helped by Michael who was happily running up and down the long catwalks. These were nice and safe as they had proper bulwarks not just wires as in *Pat*. Impressed, I stepped on deck. She was fifty-feet long and about twelve-feet wide, with a green painted hull, against which, on either side, nestled her leeboards. Being rounded at stem and stern, no stowage space was wasted, in contrast to the sharply pointed ends in *Pat*. A bewildering array of winches, windlasses and drums met my eyes, which James carefully explained to me. At the foot of the mast, both to port and starboard, were handles connected to different winches, which hoisted or lowered the mainsail, gib and foresail, as well as the leeboards. It was confusing to sort them out to begin with. Right up in the bows, where the wide deck gently sloped upwards, was a huge drum and windlass for the anchor. The decks were caulked, seasoned silvery teak, with slatted boards in the vast well-deck. A raised platform, or poop deck, aft of the well, stretched the entire width of the boat, on which one stood to steer. No wheel now, but a mightly tiller, reaching right out over the after cabin to an enormous rudder. In the well stood a handsome brass binnacle and a proper ship's bell. I could hardly take it all in.

James, who had recovered from the ordeals of the trip, kissed me, saying eagerly, 'Now – wait till you see below.'

We went down the companionway steps to the after cabin first, under the poop deck. It had a fitted carpet and blue chintz covers and I exclaimed in delight, 'But it's the prettiest of cabins!' Swiftly he said, 'Wait till you see the rest of her.' That cabin was lit by a skylight and two attractive scuttles in the stern, one on either side of the rudder. A settee ran the length of the port side, with mahogany fitted cupboards above and lockers below. Between the scuttles was a dressing table unit, consisting of shelves and a mirror, with electric light. James switched it on. I was dumbfounded, 'Electricity!' 'Yes,' he said, 'Throughout the boat – run off the generator which is charged by the engine. I only need to run it once a week.' The bunk, a small double one, ran the length of the starboard side, being slightly narrower one end. A handsome mahogany chest was tucked in beside the steps from the well, which contained a basin and water, and best of all, this lifted up to reveal a loo! The whole cabin was self-contained.

Unbelieving, as though in a delightful dream from which I would wake if I moved too fast, we went back up the steps, crossed the well to the main body of the boat. A full-size mahogany door opened onto steep steps leading down into a palatial saloon. It must have been about twelve feet long, and stretched the entire width of the hull. There was room to stand up everywhere, even for the 6 ft 2 in James. A patterned fitted carpet matched the curtains over the scuttles and the huge skylight flooded the cabin with light. Directly to port and starboard at the foot of the companionway were two doors, one leading into a proper loo with a flushing pump, the other into a small cabin. This too, had a fitted carpet, plenty of headroom, a basin and a bunk stretching athwartships – Peter's cabin.

In the saloon, a Rayburn-type fireplace with doors, stood in the middle of the starboard bulkhead, flanked by beautiful mahogany cupboards with shelves in front of them, edged by 'fiddles', as the Navy calls them, or galleries to the layman. They looked like exquisitely carved little bannisters – preventing books, clocks, etc. from falling out. Large scuttles (portholes) on either side of the fireplace, coupled with two more on the opposite side let in lots of light. A long settee took up most of the port side, covered in the same pretty chintz as an armchair and the diminutive curtains; beside it was a decent sized table, bolted to the deck as in *Pat* and with flaps. Going for'ard, two doors led out of this lovely saloon, one into a cabin on the port side, the other into the galley. Our cabin also had a washbasin with shelves

and a mirror, a hanging cupboard and good locker space under the double bunk. The headroom ended just before the bunk, where the cabin top stopped, but one could just sit up in bed. It all seemed like a four-star hotel.

The galley pleased me most of all, Not only was there a proper cooker, with rails round it and an oven, but next to it stood a fridge, worked by Calor gas. These were side by side on the starboard side of the long, narrow galley; past them, unbelievably was a blue mini-bath! It was like an Aladdin's cave. To port stood a sink flanked by a plate-rack with a gas heater above it, next to which a little work top let down on a chain. What more could anyone wish for? Imagine not having to heat a kettle any more to do the washing-up or the nappies; to be able to run hot water into a *bath* by means of an extending rubber hose. I could not wait to move in! There was still the cabin in the bows to explore, where Michael would sleep. There was no headroom over the bath or further for'ard, as this was under the foredeck, but Michael would be able to stand up. His bunk was along the port bulkhead, while all the ship's stores, pots of paint, coils of rope, spare sails, wire halyards and stays were stowed on the opposite side. Many, many years later, he told me how spooky and frightening the little cabin seemed. Admittedly it was dark, with only a hatch which could be propped up, but he never complained during the years he slept there.

'James,' I murmured, after gloating over everything, 'What a beautiful boat and home. I'm so happy, let's begin moving stuff over at once.' Patricia appeared to come and help and we proudly showed her her cabin. She never showed a lot of enthusiasm, but nevertheless was pleased with it, quietly getting on with carrying the endless paraphernalia from *Pat* on board. In between feeding and bathing Peter, cooking and washing nappies, I helped too. Soon it seemed like home, with Tilly and Pinky curled up on the end of the settee busily licking themselves. As it was a steel hull, at least an eighth of an inch thick, I wondered if there would be any mice for them! Jake sniffed everywhere energetically, finally lying down under the table approvingly. By the end of two days more or less everything was transferred.

May was a beautiful month. I knew James was longing to take *Elsa* to sea again, but a lot of maintenance work was needed on the hull, plus the fact that we had to sell *Pat*. One day a nice couple, in their thirties, came on board and told us they had seen the advertisement for *Pat* in *Yachting Monthly*. I showed them over her, then asked them back for a cup of tea while we waited for James's return. They were

keen to buy, and once James had explained how she sailed, so easily now, only needing one man, they were totally convinced; buying her there and then, deciding to live on board just a short distance astern of *Elsa*. Funnily enough, we never went aboard again, possibly because of the two small boys, possibly because the couple were considerably older than ourselves. It was fun to watch her being sailed, very expertly too, as they explored the creeks in the Medway.

The health visitor came again, vastly relieved to find the six-week-old baby in a proper cabin all to himself instead of dumped in a carricot on the tin trunk in a damp and smelly cabin! In fact, as I had explained to her the first time, he had plenty of fresh air, was perfectly healthy, fed by me, and I was even ironing his nappies, in those early days, to soften them; but she had definitely registered disapproval as she slithered down the gangplank, shaking her head and muttering.

James unfolded his plans for the summer one evening, 'After I've removed some of the rust from the keel strakes, and we've had a practice weekend sail, don't you think it would be a splendid idea to take her back to her birthplace, Lekkerkerk, in Holland, and explore some of the canals?' Bravely, but with a sinking heart I agreed, 'Yes, darling – the canals and rivers or inland waterways would be lovely – nice and calm – but won't the North Sea be nasty?' He reassured me, 'Don't worry, Toni. We'll obviously have to have a crew. I'll find some chum on board, so you won't have to keep any watches.' Plaintively I asked, 'But I'll still have all the cooking and cleaning to do won't I?' He thought for a bit them came up with a bright idea, 'We'll ask a *couple* to come with us, then the girl friend – or wife can help you. There – all fixed.' I had no option but to agree, despite misgivings which I dare not give voice to.

In June, young Peter was christened in the little church near Rainham, where Nelson had been baptised. His godfather, my cousin, came down for it, representing all the rest of the family who could not possibly come that far. For some reason I had been feeling low and depressed, partly due to being unable to regain my figure, aggravated by what must have been post-natal depression. It cheered me up enormously to see a close member of my family, making the little lunch party a real celebration.

James bought or acquired old charts of the North Sea as well as the Dutch and Belgian coast, pouring over them on the saloon table in the long light evenings, whilst at the same time arranging a weekend's sailing. He had already asked a brother officer from *Berryhead*, who accepted with alacrity,

wishing to bring his fiancée too. It seemed ideal, both of them being a bit older than us. Even for a mere weekend, with five adults, for Patricia was coming too, plus Michael and Peter, the catering and organization were formidable.

They arrived on the Friday evening, instantly reducing the size of the main cabin for George was a big, fairly stout man; Deanne was tall, dark and slim, both charming and helpful. While James instructed George in the complicated workings of the various windlasses, Deanne unpacked in Peter's cabin, full of admiration for the spacious boat. 'Her lines are so beautiful, like a bird – how lucky you are to live on board.' Proudly, I agreed.

We had no particular, clear cut plans, just to try out all her paces, see how close to the wind in calm weather we could sail her, and possibly to take her into Whitstable for Saturday night. The weather was magical – a hot July. By 5 a.m. James was up, waking George, in order to catch the ebb. Kissing me briefly, he said, 'We'll just have mugs of tea before sailing – breakfast later when we're under way.' He was excited – but never showed it.

The engine in *Elsa* had an electric starter, an amazing improvement on the wayward cranking handle on board *Pat*, though I felt a guilty twinge as usual when making a disparaging comparison. 'I only need the engine to turn us round,' James explained, 'As soon as that's done, we'll hoist the sails and hope for a breeze.' The light summer airs would only be enough to ghost us along, but with an ebb tide we should reach the open sea quite soon, where there would be stronger 'cat's paws'. 'Right, George, hoist the mainsail, ' he called. I had been standing in the bows, ready to shove us off with the boathook, if, in the confined head of the creek we risked bumping into our neighbours, who had been woken up by all our activity and were up on deck in pyjamas to watch our first venture in *Elsa*. George was obviously having trouble finding the right handle to wind in order to winch up the sail, so I went to see if I could remember what James had told me. Before he could start winding, James called for the staysail and gib to be hoisted too. One was on the opposite side of the mast, and I dealt with one of them, dashing back to the well in order to gape at the majestic unfolding of the regal mainsail. No time to stand and look though, for the sheets had to be trimmed, made fast to the cleats; and the relevant leeboard lowered. This was supposed to stop any sideways drift, but in reality *Elsa* did not sail any closer to the wind than *Pat* when tacking. How I would have loved to be standing on the bank to admire the stately, gentle, royal

progress as *Elsa* calmly drifted down the Medway.

In truth, no time existed in which to drink it all in, for by now, Michael was up, quietly playing in the well. Tilly and Pinky resignedly licked and cleaned themselves on the cabin top, having had a quick run ashore. Contentedly, in the warming sun, which now shone in copybook fashion after a spectacular pearly dawn, they stretched out a paw, claws extended before curling round to sleep. How blissful to be a cat!

There were no plans or goals this weekend, merely a lazy trying out of her paces, with an anticyclone laid on for us. Deanne was up on deck too, looking ravishing in trousers, her slim figure making me self-conscious of my 'nursing mother' plumpness. She murmured quietly, 'This is too perfect. Surely it can't last. Come on – show me where everything is in the kitchen – I mean galley – then I can help at meal times.' I was so grateful for her genuine offer, following her down the steps into the saloon, relaxed in the knowledge that Pat was keeping an eye on Michael.

The sea was calm, the breeze a caress, therefore the movement below was negligible, especially as the galley was not right up in the bows as in *Pat*. The rounded bows lifted with any wave or swell, instead of roughly cleaving through it, giving a gentler, unhurried motion. In fact, there was not enough wind to put the Boeier through her paces properly; even the tiller could be left, lashed by two ropes, from both port and starboard cleats, adjusted by pulleys. By mid-morning, the sun was beating down with unusual ferocity and heat for the sea round the English coast, necessitating a floppy white hat for the boy, and bare tops for the men. Whenever a slightly more vigorous 'cat's paw' of wind filled our sails, James would call out 'Lee-o!' and we would spring into action. George coped with increasing efficiency at letting go the main sheet at precisely the right moment, then hauling it in on the other tack, while Deanne wound the winch of one leeboard; running across the deck in order to lower the other. We practised lowering and hoisting the staysail and gib too.

At lunch time, though Peter was only three months old, I decided it was warm enough to feed him up on deck, discreetly naturally. However, a shocked gasp from George, accompanied by a worried look and a muttered: 'You can't feed him in *public!*' sent me rushing below in confusion. It has always seemed so natural and normal to me, and I had not realized how offensive it might be to some people. Deanne joined me in the saloon. 'I'm sorry about George – he has never been married, so he's embarrassed. I'm sure

he'll get used to it − its so silly of him.' She paused a moment, 'I am divorced. It was all such a mess − so squalid. Thank goodness there were no children.' I felt sorry for her, imagining in lightning flashes what it must be like; an inconceivable black hole of misery, 'Oh Deanne, I *am* sorry. What can I say?' She reassured me, 'George is utterly devoted to me and wants to marry me − but I can't make up my mind. Yet I'm nearly thirty, and I do want to have a baby before I'm too old.' Peter was sucking ravenously, and I realized how lucky I was, for if he was on a bottle, anyone could feed him, I would lose those precious twenty minutes, six times a day, of sitting down and relaxing amid the chaotic hurly-burly of the day. At twenty-five I felt a fleeting pang of envy and regret at missing out on the fun of being alone with an adored husband, and said, 'Don't be silly Deanne − thirty is not the least too old to start a family, and you will have had all the freedom and fun you want. You must be awfully sure before you marry again though − surely you *know* if you love George?' She shook her head, 'No, I'm fond of him, and I'd love the security of a home and husband. I shall never love anyone as I did my first husband. But this weekend is perfect − it'll give us a chance to get to know each other well. Luckily I'm not seasick!'

As I finished feeding Peter, a slight breeze heeled us over, and James's voice called down the companionway; 'Action stations!' George explained, 'We're going to practice lowering the sails, stand by!' With James at the tiller and George winching down the mainsail, Deanne and I stood on the cabin top clasping and grabbing fairly ineffectually at the endless folds of the great spread of canvas. These conditions were ideal; even so, it felt as though we were attempting to fold up the big top of a circus − what would it be like in a gale?

I took the tiller for a while, impressed and awe-struck at the pressure and strength of the seas pressing on the massive rudder; the apparently interminable stretch of boat ahead of me, tapered off so gracefully by the bowsprit with its net beneath. The sail quivered and flapped and I hastily corrected the course, filling it once more. I knew that in any seas at all I could not hold the tiller which would thrash about like a wild boar, despite its restraining holding tackle. For a few moments though, I was captain of *Elsa*, as Deanne and George talked quietly and seriously sitting close together on the poop deck and James smoked his pipe, keeping a watchful eye on the luff of the sail. All too soon it was time to make tea, read to Michael, and feed young Peter, resulting in my going below to get on with these

chores while the rest 'carried on sailing'.

The little blue bath was full of provisions so Michael could not have his usual splash, but we had a game with the boats and ferries on the floor, for once not feeling the least bit seasick. Perhaps it would be different in *Elsa*.

During the sail back to Otterham next day, idyllic and deluding as the day before, persuasively and innocently it lulled me into believing all our sailing days would be this carefree. James decided to ask Deanne and George if they would like to come with us to Holland. I warned them, 'It might be quite rough, and hard work you know. Do you think you can put up with two tinies and two cats for a fortnight George?' He looked reassuringly strong and kind, 'Yes – you see, Deanne and I could have a fortnight together. It would mean a lot for both of us.' At the time it did not strike me as indicative of a selfish nature. So – with great enthusiasm it was agreed they should sign on as crew on 28 July and during the next couple of weekends James devoted himself to getting *Elsa* into prime sailing condition, ready for the rigours of the North Sea.

What I had most dreaded happened – the spell of ideal, unnaturally fine summer weather ended. The wind veered round to the South-West; ragged grey clouds hid the cerulean sky and at night the familiar winter sounds of the shrouds twanging and slapping the mast would waken me from my deep, exhausted sleep. James merely remarked that a south-westerly was just what we needed to blow us across the North Sea to Holland – a soldier's wind he called it; I silenced my fears and nightmares. Jake was booked in to stay at the same kennels as before, which we hated having to do. As far as the cats were concerned, I thought it would be comparatively easy to empty and refill their box every day; for once in Holland, we would be alongside a wharf or jetty nearly every evening. No need for them to go ashore.

The weather forecasts, not as detailed as they are now, were nevertheless pretty gloomy in their outlook, with low pressure areas, quite strong winds accompanied by squally showers. In the Navy one cannot pick and choose a date for one's holiday. Leave started and ended on a certain date, which meant that in order to have the maximum time over there, we had to sail on the first day of the allotted fortnight. Deanne and George drove down as arranged, sensibly equipped with submarine sweaters, oilskins and boots, and unpacked in their cabins, while I took down the washing lines and filled the water tank, knowing we would have to use it sparingly.

It would be a long haul to Rotterdam, with not a moment

to be wasted, necessitating sailing on a tide long before dawn. With luck and a fair wind, we should reach Holland the following day, but somehow I was not that optimistic! The wind did not abate in the night, but apart from one or two anxious dreams, I slept soundly, hardly noticing James creep out of our bunk just before 4 a.m. He was so quiet even Peter, in his carricot at the foot of our bunk, did not hear him. Dimly and dreamily I was aware of softly padding footsteps on the deck above me, sounding quite romantic in the dark, followed by the quiet throbbing of the engine which would only be needed to get us out of the creek. Finally came the call of: 'Let go for'ard, let go aft,' accompanied by the heavy thud of mooring ropes thrown on deck; then for an hour I went back to sleep, eventually being woken by Peter demanding his breakfast.

By this time we were well under way, out in the Thames estuary, still in waters sheltered by the southwesterly wind, but rolling – gently and inexorably. As always I was assailed by a feeling of nausea and fear but momentarily, up on deck, in the brisk morning air, I felt better.

Geroge had the tiller, while James, who was adjusting the rigging, came towards me, grinning happily; 'Darling – just look! She's sailing magnificently – maybe a bit slower than I'd hoped – mostly because she *will* ride up each wave instead of taking a short cut through them.' I tried to sound enthusiastic, but the grey uniform expanse of sea and sky oppressed me, 'James – you must all be so hungry. I'll get breakfast. Will scrambled eggs do? Did you listen to the weather forecast? At least there are no "white horses" yet!' The tide was running with the wind, which was why the waves were not yet breaking. Below Patricia gave me a wan smile, asking if she might have a Kwell too! The noble, unseasick Deanne was already cutting and buttering bread and had put the kettle on; I was grateful for by now the mere thought of scrambled eggs made me want to throw up. She could tell by my green-white face how I was feeling and sympathetically offered to cook breakfast, but I remonstrated, 'Oh Deanne! This may well be the last meal I shall be *able* to cook – I really must try. Can you sit Michael on your lap and give him some cereal while I scramble the eggs?'

We were sailing into more open water now – the lumpy aimless tumblings of the North Sea. By the time James came down the companionway, ravenous for his breakfast, having been up on deck for hours, I called from the galley, 'It's no good. I'll have to lie down – I can't eat my breakfast. I'll just drink some tea to keep my milk supply going. I'm so sorry.

121

Deanne will look after you.' Inwardly, I raged at my total ineptitude. Deanne performed miracles in the galley, feeding the men as they relieved each other off watch. I retreated to my bunk, holding the baby close to me so that he would not get tossed about. The poor cats got quite forgotten, but stayed curled up in the sail locker, presumably trying to forget their discomfort by sleeping non-stop.

The seas became steeper, uneven and lumpy; *Elsa* did everything with them, pitching, rolling and pretending to be a roller-coaster, rising and falling as seagulls do, unperturbed. Fear, misery and nausea assailed me in turn and I was convinced that my milk would dry up for I was eating and drinking nothing. The two naval officers enjoyed most of it; James occasionally put his head round the door to ask how we were, assuring me that Deanne was coping; Patricia was feeling slightly sick, cuddled up in her bunk with Michael; and we were slightly off course because of the southerly gale now blowing.

George was strong and capable, but even so, there came a time when it took both of them to hold the bucking, kicking tiller. Both men were soaked through with the driving spray from the cascading waves, added to the squally showers, leaving piles of wet clothes on the saloon floor. The galley was awash with spilt tea and soup that had slopped over when poor brave Deanne was pouring it. She brought me cups of tea, but I found it impossible to keep anying except water down. How long would this go on for?

Towards evening the wind did drop slightly, leaving us lurching about with no way on, tending to gybe, as the sail, having spilled the wind, shook the long, long boom. Peter became furious, possibly because of a lessening of his milk supply, screaming in temper. I wished and prayed it would end. After dark, when I expected a watery grave to engulf us all, James came down to sleep for an hour or so; fully clad on the bunk beside me. He was supremely confident and unruffled as always, assuring me that *Elsa* was riding the seas like a bird – in her element. By dawn we would be just off Zeebrugge – of such fame in both world wars. Then he fell asleep despite the groaning of timbers and crashing of objects not securely lashed down. As always I felt completely safe when wrapped around by his close physical presence, though remaining incapable of helping, as I retched uncontrollably if I got up. The night seemed endless and James was still sleeping soundly when George called down that he could see the intermittent beam of a light over the horizon to starboard.

It turned out to be Zeebrugge, then George came below to turn in on the settee in the saloon, shedding more wet clothes on top of the existing dripping pile. Dawn broke, slightly less grey then the previous day; I sat and fed Peter, marvelling at how much milk I still appeared to have, despite twenty-four hours on a diet of water. The pills took effect with the gentler motion and feeling very ashamed of myself I crept up on deck, to find James and Deanne gazing in awe at the massive towering stone mole of Zeebrugge, some distance away. We still had quite a way to sail, but it would be bearable now. I thanked Deanne for all she had done, promising to make up for it once we were in Holland, adding, 'Now *I'll* go and make some tea!' She followed me into the galley apologizing for the mess. I stopped her, 'Deanne, do you realize those men would have had nothing at all to eat if it hadn't been for you. I think you're marvellous and I'm most envious. Have you had any sleep?' She nodded: 'Oh yes. I'd only just got up with all the talk about lighthouses. Its thrilling to see the coast from a sailing boat – especially a Dutch one – as we're going there.' She was right. Suddenly I felt adventurous and proud, as though I had discovered Holland myself instead of skulking below being seasick for most of the trip! Tilly and Pinky re-appeared from their hiding place, looking disgruntled and mewing plaintively. They must have smelt the land, for they went up on deck, pacing up and down the cabin top – clearly fed up. Suddenly and dramatically the sun came out, transforming the whole scene and atmosphere.

I knew James was a bit apprehensive about navigating the twelve or fifteen miles up the Hook of Holland to Rotterdam itself, wondering where we might lie in the harbour which was vast, most especially not wanting to disgrace *Elsa* in her own country. We flew the blue ensign at the stern and the RNSA burgee from the mast, so that at least everyone would know we were British, hopefully forgiving us if we made a mistake.

Our progress, helped by the tide, had been steady, implying that we should be off the entrance by midday. The coastguards must have seen us from a way off, or maybe idle holidaymakers always hang around jetties and wharves at harbour entrances in the hope of seeing some drama enacted. As we approached the impressively long, wide breakwater at the mouth we could see it was crowded with people. Sailing nearer, we noticed excited gesticulating as the Dutch crowd waved encouragement to us, impressed by

a genuine Dutch Boeier evidently all the way from England. We were all up on deck now, except for the sleeping baby; Michael held my hand and waved back. Because of the favourable wind we were able to sail really close to the mole and many people took photographs, making us feel like movie stars. Suddenly they shrieked and pointed in the sea between us and the jetty. I flew to the side in time to see two bedraggled cats swimming for all they were worth to the shore! We had not seen them jump overboard, but those watching us had done so and could not believe their eyes! Cats actually jumping in the sea and swimming – unheard of! (I have never known it happen again).

This caused immediate panic. Instead of our stately progress up the Hook waterway, we lowered the sails, started the engine which responded instantly, thank goodness, and slammed it into reverse. While Patricia took Michael below, we carefully crept alongside some steps in the jetty – magnificently executed by James. George and I threw mooring ropes up to the now anxious onlookers, only too willing to help, as Deanne ran up and down the catwalk with the fattest fender to save our beautiful paint. Frantic for the cat's safety I scrambled ashore, asking where they had gone, shaken to find I could not understand a word, but following the friendly, sympathetic pointing hand. There they crouched, alternatively shaking themselves and licking each other, dripping wet and utterly miserable. I put on my most cajoling 'cat voice' to call them to which they responded instantly, rubbing their thin straggly bodies against me. How they must have hated that crossing! Their first long sea journey – and how I sympathized! By now, James had joined me and we each picked up a bundle of saturated fur to take back on board. Meanwhile, Patricia had heated milk and opened a tin of sardines (a luxury) which they devoured after we had done our best to pat them dry. For hours afterwards they licked themselves, apparently suffering no ill effects from the salt water.

The admiring crowd still stood peering at us, presumably wondering what entertainment we were going to provide next, so I took Peter up on deck for a breath of fresh air in his carricot, which produced 'Oooh's' and 'Ahh's' from the women but somehow lacked the drama of swimming cats! In no time we were under way again, this time under power for there was not enough room to manoeuvre under sail in that hectically busy waterway. The nail-biting journey took a long time, calling for intense concentration from James and causing many anxious moments.

On our way we were boarded by the Customs who spoke English and helpfully told us how to find the yacht haven in Rotterdam. It turned out to be a delightfully quiet and secluded corner on its own, away from the bustle of the main stream, surrounded by grass and trees. We lay alongside a tidal wharf which made going ashore very easy. Michael was especially pleased to be on dry land, racing up and down to let off steam. I stayed on board to feed Peter and clear up some of the mess and clutter; the least I could do after my pathetic performance during the crossing. Deanne and George went off to explore, while James organized water, fuel for the engine, bread and milk.

As we sipped our mugs of tea, taking a welcome break sitting in the well, sounds of music floated across to us – intriguing, different music. We decided to investigate and our meandering through the old, picturesque, quiet part of Rotterdam led us nearer to the ever-increasing volume of music. There, on the corner of the street was the biggest barrel-organ or hurdy-gurdy I had ever seen. A man turned the handle and pop tunes of the day such as *Put another nickle in – in the nickolodeon*, sounding delightfully foreign, blared away. Michael was entranced, but Peter screamed his protest violently, vying with the instrument for sheer volume of noise.

That first evening on our return from the short stroll, I reckoned the cats' box of earth must be renewed. As we approached the yacht basin, we saw among the trees, a cat, 'Look!' I said to James, 'There's a cat just like Tilly.' It *was* Tilly. She had stalked unconcernedly ashore, shortly followed by Pinky. There was nothing I could do about it. They never moved far from the boat, wherever we were, and I just hoped to goodness no one would find out, because of the quarantine laws. Deanne and George returned much later having explored the cafés and bars and were ravenous.

Before leaving Otterham I had cooked a bit of gammon from the chandler's, so that apart from potatoes there would be no cooking that evening. George sat down heavily – looked at the table and as though he were in a restaurant solemnly said, 'Where's the mustard?' I nearly exploded with fury through tiredness and delayed worry, especially as there was none anyway; I controlled myself, saying calmly I was just about to feed Peter. His shocked expression stopped me and I retired to our cabin, where throughout the entire fortnight, if George happened to be on board, I had to feed the infant. It seemed so unfriendly and unnecessary, and from that moment on, relations were strained between us.

Deanne was aware of his selfishness and more than made up for it by her kindness and help.

We stayed one more day in Rotterdam before sailing up the Lek, towards Lekkerkerk, *Elsa's* birthplace. It was a tricky operation, even with naval charts, to sort out; among the myriads of waterways, rivers and canals, flowing out of Rotterdam; which one to head for, once again negotiating the ceaseless flow of boats, barges and ships of every size. James was adamant, *Elsa must* sail past her boatyard – 'Even if there is no one there to see her – it would be too humiliating just to motor past!' She had been built a very long time ago, and though we scanned the village closely, could see no signs of a boatyard, only a row of houses behind a stone wall bordering the river, and a delapidated wooden wharf. Still, honour was satisfied and as the river grew narrower, we lowered the sails and started the engine. The day was grey and sultry with hardly any wind, so that the inland waterways were calm. Michael and the cats could play happily on deck and Peter lay contentedly in the well. This was my idea of perfect sailing!

Next day we sailed and motored peacefully along the canals and rivers to Dordrecht. We had been towing the dinghy, taking great care not to let the painter wrap itself around the propeller, it gave us more room on deck, but in fact we never used it. As *Elsa* approached the occasional bridges, someone on the lookout would open it by raising the centre where it divided in two, enabling the mast to slip through, while a boy held out a bag on the end of a long stick for us to put our money in. This was quite a tricky operation, for boats, unlike cars, do not slow down and stop instantly; they tend to drift on. The first bridge caused us great alarm, for we were nearly on top of it before we realized they were going to open it and James was all set to slam the engine into reverse, but happily the near disaster was averted. At yet another we failed to get near enough to put our money in the proffered bag, but called out we would put their dues in the next bag along the line.

Dordrecht was fascinating with bustling, busy waterways – a Dutch Venice – including a secluded yacht haven above a footbridge, where we moored for two days. Typical old Dutch houses surrounded the harbour, with a church nearby, inspiring James to paint a delightful picture of the view from the deck.

It was not a long walk to the main square where the market-day stalls made gay, vivid splashes of colour, dominated by hundreds of the round Dutch Edam cheeses

with their bright deep-orange rinds. They lay in sledge-like containers slung between ropes, carried over the shoulders of two men. The Dutch all seemed immensely tall and fat to us, probably in contrast to the forcibly slimmer British brought about by severe, continued rationing.

Restaurants abounded and we pushed the pram from one establishment to another, trying to figure out what the outside menu said, mouths watering in anticipation. Obviously it could not be anywhere too grand or expensive, for even our best sailing gear was not exactly smart and the addition of a three-year old plus a baby made our strange party unlikely to expect a rapturous welcome. We trusted to luck and finally ventured into one. It proved a good choice for we were among the first British sailing tourists to travel across the North Sea and the proprietor was most excited to learn we had come in a Boeier. Conversation consisted mainly of voluble hand signals, Boeier being the only Dutch word we knew, but the proprietor translated the menu to us as best he could, while I silently prayed that Peter would not scream, demanding to be fed before I had had time to eat.

It was astonishing to see so many people crowded round the tables covered in prettily checked tablecloths, long menus on each one. We all chose veal, unheard of for years at home; in some rich, velvety mushroom sauce, and a bottle of cheap white wine. Michael got bored with the long wait and began to roam, making it impossible for me to relax, as George became tetchy and impatient at the interruptions caused by one or other of the boys. So far, Peter lay happily in his carricot but I knew it would not last as it drew nearer to feeding time. Unable to join in the conversation, in my desperate efforts to keep both little ones quiet, I nevertheless could sense the tension between Deanne and George. She had become increasingly aware of his totally selfish attitude, his ceaseless demands for different things at meal times, regardless of how many times I had to get up, and was obviously thinking that once they were married, he would quite possibly treat her in the same way that he treated me! Inevitably, she had started to fall out of love with him whilst at the same time regretting the fact.

Michael ate chicken with relish, staring around with wide-eyed wonder, never having seen so many people in one place. Apart from one or two fairly tactless, but luckily unintelligible remarks, he behaved as well as any three-year-old. Unfortunately, before the pudding, Peter reckoned he was losing out on this outing and noisily proclaimed it, making the hapless George clench his teeth and grow puce

with embarrassment and fury. Hurriedly, we gulped down the exquisite *poires belle-Helene* – the first time I had ever tasted that concoction. I wheeled the pushchair outside and waited for them, covered in confusion. Nevertheless, it had been a memorable meal and Deanne quickly joined me, apologizing for George's boorishness. It seemed paradoxical that she should be envying me whilst I envied her.

Peace descended for a tranquil half hour before 6 p.m. as we sat in the well and on the cabin top, differences forgotten, content to be in this friendly town, listening to another of their evocative barrel organs in the distance; James smoked a pipe, elbow resting on his knee, hand cupping the bowl – far, far away in spirit. The sun appeared reluctantly, in time to illuminate for us, in glorious technicolour, the town, church, boats and water – washing all in a hazy gold dust, transforming the scene into an old Dutch painting. Delicately the two cats stalked ashore, tails held high, for their evening stroll before being fed. They had become accustomed to the daily change of venue now, enjoying the peaceful sailing and being able to explore some dry land once a day.

We were sad to leave Dordrecht next morning, but after using the engine for a short while, the river flowed into the lovely calm waters of the Hollandsche Diep, where we drifted lazily, mainsail goose-winged right out to catch the merest breath of wind. That night we moored at Willemstand, just before the Hollandsche Diep branches into the Haringoliet and the Grevelingen; sailing on the following day to Wemeldinge, a tiny village. This was quite an exacting sail, sticking to the marked channels, between Tholen and Schouwen and across the Oosterschelde. A freshening westerly wind ruffled the sheltered waters without making it rough, but going about became a sluggish affair as *Elsa* had not enough way on to respond to the rudder. It was calm sailing, allowing both Deanne and me to take a spell at the tiller, while James dropped astern in the dinghy in order to photograph us. What a great shame it was all before the days of colour photography. It takes a lot of imagination to transform the sombre grey, black and white phototgraphs into the translucent, muted pastel shades of that beautiful countryside.

One particular morning was summery, a pearly dawn chased away by a placid sun in a milky blue sky; no wind to speak of, just light airs. James suggested sailing west out of Oosterschelde, right round Walcheren Island, to Vlissingen (Flushing). He was longing to be at sea again and seldom can

a day have been more perfect. I suppose, in all those four years at sea – perfect days can be numbered on the fingers of both hands. This was one of them. We sunbathed on the cabin top, soaking the tiredness away, but not quite brave enough to swim – dreading the icy coldness of the northern waters. Michael built his weird constructions of bricks, representing boats, houses or ferries. 'If only – ' I prayed inwardly, 'If only it could be like this when we sail back to England in two days' time.'

Safely tied up alongside in Flushing, Deanne came into our cabin where I was feeding Peter, 'Toni – what shall I do? I know now that I can't possibly marry George – but I can't bring myself to tell him.' Wearily I suggested that she should leave it until we reached home; but she insisted, 'He wants me to have a meal with him in Flushing – now – tonight. I can't pretend everything is the same.' I gave a smile and said, 'All right, say I've asked you to cook supper tonight and you can't go!' This plan made George more resentful of me than ever. Nowadays of course, on sailing trips, each member of the crew takes a turn in the galley – whether it's for a day or a meal – but in those 'bad old days' it was up to the 'boat wife' to conjure up interesting meals out of the same boring old ingredients, without even the tantalizing variety of today's choice of tinned foods.

By next day, even James had noticed George's grumpiness. He mentioned it early in the morning while I gave Peter his 6 a.m. drink, snuggled up in bed for once, 'Do you know darling, I think we have saved the delightful Deanne from a fate worse than. . . . !' Yawning, I answered him, 'Yes, I thought in fact that you hadn't noticed how he treated Patricia and me, expecting to be waited on hand and foot.' James stroked the baby's soft dark head and kissed me gently as I leant over, 'I know, I'm sorry I'm not very observant, and he has been a great help to me on deck. I've always had so much to do and plan when I've been below – still – he is a boor, and a prude,' he added, remembering I had had to hide in my cabin for every feed. I would have given anything to lie back in our bunk, beside James, and go to sleep cradled and loved in his arms; but already Michael and Patricia were clattering down the companionway to put the kettle on for early morning tea – and Peter needed changing!

George had taken Deanne's tea into her cabin, and we could hear their urgent voices – his pleading – and her patient gentle reasoning.

The weather had changed again, colouring everything a uniform grey. We were sheltered in the harbour and along

the canal, but up aloft the burgee streamed out, silhouetted against the leaden sky. The barometer had fallen slightly too. It was not always possible to get the BBC weather forecast due to our steel hull and atmospherics, so we relied mainly on old-fashioned interpretations of the clouds and sky; whether the wind had backed or veered, plus instinct. We felt oppressed and I kept going up into the well, apprehensive yet compelled to see whether the wind had risen.

Our lunch was eaten in silence, while George brooded. Having hardly been ashore at all, I was determined to do so in Middelberg when James and I took an hour off, leaving the boys with the others. The dignified old Dutch houses with their distinctive architecture were at their most colourful round the old part of the town, cobbled streets underfoot. We strolled peacefully, savouring our rare time alone together and I tried to quieten my too vivid imagination, already conjuring up the horrors of the North Sea. In true tourist fashion we bought some little Delft tiles and a windmill saltcellar as well as a little wooden train for Michael. On our return to the boat, with laden shopping baskets, we were told that Tilly and Pinky had tried to follow us, only being dissuaded by Patricia and Michael calling them and holding out bits of frankfurters.

After George and Deanne returned from a drink ashore, I could see he had been trying to drown his sorrow and felt sorry for him, until we sat down to the lamb casserole I had cooked, when his belligerence spoiled the meal. Secretly I hoped that James might come to bed early with me, as soon as the last feed was over – but no – George was already planning a lengthy gambling evening of poker, vingt-et-un and liar dice and I knew I would be asleep before James fell into the bunk beside me.

Next day was overcast again, but calm, enabling me to steer quite a lot of the way back to Flushing. But tension returned that night in Flushing, our last in Holland, for the wind rose. Gently at first, whispering and teasing the rigging, dying away only to return a bit stronger, causing the taut ropes and wires to sing and hum their own warning dirge. I shivered with dread. At least I could conceal my fear if not the seasickness I was so ashamed of. James had a plan to make the crossing seem quicker, 'Darling, we'll spend a night in Zeebrugge – it's only a quick dash from there.' I nodded my gratitude. The last morning had come and nowhere could the men find a stand-pipe to fill our tank – essential before a long journey. I was adamant, 'It *must* be

filled.' Eventually the harbour master suggested the Fire Brigade, who drove up the jetty alongside with a great flourish! They placed their huge hose over the funnel into the tank and turned on the pressure. Almost immediately a fierce fountain of water shot into the air, drenching us all! We had not reckoned on such pressure. I dashed to the galley to turn on the tap – but only a trickle of dark brown rust appeared. Unfortunately, the force of the water had loosened all the rust in the tank making it virtually unusable and certainly undrinkable.

I explained as best I could what had happened and the kind firemen told me to turn on all the taps in the boat – there were three – while they filled the tank again as slowly as they could, which would eventually clear it. While this pantomime was going on, James became impatient, alternately looking at the sky, the time, and the barometer. As usual there was a tide to catch – a little rust in the water would do no one any harm! 'Why, doctors even *prescribe* iron tablets to people,' he reasoned. At least by now the water was flowing freely, albeit faintly tinged with brown and harbouring minute specks of rust. I agreed with him, 'Oh, all right! We could go on like this for hours. We'll just have to boil all the water we drink – especially for Michael.'

I made sure both cats were on board and secured everything below that had rattled or rolled about on the way over, as the men prepared to cast off. With their feline sixth sense the cats had curled up in the sail locker in anticipation of the trip, glaring at me balefully, ears back. I wanted to curl up with them, to sleep until we reached Otterham Quay.

Short angry little waves greeted us as we reached the open sea. It was an onshore wind, West-South-West, so that what could have been a short run involved taking a fairly long leg out to sea in order to run back into Zeebrugge. *Elsa* did her best to go about but the steep little seas kept pushing her back on the old tack, until a final flurry of wind caught and held the mainsail enabling her to wallow around in a graceless manoeuvre. Everything crashed and slid and banged about in a cacophony – so much for my stowing! Peter slept soundly, entirely used to and at ease with this strange world he had been born into. Shouts summoned me up on deck and, holding on, I lurched into the well-deck. The truly formidable sight of the famous mole stood high against the sky a couple of miles away; silently, awe-struck we stared at the grim, unassailable towering wall. *Elsa* was sailing more easily now, as we approached and skirted the impressive length of the crescent-shaped jetty, over a mile long,

forming the harbour. Even our tall mast was dwarfed by the bleakly towering parapet. Uppermost in all our minds must have been the thought of the First World War attack on Zeebrugge by a British flotilla and the Royal Marines. What superhuman courage would have been needed to assail such an impregnable sea fortress! When we rounded the end of the mole, our gasps of astonishment were audible, as the jetty's massive thickness of nearly one hundred yards made us shake our heads in disbelief. The harbour was still closed to shipping in 1950, as a result of it being blocked in 1940 and blown up in 1944, but with our shallow draught we were able to motor between the buoyed channels to the yacht basin near the mouth of the canal leading to Bruges.

By some miracle the wind lessened overnight, to an acceptable Force 4 to 5; nevertheless it was a headwind which would mean a slow crossing. Both wind and seas were kinder to us on the way back; or it may just have seemed so in comparison with my forebodings. Deanne and I took the tiller for about half an hour each as *Elsa* thundered along on the port tack. She did not confide in me any more about her future plans or what she would be doing about George, but there was a resigned acceptance is his attitude which seemed conclusive.

It was the morning of the 13 August and leave was up, so that our neighbours in Otterham creek were expecting us, as, sailing past graceful Thames barges, whose crew waved cheerfully, we finally lowered the sails and motored up our tiny creek. They took our ropes and made fast. We were happy to be safely home again. Tilly and Pinky were even more pleased, jumping ashore before we had time to tie up; they hunted for a long time, making up for many lost mouse-catching hours.

While Deanne and George packed their zipper bags, James went to collect the car from the shelter of the boatyard and I made us all a last mug of coffee. They had enjoyed some of the trip I think, though I knew that George's patience had been sorely tried by so much domesticity. Suddenly, like waiting at a station, there was nothing to say; no longer were we a cohesive crew, belonging to the boat, but separate and very different individuals. My gratitude to Deanne was immense for all she had done, especially on the trip out, and as I kissed her goodbye, in my heart I wished her happiness. It was difficult to find anything warm or kind to say to George, as he shook our hands, politely thanking us for the sailing trip to Holland. Then James drove them to the station and we never saw them again.

On his way home he picked up Jake the spaniel from the kennels and I could see immediately he jumped out of the car how strangely changed he was. His tail was between his legs, and though he came to me willingly enough, his *joie de vivre* and wriggling bounce had gone. 'James – what's happened?' I exclaimed, as Michael rushed forward to hug his old friend and Jake cringed, lips curled in a near snarl. I could not believe it. James held Michael whilst at the same time fondling Jake's ear; 'Darling – it's terrible – apparently somehow he had a fight with a very vicious alsatian which attacked him, and though Jake wasn't badly hurt, he's been affected mentally – I don't know what we're going to do.' I stroked his silken head, tears in my eyes, for he was a different dog to the loving, affectionate Jake we had left only a fortnight before, 'Oh James! It's heartbreaking, but maybe he'll recover now he's back with us. We'll be gentle and careful, and not let Michael play with him. . . .' I stopped, for I knew how impossible that would be. 'We'll try everything we can.'

Somehow, in the bustle of settling back into the daily houseboat routine Jake appeared to recover. He would jump up on the settee beside me, eyes wary, but tail wagging gently, and I gave him lots of love. If Michael joined us, he would slink away, as though afraid of what he might do and on our afternoon walks, he stuck close to my heel as I pushed the pram – looking over his shoulder apprehensively.

Patricia had a fortnight's holiday due which involved me in being up on deck and below at the same time, in order to keep an eye on Michael who wanted to play on the bank and Peter who kept trying to climb out of his carri-cot. The three-year-old was puzzled by Jake's behaviour, trying to coax him onto the settee, or stroke his velvety head. It was impossible to explain, as I could not understand what trauma the dog had gone through, but the strain of curbing the boy's instinctive affectionate behaviour was worrying, though necessary, as I could see the beginnings of a snarl each time. For a few weeks we managed, despite Jake barking at the carricot every time Peter cried. Admittedly he did not cry often, but the hysterical yapping only made him worse.

The autumn was hot and beautiful, with a wealth of blackberries along the path to the end of the creek. Patricia came back, rested and happy after her holiday, and we would all set out, with the pram and containers for the luscious fruit, followed at a distance by the cats. They too were upset by the spaniel, used to curling up beside him, a furry trio. Now they eyed each other suspiciously.

CHAPTER SEVEN
Christmas on the Move

James's new appointment became known about this time. He was to report to *Plover*, a minesweeper based at Portsmouth, necessitating a search for a new berth for *Elsa*. He was naturally full of enthusiasm: 'There are so many lovely harbours on the south coast – lots of places to explore and the calm waters of the Solent to sail in.' I asked when he was due to join and his reply chilled me, 'Not until January, which means we can sail round during the Christmas leave.' My whole being revolted at this idea and I exploded violently, 'Oh, no! It will be much too cold and blowy in December.' Firmly, he went on, 'Cold, yes. But the weather can be lovely in December – no more gales than the summers we've known.' I had to admit the truth of that, and asked, 'Where had you thought of going?' 'Perhaps Bosham in Chichester harbour, or Hayling Island – I don't know yet. I'll go down one weekend and have a recce.'

We got out the map and poured over the myriad rivers and harbours. Certainly it would be more fun, with greater sailing scope than in the muddy Medway. He went on, 'Think how much easier to be able to sail when we want to. We'll always be afloat instead of sitting on the mud waiting for the tide.' I was forced, against my will, to agree with his irrefutable logic. I changed the subject, 'I'll start weaning Peter at six months, then he'll be over the difficult stage by December.' Absent mindedly and uninterestedly, he agreed with me.

For my twenty-fifth birthday in September, the equinoxial gales for once did not blow up the river to flood the bank, so that Patricia was prepared to stay on her own with the little boys while James took me out for a celebration dinner. It was a wonderful, unheard-of treat, to be alone with him,

eating what was probably an ordinary meal, but with a bottle of wine to loosen our tongues. I had to voice the fear and doubts that had been gnawing at me, 'James – I love you so – I wish I was a better sailor. You will always love me won't you, despite it. I'd die if you stopped loving me.' The eyes which could pierce like a gimlet, softened as he put his hand over mine, 'Of course I won't stop loving you.' I persisted, not aware how distasteful the subject was to him, 'Yes, but if you do, will you promise to tell me?' He promised, casually, then deliberately changed the subject. So we made plans about the journey and he assured me, 'We'll be able to put in somewhere every night and it's not very far, so if we don't like the weather we can stay put for a day or two.' Lulled into a sense of false security, thrusting my intuitions to the back of my mind, I complied with his wishes and we drove back to the boat, drowsily content.

In the saloon Patricia sat reading; a worried look on her face. She greeted us; 'Oh, I do hope you had a marvellous meal – but something's happened. . . .' I interrupted her, 'Not the boys?' 'No, no – they're fine – it's Jake. He growled at me and then he sat in the well and howled and howled. Now he's gone ashore and he's been gone for ages.' We comforted her and James fetched the torch to go and look for him while I started to feed Peter, nodding sleepily due to the wine. It seemed ages before he reappeared, with Jake. 'He was right down the footpath – maybe he tried to follow us.' James was as puzzled and frightened as I was by the schizophrenic behaviour. The persistent nagging fear in our minds was that Michael might become afraid of dogs.

The autumn weather brought rain, so that nappies no longer flapped round the rigging in a perpetual surrender; instead they draped over the big guard round the stove, where Jake curled up, warily watching Michael play with his bricks. The inevitable happened; Michael pushed one of the constructions too near the spaniel, who turned on him and snapped. Both the boy and dog were terribly upset. Michael merely had a nasty fright, whereas poor Jake slunk away, to hide in my cabin, feeling so guilty, his tail between his legs. We discussed the problem again, decided the risk was too great and that we would give Jake to an elderly couple with no children. He was only four and we loved him dearly, the decision was heartbreaking.

One weekend James went down to Chichester harbour but the quay at Bosham seemed too public, so he drove to Hayling Island and found a wonderful boatyard at Mill Rythe, with many wooden jetties. These were reached

through the boatyard so that one was not at the mercy of any casual passer-by. He duly arranged for us to berth there around the end of December.

The weather at the end of October was perfect, with clear blue skies and moderate winds enabling us to sail to Garrison Point and Queenborough one weekend, with a splendid crew, called Bill. He was a brother officer, unmarried but fond of children, kind and thoughtful, even offering to peel potatoes up on deck, make pots of tea, in short any odd job that needed doing. He was a real blessing, for now Peter had completely outgrown his carricot, sitting up and climbing out of it onto the bunk on which it was placed. As yet, this had no side to it, so I had to watch him constantly for fear the rolling of the boat might tip him onto the floor. James soon made expert wooden railings which slotted into the side, transforming the bunk into an effective playpen/cot. This was just what Peter had been waiting for, to pull himself up and try to stand.

When I went into his little cabin, the expression of sheer concentration on his face was impressive, as, trammelled though he was by a fluffy blue sack-like dressing gown, he gripped the rails and hauled himself up, if only for an instant. A big grin would greet me, then his fingers would loosen, and chuckling he would fall over, holding out his arms to be picked up. His ceaseless activity helped to ease the painful sorrow of losing Jake, who had settled down quite contentedly with the ageing couple, going for walks and leading a well-ordered life. Michael was extremely patient with his younger brother. He spent ages laboriously constructing a splendid ferry on one of the locker boards, only to have it meet head on with a fast-crawling devil, hell-bent on sinking ferries. As I tactfully removed or distracted Peter, allowing his elder brother a chance to reconstruct the complicated edifice, I was thankful that Jake was not there to be plagued by them both.

We bought a highchair and a harness. Unlike the placid Michael who had stayed put, Peter had only one ambition in life, to climb out of everything. Now that Michael was three-and-a-half and old enough not to fall overboard when up on deck, Patricia went back home, just coming over for a couple of days a week so that I could go shopping on the bus into Rainham without a toddler and pushchair. I felt much stronger, too, now that I was no longer feeding Peter. The two brothers were close friends, despite the sinking of ferries, and there was nothing the cats liked more than to cuddle up warmly in the pram in the well. No matter what the two boys

did, either inadvertently or on purpose; whether their tails were pulled or their soft furry bodies hugged too tight, Tilly and Pinky behaved with utmost decorum and devotion. Sometimes, in a huff, they just padded away. Once, Michael, in order to impress his younger brother *did* pull Tilly's tail too hard, after being told not to. For the first time I smacked the astonished boy – hard – on the leg. Tilly had leapt ashore in pained astonishment and sat there, tail twitching, staring hard at me, disapprovingly. Michael's tears brought her back into the well, where she robbed her soft body against his legs, forgivingly comforting him, making me feel guilty, but her tail was never pulled again.

The weeks flashed past, with weekends mainly spent in overhauling the rigging, main sheets, anchor cable, rudder pintles and, for the first time, the sea anchor. This was a cone-shaped canvas bag with a wide mouth and a small opening at the tail rather like a wind-sock on an aerodrome. Theoretically it would be lowered over the stern, in really bad storms, to make the boat lie head-to-seas, with only a slight drift astern. Only the mizzen sail or bare mast were needed in severe gales to keep her head on, with a long warp trailing the sea anchor. Needless to say, this conjured up horrific pictures, both imagined and remembered from the many true sailing books on our bookshelves.

My father was now living on the Isle of Wight, having remarried. Because of living at the opposite ends of the country we had not yet met by step-mother, but it was a relief to know that he was being so well loved and looked after. I wrote to them with the good news of our sailing round to Hayling Island, adding that it would be fun to be so near that we could sail to Yarmouth quite easily for weekends. My father, astounded at our venturing to sea in December, exploded with literary rage, very nearly forbidding us to do so! But as I explained by letter, James could only sail during leave periods and Christmas leave was the only possible time for otherwise it would mean leaving the boys and myself alone 'up a creek' until Easter. A stormy silence ensued!

Bill was to be our crew, a comforting thought, whilst Patricia agreed to accompany us on the way round, providing she could return home for three or four days over Christmas. James agreed immediately, 'That'll be easy. I expect we shall tie up in some harbour for a few days and as I'll be on board of course you must go home for Christmas.' The stove kept the whole boat warm, staying alight all night with coalite. We had put a paraffin heater in the after cabin

for Patricia. The coalite posed a small storage problem, which we overcame by converting the paint locker up for'ard. As there was a hatch it would be easy to buy a sack or two on our way round, merely adding to the general procedure of refuelling.

The last few days at Otterham Creek sped by, as we peered at the barometer – avidly listening to every meteorological report and, most reliable of all, scanning the sky and clouds. In those far off days only the immediate next few hours could be forecast, and as we were to find out, not always accurately.

One of the main drawbacks was going to be the very short daylight hours but that did not worry James, 'As long as we've got plenty of searoom it's just as safe in the dark.' Secretly I always felt that sinister happenings lurked behind the cloak of darkness. If we left before dawn on the morning of 16 December we could make Ramsgate by that evening; knowing the harbour so well by now, it would be easy to enter.

That night the wind blew steadily but not too strong and I went to bed early after washing up and changing Peter, leaving the two men to plot our course on the chart. Mentally James was miles away as he called: 'Goodnight darling – the tide will be just right at 0600 – can you give us a hand with the mooring ropes and holding a torch?' The strange mixture of excitement, fear and the mystery of an unknown destination had me in its spell; half of me wanting to be like him: 'Of course. I wouldn't miss the start of this journey for anything. We'll have a mug of tea about 5.30 and breakfast under way.' Coming back down to earth, he kissed me, murmuring: 'You're wonderful.' Admittedly I thought so too – if slightly mad as well – for what other sane, sensible, normal housewife would agree to such folly. I had become his Svengali.

It was strange and momentous to be leaving this muddy creek after so long, for the last time. The boys and cats were still fast asleep when I tipped a hod full of coalite on the stove, grateful for the delicious warmth of the saloon. Bill was already up and dressed; 'I've put the kettle on. Where's the skipper?' James was filling the water tank, bringing our length of hose back with him, 'I'm afraid this will have to join the rest of the junk in your cabin Bill, but as you'll be sleeping on the settee in the saloon most of the time, you don't really mind do you.' Bill laughed, 'Fat lot of good it would do me if I *did* mind!'

I switched on the navigation lights, so simple in comparison with *Pat*, for they were electric and run off the

battery charged by the engine – no messy paraffin. The engine responded with a roar and James put the tiller hard over as he slowly reversed *Elsa* until she was at right angles to the bank. 'Let go for'ard!' he called to Bill, who clambered on board as we completed our turn and were facing down the creek.

The forecast was due at 6 a.m. so I tore below to listen. '. . . Thames, Dover, Wight. . . West-North-West, Force 4 to 5, rising, visibility good. . . .' Excellent news. Bill and I coiled and tidied ropes; retrieving the fenders too, while James, who always seemed to be able to see in the dark, carefully followed the compass course. We had slipped our moorings so quietly and quickly there had been no time for nostalgia.

Once we were out of the Medway, safely off Sheerness, with the dawn breaking, Bill hoisted the mainsail, jib and foresail on the port tack as I lowered the port leeboard with the winch. James switched off the engine. Clear of the lee of the shore, we felt the full impact of the wind as *Elsa*'s great mainsail filled joyously, heeling us over gently. The mouth of the Thames was calm because of the offshore wind and to my inexpressible delight I did not feel sick. It was cold, very cold, with occasional showers as darker grey clouds raced across beneath the uniformly grey sky. Obviously it got much rougher as we lost the protection of the land and sailed into the Straits, but we were slipping through the water like a racing yacht and the exhilaration buoyed me up. It helped too, being able to keep on the same tack. We dressed Michael up warmly in his snow-suit so that he could play in the well, putting a harness on him with a line attached to the binnacle to stop him falling overboard by mistake. Bill was so good with him, holding a serious conversation, unlike George who had never spoken to the boy.

That first day we played safe, sailing into familiar Whitstable before dark, for there was no need to hurry as we only had half the distance to cover that we had sailed in the spring of 1949. The wind stayed in the North, occasionally backing to North-West by North or veering North-East by North. I had not appreciated what a difference not having a southwesterly gale would make to the sea; especially the absence of an underlying swell. Perhaps I was fitter, the net result being a seasickness one could live with – nearly controlled by Kwells – vastly relieved by being sick without the accompanying dizziness and headaches.

Tilly and Pinky only woke to drink a little milk, eat their

cat food and use their box. Tilly tried to slip into Peter's bunk for warmth, as they could not get anywhere near the fire, but I dared not let her stay for long because of his bear-like hugs. I began to realize James was living in a world of his own, while we existed only on the extreme outer edge. I did not have the time to put this into words or even coherent thoughts; let alone philosophize about it, for mentally and physically I was totally absorbed in the boys' welfare.

The first four days or so sped by uneventfully, except for the usual panic and chaos when entering harbour and going alongside. Sometimes a mooring line, no matter how skilfully thrown, would fall short of the jetty, where some kind person nearly always stood waiting to catch it. Then *Elsa* would carry on her majestic progress regardless, occasionally causing embarrassment as when the bowsprit seemed in danger of colliding with some fishing boat or other obstacle. Sharp shouted instructions, well larded with expletives, would ensue, as we bustled about with boathooks and fenders, tripping over hastily lowered sails, odd ropes and each other. The wind still held and the forecasts were without severe gales or even fog – equally dreaded. In Dover, James called me to him. 'Our next leg is a long one. Do you mind if we just spend one night at sea? I'd like to get right round Dungeness and Beachy Head with plenty of searoom, before putting into Newhaven.' Feeling more confident than usual I agreed, 'Yes darling – just this once – of course. Will we be able to stay in Newhaven over Christmas?' He replied with an affectionate lop-sided smile, 'Actually, that's what I'd thought. Bill can go home for a few days, Patricia too, and as I'll be here all the time we'll have a tree and a proper Christmas together. After all, that's the point, it doesn't matter where the boat lies – it's our home.' I sat beside him, and took his hand, 'I've done nothing about cards and presents – how awful.' He laughed, 'Well, we'd better sail into Newhaven pretty fast, so that you can catch up.'

That first evening at sea in winter, dusk and night were kind to us. *Elsa* sailed on unperturbed by the dark as though she could see in the gloom, swishing and bubbling through the phosphorescence of the tamed waves. The night itself was starlit and clear, though eerie, all sounds strangely changed in the dark.

The following day, we put in at Newhaven which was one of the few ports or harbours on the South Coast we had not yet sailed into, so we were relieved to be doing so in daylight. The long, long entrance between the two jetties caused a phenomenal swell, or send, rather like the Severn

'bore', and we found ourselves swept up on one of its waves, coasting along at a tremendous rate, until we reached quieter waters further up. A trot of fishing boats lay alongside a pontoon and we nudged our way in beside them.

After a hurried meal, Bill and Patricia went off to catch a train. It was only 20 December so they had a good holiday to look forward to. Before leaving, she hastily put some little parcels on our bunk, saying 'Have a very happy Christmas all of you. These are just some little things for the boys.' I was overcome and apologized to her: 'Oh Pat, you *are* kind – and I feel awful. I haven't done any shopping yet at all – not even for the boys or my husband.' 'I know,' she smilingly answered, 'You've been rather busy recently!' adding, 'I'll see you on the 27, for the last leg of the journey. I do hope it isn't too far from the boat to the shops for you, but your husband will be there to help.'

Once James had seen the harbour master and explained the position with two little ones on board, we moved to another berth. The movement was extremely lively, for the rise and fall was tremendous – at least twenty feet – whilst the send and swell made us career up and down like a lion pacing his cage. We put out all our fenders to protect the side as we surged to and fro, especially at high tide, when the slack of the mooring lines gave us full rein. I could only get ashore with the pushchair and Michael at high tide when the gangplank was horizontal. Having made sure *Elsa* was secure, we all went shopping next morning, in a fever of Christmas excitement, to buy belated cards and presents, a tree, our first few decorations and tinsel; plus, more prosaically, to organize fuel, water and the mundane everyday necessities.

Soon the saloon was cleared of damp clothing, swept and dusted, warmed by the stove and lit by the soft glow of the paraffin lamp. It was transformed from sailing boat to home with James trying to explain the sacred mysteries of Christmas to Michael.

Despite the long walk from the harbour to the town for the day-to-day essentials (delivered to most people) I was happy. Let it blow as much as it liked; James was with me and I had him all to myself. The glowing moments were rare and not reciprocated. I knew he must be bored and wished I could astonish him one day with some stupendous achievement – or at least make him perceive his luck in having a wife willing to live – and nearly *enjoy* some of it – this diabolical life.

*In return, yes, I was demanding. I needed – craved –
affection – love both physical and verbal – wanted to be
told this or that was well done – kissed – made love to –
childish maybe. But because I wished to show and share this
side of our relationship, I presumed, in crass but
understandable ignorance, he must feel the same – unless
of course, he had stopped loving me altogether, and yet I
could not bring myself to believe that this had already
happened.*

These fleeting thoughts were put aside for the magic of
Christmas. Peter's own present to us were his first steps, at
nine months, and I did not voice my secret thought it it
would have made life simpler had he left this accomplish-
ment until he was fifteen-months-old like his elder brother
had done. Michael's eyes were wide with excitement and
wonder at the little tree and his stocking; the Christmas
chicken and apple crumble tasted delicious.

The weather grew colder, but as the wind eased it did not
appear so cold. Soon the peaceful interlude was over. Only
one more short sail and we would be safely moored in our
new surroundings.

On the day after Boxing Day, shouts of, 'Ahoy!' followed
by the thud of footsteps on deck meant the rest of the ship's
company had turned up. Patricia was given a rapturous
welcome by the boys. She hugged them both, then holding
her hands to the fire, exclaimed, 'Goodness, it's cold!
There's snow in the air. Did you manange all right over
Christmas? I had a happy time at home, but believe it or not
– I missed you all!' I assured her that we had missed her far
more.

CHAPTER EIGHT
The Blizzard

James was pleased and relieved to have his crew back on board and they immediately got out the chart, though as Bill said, 'It's so near, we hardly need to plot a course!' James smiled wryly, pointing out that it was as well to know what rock, sandbanks and buoys to miss, adding, 'There's still Selsey Bill to get round – quite a nasty race off that point. I want to give it a wide berth.' Bill asked when we would sail, and I gave a gasp as I heard James explain, 'I thought that as the wind is from just the right quarter, East-North-East – ideal in fact – we might leave tonight.' I interrupted, furious at his betrayal of trust, 'James, you said we would definitely never sail again at night.' Ignoring my interruption he went on, 'We wouldn't sail till about 11 p.m. in order to catch the tide. I definitely want to enter Chichester harbour for the first time in daylight. It's a tricky entrance with a bar. That way we'll have two days left to the end of my leave to settle in and get ourselves organized.' Annoyed with myself for such a display of temper, I had to pretend to agree. After all it would only be half the night and into harbour by lunchtime.

The maintenance work had been dealt with during our spell in Newhaven, so there was little preparation necessary. *Elsa* had not sat still for a moment owing to the swell, therefore my sea legs had asserted themselves – no fear of being sick. We all listened intently to the 6 p.m. weather forecast, '. . . Thames, Dover, Wight winds Force 4 to 5, gusting to Force 6, East-North-East. Visibility good. . . .' Perfect – a soldier's wind, albeit fairly strong, but the seas would only be slight being off shore. The stove had been filled with a hod to last the night, supper cleared way and we stood in the well, leaning against the cabin top, sheltered by its height, mugs of cocoa warming our hands, waiting for the

tide to turn. It was a magnificent, clear, bitterly cold night; the sky was dense with unnaturally brilliant stars. Bill saw a shooting star plummet down and we scanned the sky for more; if we could count seven we decided it would be a lucky omen. Never before or since have I seen so many plunging glittering trails as the unearthly firework display given by falling stars that night. Before James started the engine, about 11 p.m. he tapped the barometer which was just starting to fall slightly. We dismissed it as irrelevant – surely we would have reached Chichester before any significant change in the wind or weather.

We stood by to let go for once we were clear of the entrance, close hauled on the port tack, Bill was to take the first two-hour watch, well muffled up, after which James would relieve him. '. . . Unless you are too cold to hold the tiller, in which case give me a shout sooner.' Soon we slipped out of the harbour, rolling about a bit until the sails filled and steadied her, whereupon we seemed to fly along like a racing yacht. Patricia went below to curl up beside Michael in the after cabin and James and I lay down together on the settee to snatch a short rest. As always, James fell asleep straight away, with a sailor's ease, but I lay beside him, fearful and apprehensive, at the same time ashamed of my lack of confidence in his superb seamanship.

The sound of the hull swishing smoothly and crisply through the comparatively calm seas lulled me into an uneasy doze, helped by the warmth from the glowing stove. The hiss of the boat seemed to increase as we sped along; at this rate, I thought, we would be off Chichester before dawn. *Elsa* heeled over in response to the increasing strength of the wind, and at that moment Bill's voice could be heard above the roar of the wind and waves as he opened the companionway door and called down, 'James. It's snowing and gusting a bit. Can't hold her on this course any longer.' James was up on deck in a flash, pulling his bobble cap down over his ears and buttoning up his oilskin. I followed in my short duffle coat and was filled with awe and disbelief at the full impact of the wind's increasing ferocity and whirling, driving snow.

The scene was diabolically beautiful, with the mast and rigging covered in snow where it settled and stuck as it does on trees. Bill had not noticed, as he steered, that the wind had veered easterly and increased whilst *Elsa* blithely sailed along; nor did he wish to waken James unnecessarily. The bitter east wind cut through clothes like sharp cold knives; stark terror took hold of my heart and mind. James, as ever,

was to all outward appearances quiet and confident, though instantly aware of the danger. Glancing at the compass and sails, he briefly eased the tiller over, bringing her onto a close reach, while he thought with lightning speed what should be done.

Already our fingers and faces were numb. The snow was blinding, as thicker and faster the flakes tore past us, eerily lit for an instant or so by the light from the saloon skylight. Within minutes the full easterly gale was upon us. James had to shout to make himself heard, 'Bill, can you and Tonia lower the mainsail. I'll point her up into the wind to empty the sail. We'll lose it otherwise. Then I'll start the engine. The jib and foresail will keep enough steerage way on her.' Spray from the short breaking seas was already freezing and coating the cabin top and sheets with ice. Profound dread replaced the exhilaration of the first carefree hour. Bill took his lead from James, working as fast and as calmly as he could, while fear inspired me with a desperate strength, forcing my numb fingers to claw at the rigid frozen sail in its wildly drunken flapping, while my gumboots slithered on the lurching slippery deck. Bereft of the steadying influence of the sail, *Elsa* pitched and rolled in the short steep waves, as James strove to control the massive tiller. Each breath was agony, for the raw, icy gale filled one's lungs with frozen needles. My brain was paralyzed, filled with one all-pervading thought till I felt it would burst. The boys. What would happen to them? One split second in that cruel cold sea would kill them. Why had I not *insisted* on waiting till dawn? Look at what my meekly giving way to his 'superior judgment' had done.

'Lash the boom – quickly – or it will snap off!' yelled James. He started the engine in a desperate attempt to keep us clear of the Isle of Wight. The sail lay in bundled, billowing folds any-old-how on the deck, with no hope of trying to lash it tidily under those conditions. Vainly, slipping about in the well, we tried to throw a rope up over the boom, for by now it was too icy and dangerous to stand on the cabin top in order to reach it where it swung wildly to and fro. Patricia's white and terror-stricken face appeared in the hatchway to her cabin. James tried to reassure her, 'We're rolling about a bit because it's snowing and we've had to lower the mainsail. Keep warm in bed with Michael.' Obediently she disappeared. He then got Bill and me to hold the tiller, eventually succeeding in securing the ice-covered boom himself, lashing it down amidships as hard as he could. He shouted to make himself heard, 'We're travelling much too

fast – and heading straight for Bembridge rocks with this shift in the wind. We'll have a send up a flare and hope they see it and send out a lifeboat.'

How could our ineffectual, one-screw engine struggle against this nightmare tumultuous sea? I was too numbed with shock and fear to cry, but every nerve in my body exploded with horror as I imagined us crashing onto the rocks; breaking up, while the blue, lifeless bodies of the small boys were smashed and rent. I moaned. 'Oh, James!' Briefly he pulled me to him, 'Pray very hard my darling. I will do all I can. I am shattered by this – forgive me. But this blizzard was not forecast.' My lips were too stiff to answer, but inwardly I loved and trusted him implicitly. Holding on tightly I staggered down the steps, looking into Peter's cabin on my way to the galley. Unbelievably, he was still asleep. Fearing that he might be thrown against the wooden bars of the bunk side I grabbed a couple of cushions from the settee to pad the inside of the wooden bars.

James left Bill to hold the tiller, secured by ropes and pulleys, while he fetched the flares. As I reached the galley, my fingers started to thaw out, resulting in excruciating pain and I cried out, astonished at the intensity; unable to use them until the blood circulated again. Now and again the faint whirr of the engine could be heard bravely battling against the elements, out of the water most of the time. The effort and concentration needed to fill and hold on to the kettle while it boiled, bracing myself by pressing by back against the bulkhead, wedging a foot at the same time as holding on with one hand, made the fear and dread recede for a while. Putting some biscuits in my pocket and grabbing one mug, I painfully hauled myself back on deck in time to see and hear one of the flares shoot up with a whoosh – soon lost to sight in the whipping blanket of snow. The hot drink was cold before Bill could put it to his numbed lips. I went back for some for James, who by now had lashed the tiller amidships and was up for'ard, lowering the jib and foresail. I screamed at him, as loud as I could to tie a rope round himself. In those seas, rearing and wicked, invisible until right alongside us, if he slipped in, we would be powerless to save him, as *Elsa* was now their plaything. The blizzard picked her up and shook her like a toy, forcing her to cavort like a crazy mechanical object whose tightly-coiled spring had suddenly parted.

Occasionally, above the crashing of blocks and tackle and the shrieking of the wind, we could still hear the mad racings of the engine as the propeller, lifted right out of the water as

we slithered down a trough, whirred uselessly. Soon the strain on it became too much and it stopped. We were now truly helpless, out of control, and despite our three flares, no sign of any response. We had no idea how far away we were from the Isle of Wight and the infamous Bembridge rocks, but no one, in that dense blizzard, could have seen them, even close to. James had released the flares to boost our dwindling hope and morale. None of us could move our lips by now, so stiff with cold and ice they were, but I managed to persuade Bill to come down into the saloon to thaw out, leaving James vainly trying to pierce the immediate whiteness, etched against the black night; praying he would not see the darker shapes of the headland; straining too, to hear the particular roar of the shallows – yet praying with all my soul and strength not to.

Luckily Bill had great big naval watch-keeping mittens on and a long enveloping oilskin. His and James's were the only two on board. Even so, he was frozen right through and sat on the floor in the saloon by the fire, miraculously still alight. It must have been about 4 a.m. Being December, the night was endless and we knew no dawn would break before 8 a.m. As soon as some feeling had returned to his numbed body he insisted on keeping watch so that James could come below. Love, grief and appalling fear made me lose control as I saw his snow-covered face and figure climb stiffly down the steps into the saloon and I sobbed as I clung to him hysterically, ashamed, yet unable to stop. He was too shattered and frozen to speak but his eyes were steely and determined. I admitted my great fear to him and when he had drunk a hot mug of tea and eaten some biscuits, a little colour returned to his face and he quietly said: 'We have done all we possibly can – we don't know what lies ahead – but now we must get some sleep if we can. Save all our strength for when it's needed. Bill will call me if there's any change.' How I admired his incredible control, courage and determination. Having given me a brief hug, he lay down on the floor in his oilskin, ready for instant action and within no time at all was fast asleep.

I pulled myself together, forced myself to calm down, inspired by his example and lay down beside him, comforted as ever by his presence. The physical effort required to prevent oneself from being hurtled and rolled about on the floor stopped my sleeping, so I lay there waiting for a louder crash, jolt or shock which would mean the end. I could picture the scene in my mind, imagining that if we were flung far enough up on to the rocks, it might be possible to wrap

the boys up and carry them to safety. After a while, too fearful to rest any longer, cramming my bobble hat on my head again I hauled myself up the companionway to look for Bill. For a sickening, awful moment I thought he had vanished overboard, but peering up for'ard through the snow I could just make out his silhouette as he held on tightly to the snowy rigging, straining his eyes for a glimpse of the killer rocks.

By now the entire boat was thick with snow and ice. Icicles hung from the boom and rigging; it looked like a diabolical Dante engraving or one of those encapsulated snow scenes. Would morning never come? The tune of *Eternal Father strong to save* played itself over and over in my head – a wordless, yearning prayer. Slipping and sliding, I reached the poop deck and opened the companionway an inch or two. The little bulkhead light by her bunk showed Patricia and Michael fast asleep, one head each end, somehow giving an illusion of safety, normality and warmth. I crept back again. Even that short sortie had turned by fingers dead white again and I moaned gently as I pressed them under my arms, between my legs, anywhere to bring them back to life, despite the pain it caused. When James work up a little later the blizzard was still raging but he was more optimistic now as he was certain we must have avoided Bembridge and the Isle of Wight too. He had no idea where we might be, but the constantly backing and veering East-North-East gale must have blown us way out to sea, where at least we ran no danger of going aground.

He relieved the snowman-like figure of Bill; the careering nightmare sail in the blizzard and dark wore on. I dozed through sheer exhaustion, woken by the intense cold and realized that the comforting warm stove had gone out. It would have been impossible to light it again under those turbulent conditions where we were being tossed about in all directions, driven inexorably further out into the Channel, sailing under the bare pole of our towering mast.

At long last, a barely perceptible lightening of the horizon heralded a bleak dawn. The wind increased to Force 8, but the snow had stopped and in its place an icy brilliant sunlit dawn burst upon us as we pitched and rolled at the mercy of pale emerald green seas of amazing cruelty. The sky too, a faded clear turquoise, mocked our helpless plight. Our teeth chattered uncontrollably and we shivered in our wet clothes. Peter woke, hungry and furious at not being able to stand up. It was so lucky that I had padded the comfy bunk for he could come to no harm even when tossed about.

Somehow he managed to drink some milk from his mug, settling down to nibble a biscuit – the only breakfast I could offer him. Changing his nappy took ages; his little body so warm I would have given anything to climb into his bunk and hold him to me in order to thaw out, but I bundled him back into the fluffy blue dressing gown and left him happily if messily chewing a second rusk.

Patricia appeared, as frightened and shaken as I was, but brave, determined to take some milk and biscuits over to Michael. We drank some tea, for with two people it was possible to pour the boiling kettle onto the pot, each one holding on with one hand, and the teapot or kettle with the other. Poor James and Bill looked haggard with bloodshot eyes. As they drank the hot liquid, an ominous banging reverberated against the side, Terrified, I shouted, 'What's that? Have we hit something?' James was already on deck, Bill at his heels. I followed, in my flimsy duffle coat, in time to see him peering over the side. It was the massive, thick starboard leeboard, having sheered through the wires that lowered it. Still held by its pivoting great bolt which rivetted it to the side, it crashed against the rubbing strake. James shouted, 'Quick! The axe. It'll stove us in if we don't cut it clear.' It took ages to find the axe, hidden at the bottom of the sail locker, disturbing the sleeping cats to get at it. They burrowed deeper. In my agony of fear I had completely forgotten them.

It was a hazardous task for James to hack away at a constantly moving target, in imminent danger of being washed overboard as his boots slipped on the icy deck and he leaned over the side. Eventually it broke free, whipped out of sight in a split second. I wonder where its massive great bulk landed up. They were made of solid three to four-inch thick seasoned oak, about seven-feet long, shaped like a wing, the wide after end being roughly four to five feet deep.

The snow had blown away, leaving a coating of ice over every surface which gave the appearance of a boat made of brittle glass, dazzling to the eyes, reflecting all the colours of a diamond or rainbow. No land was in sight and our plight was serious, for with no sail or engine we could only drift helplessly, lurching and bouncing over the waves. Even in her distress *Elsa* sped on with dignity, rising and falling like a bird on the turbulent seas. Her remaining wing, or leeboard, suffered the same fate as the other, clanging and battering against the side, until James hacked it free. We all felt ashamed at submitting her to such wounded pride.

Suddenly and unbelievably, on our horizon appeared a

speck – a boat – rescue! Would it see us? We were so camouflaged, a green boat tossing in a green sea. Slipping and sliding we waved and stupidly shouted and to our immense relief a cargo ship – or lighter – approached us to within hailing distance.

She could not get near us as she was out of cargo, high in the water and as the seas were so huge her sides would have crushed us. I had some notion that if a boat is rescued as a total loss, the vessel that has come to her aid can claim 100% salvage; therefore, in order to prove there was nothing seriously wrong, I stood on the cabin top, clutching the ice-covered boom with my bare hand, waving cheerily with the other, while my mouth froze into a grinning welcome. James hailed her, briefly explaining our predicament, engine broken down and no leeboards, meaning that even if we did hoist the sails, once it had all thawed out, we would only drift sideways. They asked if we would like a tow, pointing out that we were in mid-Channel, well south of the Isle of Wight. We accepted eagerly and a brief discussion ensued as to where we should attach it.

Meanwhile, she circled us, great rusty sides towering above us one moment, then as she rolled crazily, her whole upper deck was in view. The cold was piercing, my lungs seemed full of icicles and I decided my role was over, and that I could go below to put on a kettle. Horror-stricken, I realized my hand would not leave the boom. There was no feeling in it. It was stuck fast. Bill saw my plight and swiftly removing his great mitten put it over my bare hand to thaw it out, releasing it from the boom. This only took a moment and unaware of the damage done, I stayed on deck a while longer to watch the manoeuvring to get a tow-rope on board. It was decided to tie it round the base of the mast. They duly pulled ahead, steaming very slowly, then shot the tow-rope by catapult towards us. It fell short. James and Bill were getting soaked by the icy spray up for'ard as they crouched ready to catch the catapulted rope. Time and time again the lighter hauled it back and tried again. Once indeed it landed on deck, and the two men tried desperately, with numbed fingers, to attach it round the mast, but the lighter pulled away in the heaving seas and the rope whipped back over the bows. It was a hopeless task.

James spoke again through the loud hailer, 'You are most kind and we are very grateful but I don't think this is possible. Can you please sent a radio message to the signal station, or lifeboat station at Portsmouth and ask if a tug can come out and tow us in. We have two very small children on

board.' They replied that they would do so and stand by us until help came. We then went below, disappointed at our failure but with real hope of an end to our near shipwreck.

It was when I reached the galley that I saw my dead white fingers on both hands. They would not come back to life. Eventually, with James rubbing them and breathing on them, such an excruciating pain shot through them that I screamed out loud. I shook and shivered in torment. Patricia came over, holding a mug of tea for me to drink, for I could not even use my swollen, frost-bitten fingers. They went a very funny colour, but in time the pain eased.

It took a day for the tug to reach us, but during that time, the lighter stayed by us, circling slowly, ready to give assistance should we founder. We were immensely touched by this warm-hearted seamanlike gesture, greatly comforted by their presence. The gale never abated, but somehow James and Bill managed to relight the stove, though we ate nothing but biscuits all day, with tea or Bovril to drink and milk for the boys who remained warm and mostly sleepy. Patricia came over from her cabin, insisting that I go and lie down in her bunk with Michael to warm up and get some sleep. 'I've been warm most of the time and I'm worried about your poor hands. How do they feel now?' The silly sausage-shaped objects behaved as if they were half paralysed, but it never occurred to me that it was real frost bite – that only happened at the North Pole! I nodded gratefully, close to tears after the strain of the day, 'Yes, that would be marvellous. Let's finish the biscuits and make another hot drink – and give some more milk and an apple to the boys. Do you think you can change Peter's nappy? I don't trust these fingers with pins!'

The sheer adaptability of children is truly amazing. Peter had played with his rattles, cuddly toys and teething rings and calmly gone back to sleep, blissfully unaware of the drama surrounding him! When *would* the tug arrive? Bill came below for a quick sleep on the floor by the stove, leaving James to watch out for it. A new fear was that the rudder pintles might snap, which would leave us wallowing beam on to the seas, when the resulting rolling might easily dismast us. I dragged myself up into the well. James's beloved face was gaunt and unshaven, his eyes sunken and hollow as he nursed the great tiller which was at least keeping us head on. 'The wind is easing a bit at last.' He said thankfully, as he grasped the hot mug, 'Thank goodness, for it would be an awfully uncomfortable ride, being towed along by a tug through these waves.' Guiltily, I said, 'Darling,

I'm sorry I was so terrified. But at least I wasn't seasick!'
He spoke indistinctly with a voice blurred by tiredness,
'I was terrified too.' 'I know,' I said, 'But you never show
it.' He went on, 'I must get some sleep because I'll have
to stay on deck and nurse her along while we're being
towed.' I told him, 'Bill has had nearly an hour – it must be
mid-afternoon by now. It'll be dark soon. I'll wake him.' As
I said this, the lighter hailed us to say they had received a
message from the tug which would be here in half an hour
or so and they wished us farewell, safe return, adding that
they would leave us now. James thanked them warmly and
we waved to the valiant crew who must have spent some
very uncomfortable hours rolling their guts out circling us,
as they were out of cargo.

I snuggled down with Michael, who had been playing with
his Matchbox cars on the shelf above the bunk. They raced up
and down with the movement of the boat, 'Like real cars,
Mummy,' he spoke seriously. Occasionally they spilled onto
the eiderdown which had been transformed into a mountainous track, 'I'm hungry,' he added. I produced biscuits
and an apple from my pocket and he chewed away
contentedly. Before I went to sleep I heard the clatter and
welcome arrival of the tug. The relief was overpowering. It
could all so easily have ended in disaster. James popped his
head in the companionway to the after cabin, 'We've fixed
the tow-rope. They'll go slowly, but it may be a bit bumpy.
Bill will steer for a while and I'll sleep. I'm afraid it'll take a
good few hours to reach Portsmouth.' 'Never mind. Thank
God we're safe,' I murmured. Before I had time to formulate
a really heartfelt prayer I was fast asleep.

The feeling of safety, responsibility relinquished and fear
a fast receding memory, induced a deep, exhausted sleep as
though drugged. Michael's warm little body nestled up to me
and slowly the healing warmth returned in comforting
ecstatic waves. I was useless, hoping they could manage
without any ineffectual attempts to help from me. I did not
even wake up when, long after dark, the tug plus willing
helpers manoeuvred us into the naval basin at Portsmouth.
Patricia had looked after Peter, giving him a warm drink of
milk and rusks after were were safely moored.

We all slept on late into the morning – that is to say, late
for us – at least 8 a.m.! Patricia lay on the settee, with Bill
dead to the world on the floor by the stove and James fully
clad on our bunk. The wind had dropped and an innocent
sunny morning made us wonder whether it had all been a
horrendous nightmare. I stood in the well, with an excited

bouncy Michael, surveying the shambles that had been wrought. Poor *Elsa*. Her decks looked like the emptied contents of a giant rubbish bin, with the torn bowsprit net hanging forlornly in shreds up for'ard. Cautiously, the cats appeared, whiskers twitching in anticipation of a run ashore. Not liking to appear too eager, they stretched extensively before stalking over to inspect the gangplank and jetty. I stretched too, making every muscle in my wracked body ache.

A dockyard workman came past, looked at us disparagingly at first, then speculatively, finally shaking his head, as he said in a disappointed voice; 'I thought you'd been dismasted – the papers say you've been dismasted – rotten b . . . .g papers – can't believe a word they say, can you?' With that he was gone! Panic seized me, 'Oh, *no!* I thought, 'My father will see it and be terribly upset – and all we've lost is our leeboards.' Leaving Michael well wrapped up, to play in the well, I went below to start breakfast, stepping over the sleeping Bill. I was ravenous, light-headed with relief.

When I picked up the matches to light the gas, I had the strangest sensation. Though I had full use of my fingers, they could not *feel* what they were holding. Presumably this would wear off. The smell of chandler's bacon and coffee woke the other three up. Poor James and Bill, their eyes were red-rimmed and running, but otherwise they were in good shape. Patricia, though, had a bad cold, and was suffering from delayed shock. Once she had eaten her breakfast we made her go back to bed. I told James about the article in the newspaper and he said he would go out immediately and buy one. Baldly it stated that *Elsa,* a Dutch Boeier, belonging to Lt Commander J. Renton, was dismasted during yesterday's blizzard and had to be towed into Portsmouth harbour – or words to that effect.

Presumably the journalists hang around lifeboat stations, and rescue services, during stormy weather, waiting for interesting items of gloomy news. That I could understand, but felt very strongly that they might have got it right. Once James had eaten and we had tidied ourselves, he and I went in search of a telephone to reassure our parents. My father was beside himself with fury. Vainly I tried to explain, 'But Daddy, – dismasted is much, *much* worse than losing your leeboards.' He just kept repeating, 'I don't know or care what a leeboard is. You should *not* have put to sea in December.' I knew he was right, yet had to be loyal to James and tried again, 'We had perfect weather until the blizzard hit us and

that wasn't forecast.' He went on spluttering and muttering about the 'downright, selfish irresponsibility of the young' and so on and so on. James got much the same response from his own father.

As we walked back to the boat we discussed what should be done. James remarked sadly, 'It's going to take a long time to get her seaworthy again. There's so much to repair. We'll even need new sails. The mainsail split badly before we lowered it.' I said firmly, 'We can't possibly live on board while this work is going on. Where shall we go?' He agreed, 'No. We'll have to go to a guest house. Make a nice change for you anyway. First though we've got to get her round to Bosham while we find a boatyard prepared to undertake the work.' My relief was overpowering. Perhaps – at last we might think about a home on dry land and sell the lovely *Elsa* once she was whole again. Now was not the time to discuss such a major upheaval; I would talk to him when we had got over our shock.

With some minor tinkering, the engine coughed into reluctant life. Obviously we could not stay in the naval basin a moment longer than necessary. Various forms had to be filled in and signed, by the tug owners and James, for insurance purposes and once this was done we prepared to motor round to Bosham. Bill's leave was up, so he went off to catch a train, saddened at leaving us in this sorry state. The journey had shaken us all more than we realized. Even the resilience of youth has its breaking point.

Slowly, we limped round to Chichester harbour with a feeling akin to humiliation and shame for *Elsa*, as we tied up alongside the deserted winter jetty at Bosham. She looked like a raddled old hag instead of her usual full-blown, majestic appearance. I hated and resented it when the odd person stared at us.

As usual leave was over, so that during the day I was on my own, as well as the nights when James was duty officer. He arranged for us all to stay at the Critchfield Guest House. Thank goodness it was out of season and though a haven for elderly couples and spinsters, they made an exception for us four homeless waifs and strays. Tilly and Pinky went to a very superior cat kennels. Before we moved in, a boatyard had to be found which understood about Dutch Boeiers – a bit of a rarity in 1951.

It was lucky that we were insured for winter sailing and not just winter mooring – quite an appreciable difference, even in those days. We were not down as a 'total loss'

despite the tow because, as we pointed out to the insurance representative, it we had waited for the weather to calm down, we could have got the engine to start and once the ice on the boom, rigging and sails had melted we could have hoisted them and limped in somehow. That delay however would have been foolhardy to contemplate with two very small children on board. So, after the legalities had been sorted out, we 'abandoned ship'; packed our personal belongings and ferried ourselves, the pram, highchair and toys to the Critchfield, who could at least provide us with a cot.

CHAPTER NINE
Fair Solent and Foul Channel

James hated the communal life at the Critchfield, with no privacy; but for me it was like an enforced holiday with only the children's washing and ironing to see to. It was a rare treat to have unlimited water and I revelled unashamedly in the comparative lack of hard work, coupled with no cooking or shopping. The boys had to be kept quiet and amused, obviously, so as not to disturb the senior guests, but this posed no great problem for they slept soundly all night, as well as in the afternoon rest; during the day I took them for walks, or played with them or read to them, which I had little time for on board. Our belated Christmas present to Michael was a red pedal-car, very grand and shiny. Being nearly four, he could easily work the pedals, and his happiness was complete as he tore up and down the flat concrete driveway to the guest house.

As soon as we had got over the shock of the blizzard and knew that *Elsa* was being repaired satisfactorily, I determined to try and insist that a life ashore would be eminently more suitable; being careful to choose what I hoped was an opportune moment. If I left it too long, the horrors would have receded; if too soon, it could be put down to reaction – so it was a fortnight later that I started, as tactfully as I could, one weekend in the evening after supper, in the corner of the little sitting room, after the old dears had gone off to bed: 'James, don't you think that now the boys are older and need more room to play in, it might be a good idea to find a little cottage?' He looked thunderstruck, 'Why? They're perfectly happy – lots of deck space, boatyard or somewhere to play in – they're jolly lucky living in a boat – most boys would give anything to be where they are.' I tried again, 'Yes, but they're too young to realize there's anything so special about a boat – they've been brought up to it and take it for granted – but

what I really mean is – I was so frightened they might have
. . . .' I could not bring myself to say the dreaded word
'drowned' and James finished the sentence for me;
'. . .drowned in the blizzard. But don't you see how truly
exceptional that was – and no one would *choose* to go to sea
in December. If a blizzard had been forecast at 6 p.m. then
obviously we wouldn't have put to sea.' Annoyed he added,
'Anyway, the boys were the best off of any of us – snug as
bugs in a rug, tucked up in their bunks.'

I persisted, 'But James *I* was frightened and cold – and I'm
fed up with having no constant water – hot or cold – or
proper bath that I don't have to pump out, and gangplanks,
and prams, and oh, *everything*!' James was quiet for a
moment and his eyes were cold, 'But you thought she was
perfect – and if we lived in a house we'd never see each
other.' Quickly, I replied, 'We could get a naval hiring near
wherever your ship or shore base was – like other naval
couples. . . .' He interrrupted to say coldly and firmly, 'There
would be no sailing.' 'Surely you could have a dinghy or sail
one of the Navy's yachts.' Again he interrupted, 'Then we'd be
apart at weekends and anyway we'd probably hate being
surrounded by a lot of naval wives and children.' I did not
agree, 'Well, I think it would be very nice for the boys to have
some friends – they've never even *met* any other children –
and I never go out or see anyone. . . .' There I stopped short,
aware I was sounding like a whining fishwife.

He went on, 'We could never afford it in any case – and we
wouldn't get much for *Elsa*. That, of course, was undeniable
– *who* in their right minds would want a large, wallowing
slow family boat. A twinge of disloyalty to *Elsa* clouded my
arguments. After all she had brought us safely through a
blizzard – even if we should not have been out in it. James
finally clinched it by saying how different it would be at
Hayling Island with no beastly mud and a proper boatyard to
see to everything. My second rebellion had failed too, not
only through a lack of determination, but an inexplicable
human attachment to *Elsa* herself. A boat is not like a house.

In March, James drove us to Itchenor at weekends, where
our sailing dinghy lay, sorely needing a refit too. While the
boys played on the foreshore we scraped and sandpapered
the old varnish inside and out, as well as the little mast.
Meanwhile work progressed slowly on *Elsa* in her
Portsmouth dockyard.

Patricia had returned home; understandably she did not
want to put to sea again, though she was sad at leaving the
two boys she had grown so fond of.

At the end of a month, having given in over the boat, I tackled James with the idea of a mother's help for me; as I explained: 'It's not that I can't *do* the work of looking after the boat and the boys, but sometimes I can't even get ashore with two of them, and it's dangerous for one of them to be playing on deck at that age without some sort of supervision.' He thought for a moment, then said, 'You're right. We couldn't have managed without Patricia when we were sailing. Someone has to keep an eye on them constantly and someone else has to cook and make cups of Bovril!'

We advertised in *Yachting Monthly*, the wording was roughly as follows 'Unusual career – young girl needed, fond of children and sailing, to share chores on a Dutch barge. Sense of humour essential.' We did not have to wait long for the replies, one of which sounded hopeful, from an eighteen-year-old in Cheshire. 'Goodness, that's a long way – what about her weekends James.' He thought that a long one every other weekend might solve that problem and reasoned, 'She sounds far the best – and her letter is really funny. Let's meet up and see if we all like each other.' I agreed. We all liked her enormously and as she agreed to give it a trial period, we presumed the feeling was mutual. Her name was Sarah Murphy. She was fair, with blue eyes and a round smiling face. She explained, 'I'm sorry I can't come down permanently until the hunting season is over and I've arranged for someone to take over and ride my unruly mount.' That suited us perfectly because it would be another month at least before *Elsa* was ready; so we fixed a date in early April for her to 'join'.

Michael had overcome his shyness early on, offering a Dinky car for her inspection. She spoke to him in a completely grown-up way which he appreciated as much as I did, neither talking baby talk, nor condescending. Peter, of course, flirted outrageously, doing his best to attract her attention away from his brother by throwing the odd toy in a provocative fashion, snatching Michael's car from him. Sarah neither ignored nor encouraged him. This was unbelievable and quite wonderful; the sooner she could join the better. We showed her photos of *Elsa*, which was, meanwhile undergoing a major face lift.

James's new ship, the minelayer *Plover* was often at sea on exercises, involving periods of a week or a fortnight, when he would be away. I dreaded the separations, especially as I knew no one and the prospect of coping single-handed on the boat pending Sarah's arrival terrified me.

Finally, *Elsa* rose, phoenix-like from the devastation of the

blizzard and it was with very mixed feelings that I packed up our things again. Obviously it would be wonderful to be in our own home again, but Michael seemed unwell, fretful, with a heavy cold, and, as yet, we had no doctor. He tossed and turned, waking up at night and crying, which was unusual for him. Unalterable plans had been made, involving James sailing *Elsa* round with a friend from *Plover* one Saturday, picking us up on the Sunday and installing us back on board before going off to sea. Serenely detached, kind yet remote, he was not worried about Michael, reassuring me by saying all small children catch colds.

After settling on board again, Michael became listless, complaining that his head hurt and he did not want anything to eat. I felt his forehead which seemed very hot and tucked his up in the bunk up for'ard feeling both worried and guilty as the cabin was damp and dark. As I prepared James's supper I decided, 'If he's not better in the morning I'll get the name of a doctor from the office.' James agreed.

We were all up with the dawn after a wretched night. Michael coughed and needed comforting; as I changed his damp pyjamas I noticed a blistery spot on his chest, were he was scratching frantically. Chickenpox! The first of the childish ailments. How had he caught it, isolated as he was from other children? The relief at knowing what was wrong with him made me feel happier, I asked James if he had had it. He was sure he must have and I presumed I had too. Apart from keeping him warm and giving him lots to drink there was not a lot one could do, except to put a soothing lotion on the spots.

Early in the morning, before returning to Portsmouth, James fetched the cats, who picked their way delicately across the freighter's deck, while I stood in the well, calling in my 'cat voice'. Tilly butted me with her soft head and the purrs from both their throats sounded like the engine on a good day. They inspected *Elsa* from stem to stern; nose, whiskers and ears twitching violently at all the strange new smells. Then they went below to see the boys, touchingly pleased to be back after all those weeks. Peter was crawling and walking round the saloon, and they rubbed their faces and bodies against him, knocking him over in their enthusiasm, skilfully avoiding his clutching fingers, as they trotted into the galley where I had put out their saucers of milk. Michael called to them and they scampered through to his lair in the bows, jumping up beside him where they settled down for a mammoth wash.

By the time I had finished all the chores I felt unnaturally

tired. While *Elsa* had been in the yard, the workmen had been careful, but inevitably the dust and dirt from weeks of neglect lay thickly everywhere. I was extremely cross and annoyed that after my long enforced rest at the Critchfield I should be feeling so rotten. My head ached, my throat was sore; it was obvious that I was starting a cold. The little ones played quietly with cars and bricks as I alternately dozed on the settee and dabbed more lotion on the thickly clustered spots. That night I tossed and turned, feeling hot and shivery in turn, reluctantly forced to take my temperature. Usually it is well below normal, but to my horror the thermometer pointed to an improbable 102 degrees. I wished I had not taken it, immediately feeling much worse. My skin felt tight as though it would burst. The burning sensation localized itself and I started to scratch; looking in the mirror confirmed my fears. My face was covered in spots and I felt ghastly.

My one thought was to contact James and ask him to come back, for I knew I could not look after the boys feeling as dizzy and ill as I did. Once I knew the boatyard office would be open, I staggered along, my eyes nearly closed by blistery spots. Tapping on the window I managed to shout hoarsley and feebly, 'Have you had chickenpox!' Susan the secretary, took one horrified look at my white disfigured face and answered, 'No, I haven't. Have you Jim?' Jim Rendell, the owner, replied he had no idea, but perhaps it would be better if I stayed outside! I relayed my messages though the window. I asked if they could send a telegram to my husband on board HMS *Plover*. The rest of the day was spent in a delirious haze, using all my will-power and physical strength to drag myself out of the chair if I sat down. Such a silly childish complaint could not be expected to arouse anything but amused laughter, nevertheless I felt unbelievably ill, hot and shivery with a wracking headache and an ever-increasing crop of spots.

Suddenly a voice called down, 'Ahoy there – anyone aboard?' I leapt into the well, eager for what I was sure would be news from James. It was. But not the expected announcement of his return. The telegram Susan had kindly brought along the path, in her high heels, merely stated that owing to extensive exercises at sea he could not possibly get back – for chickenpox. A joke of an illness! A letter was on its way. With that I had to console myself. The days to Sarah's arrival passed in a blur, culminating in Peter developing it too. I wore a beret to stop myself scratching the scabs off the spots I had rubbed raw and hardly dared to look at my white scarred face where the worst ones had half closed my eyes!

Michael had been so good, making a real effort to leave his

spots alone, but Peter ... at a year old it was virtually impossible to stop him. His little body was covered and he would not stay still for me to daub him with the calamine lotion; tearing up and down the cot-bunk while I dabbed parts of him as he passed! I felt very sorry for myself, resenting bitterly James's absence at this juncture, berating him and the Navy. A passing cloud of a thought flitted by. Someone else could surely stand in for him. Perhaps there was another reason. I dismissed this utterly disloyal idea, but nevertheless resented bitterly my plea for help being ignored or cavalierly dismissed – surely he knew me well enough to know I would not appeal for help unless desperate.

One cheering event was the arrival of Jim Rendell to motor us round to the now vacant berth at the end of a jetty very near the office and buildings. It was the best position and such a relief to be near the rubbish bins, the coal bunker, waterpipe, milk delivery point and many other facilities.

I had thought a great deal about Sarah, aware that I should have written to ask if she had had chickenpox, but never getting round to it, feeling so ill and dispirited.

The day she was due to arrive I somehow managed to do some housework and make the confined space seem bigger; sitting miserably sewing at some overdue mending when I heard the long-awaited steps on deck and the hatch over the companionway pushed back, as a cheerful voice called; 'Hello!' Quickly I called up to ask, 'Have you had chickenpox?' 'Oh, yes!' she called airily and I could have wept with relief. Having been an under-matron at a prep school, she took small boys, sewing and childish complaints in her stride. She had even done a domestic science course so I was looking forward to learning some cookery from her. James was due back the following weekend. In the meantime, how wonderful it was to have someone to talk and giggle with. Young though she was, merely eighteen, she was also extremely practical, organizing a routine, as we discussed how we would share the day's chores.

Luckily the mud was flat where we lay, allowing *Elsa* to nestle her broad beam comfortably and remain upright. This was only for two to three hours of each tide anyway. Peter was still confined to his bunk and the saloon for a couple more days, but Michael was delighted to have somebody to take him for walks in the spring sunshine. At last the weather became really warm, with a soft wind smelling indefinably of spring, wiping out all memories of the blizzard. Sarah and I swept the decks and sluiced them down carefully, making 'cheeses' of the loose ends of sheets and ropes. She found

Elsa quite beautiful; eager to sail, never having done any. I assured her; 'You won't have long to wait. We'll have a long weekend soon – probably Whitsun – then we can sail in the Solent – nice and calm.'

By the time James came back I was quite fit, even looking normal, apart from a few scabs and scars. He hugged me to him, 'My poor darling – it must have been dreadful. How are the "horrors"?' Peter was busily climbing the companionway steps and James grinned as he said, 'We'll have to rig up a line from his harness to the binnacle just long enough for him to climb into the catwalk, but not over the side!' The long winter nightmare was over; happiness was tangible and complete now that James was back in the evenings, for a while anyway.

A young Canadian naval officer on lease-lend from the Canadian Navy was very keen to do some sailing and, having no family in this country, was available to come with us any time we wanted. Soon it would be Whitsun and James was eager to try out the handsome, new, tanned sails and solid, beautifully carved leeboards. Life seemed secure, permanent, contented. My doubts and fears temporarily allayed.

One afternoon, a fortnight or so after her arrival, Sarah went on her walk with the boys, followed by the cats; they shortly returned, white faced, with Michael sobbing by her side. A dog had chased the cats. Tilly had bounded back towards the boatyard; but poor Pinky had tried to race across the road – in front of a car. Sarah was utterly distressed, haltingly recounting the tragedy. Pinky had been killed outright, by no fault of the driver, who, kindly taking pity on poor Sarah and the little ones, had removed the furry, limp and lifeless body. We were deeply saddened, missing the ginger tom; Tilly showed no sign of grieving, though she never went on a walk with the pram again.

The preparations for Whitsun left no time for mourning. Summer had arrived, before her time, as so often, filling one with languor and wellbeing, bringing out our summer dresses and inviting us to sunbathe on deck during the afternoon siesta. Peter and I became quite brown, but Michael and Sarah had the milk white skin that merely turns a reluctant pink. We bustled around in the usual pre-sailing fever, everything so much more fun and exciting than when I had done the preparations single-handed.

James and Vernon arrived on board one Thursday evening, laden with extra food and bottles of wine. Vernon was a serious young man, quiet and sensible, without much sailing sense, but so willing, albeit lacking any humour. The heat of

that Friday morning was more suited to July or August, rather than May, with not a breath of wind. Even I was looking forward to the flat calm of a 'motoring' weekend; but James kept searching the sky or peering at the barometer to try and conjure up a breeze or light airs at least – not however resorting to whistling for one, for that is a known taboo among sailors.

We slipped our moorings mid-morning, both boys safely in the well and motored into Chichester harbour, anchoring off East Head, to wait for the right state of the tide to go across the treacherous bar between East Pole and West Pole at the narrow entrance. We were towing the dinghy so the two men decided to row ashore and collect some beer for the weekend from the little sailing club at the end of the spit of land. It was all unbelievably beautiful; the sea shimmered, glassily calm, reflecting a dazzling heat, the shore merging into a blue heat haze. Sarah went below to put on her bathing suit, saying: 'It's too hot – the water looks perfect – I'm going to have my first swim.' I agreed, cursing the fact that I had to stay on board with the boys, yet guessing at the iciness of the water so early in the year. I warned her, 'Don't stay in too long. It's deep here and jolly cold.' She answered gaily; 'Oh! don't fuss, I shan't *stay* in – just a quick dip to cool off.' I had meant to stay on deck to watch her, but an agonized wail from the saloon warned me that the brothers were having one of their rare fights over toys and I hastened below to smack the offender and comfort the aggrieved party – Peter being the habitual tease.

A faint call brought me back on deck and I looked round for Sarah. The tide was still flooding and Sarah's anxious face, a few feet astern quickly told me she could not get back to the boat against the tide. Panic-stricken, I untied the lifebelt with its long line; using all my strength I hurled it in her direction – but it fell short. She was rapidly getting cold and tired, so I shouted to her to float on her back while I got the men with the dinghy, as she drifted ever further astern. Furiously I rang the ship's bell, hoping and praying they would hear it from the shore. I continued to jerk the bell rope making a terrific clanging until I could see the two men appear over the sand in the distance. Presumably they just thought we had become impatient waiting for them. Sarah was receding fast and I was petrified the cold might give her cramp. I jumped on the cabin top, waving a jersey to attract their attention, then dashing back to the bell, rang it again with all my might. As soon as they reached the dinghy I stood on the poop deck, pointing astern, calling 'Sarah! Sarah!' at the top of my voice.

In a trice they had spotted the problem, leaping into the dinghy and rowing as hard as they could towards the hapless girl. There was no hope of getting her inboard, with the tide carrying them further and further up the harbour, so she held on to the stern while they took an oar apiece and rowed for all they were worth, using every ounce of muscle and strength against the tide back to the boat, towing her inert weight behind them.

It took all three of us to heave her numbed body back on deck and I threw a big towel round her, rubbing hard to bring back the circulation. She was infinitely brave, smiling through chattering teeth and making light of the whole incident which might well have been disastrous. A mug of scalding coffee brought some colour back to her white face and soon the sun warmed her enough to stop the shivering. It was entirely my fault, for I should have realized that we were only waiting for high tide in order to sail over the bar; therefore being anchored, the flood would carry anything past us. Sarah would have none of it, dismissing a near tragedy as trivial!

At high tide there was still no wind, so we motored over the bar hoping to pick up a breeze outside the entrance. Even in flat calm, the shallowness of the water over the sand bar caused little ripples and eddies as the tide swirled over it, like a microscopic race. Stories were told of how, with the wind from a certain quarter, probably South-East; the sand could be seen between the rollers. Thinking back to that December night, even if we had reached Chichester harbour we might well have come to grief on that bar, being pounded and pulverized by the ferocious seas on the hard sand. However, on that May morning, we might have been in some tropical country. The teak decks, baked silver in the sun were nearly too hot to walk on and Sarah and I in our bathing suits sat on the cabin top, sunbathing on towels at the same time as keeping an eye on the naked boys. The sun would heal the scars from the chickenpox scabs still dotted all over their bodies. I lazily held the tiller while James and Vernon hoisted the new sails. They looked beautiful and somehow very romantic, the deep tan complementing the dark green hull. There they hung, in peaceful undramatic folds. Inwardly I admitted to myself that this was my idea of perfect sailing weather, but I knew how disappointing it was for James, so I put up a pretence of wishing for just a breath. Even the little sailing dinghies in the Solent were becalmed.

We put the steps over the side and clambered down into the dinghy in turn, just to admire her, languidly rowing round her

as she drifted gently with the turning tide. Both the mainland
and the Isle of Wight were shrouded in a blue heat haze, so we
decided to anchor off Sandown beach and row ashore for a
swim before having our picnic lunch on board. The water was
translucent, of the palest aquamarine as we glided up onto
the beach, where James left the boys and me before going
back for Sarah and Vernon. 'Bring a wooden spoon back with
you and one of the buckets,' I called after him. For though we
lived in a boat, near beaches, we were never close enough to
go to them and having no car, this was the first time the boys
had played on sand.

They were enchanted with it all, not very adventurous in
their paddling, but happily digging, while we lay soaking up
the warmth, after one quick dip. The water still retained its
winter bite. Sarah murmured, 'What an idyllic life – it's
better than horses and riding any day!' I had to put things in
their right perspective though, saying quietly, 'You won't
believe this, but today is the first time we have ever had
weather like this *and* been at sea, as opposed to tied up
alongside.' We sat hugging our knees, silently admiring *Elsa*,
looking exactly like the original 'painted ship upon a painted
ocean'. Before leaving her we had furled and neatly tied her
mainsail which lay arched in a graceful curve just above the
boom. The new paint gleamed and the burgee and the blue
ensign hung limp in the sunshine. James was impatient to be
back, 'If you children have finished swimming and making
sandcastles perhaps we can get on with some sailing,' he
commented wrily. We smiled. It was lunch time anyway. The
merest breath greeted our return, so while Sarah and I
produced lunch, up went the sails once more, gently ghosting
us along. The *Queen Elizabeth* overtook us some distance
away, majestically making her way into Southampton Water.
In those days there were far fewer dinghies in the Solent;
those that came near all waved in a friendly manner.

Slowly, calmly, and in a dignified way we sailed – no, you
can-not call our drifting with the tide 'sailing' – west past
Cowes into the Solent proper, towards the Beaulieu River,
reaching it as the sun was sinking. The transition from lazy
calm to fast action was instantaneous. We lowered the sails,
started the engine and nosed our way up the peaceful river,
looking for a free mooring buoy. Vernon stood in the bows
with the boathook ready to pick one up. It is a tricky
operation even under those ideal conditions. Having never
done it before, he failed at the first attempt, forcing James to
take a great sweep round again, before approaching with the
minimum necessary steerage way. This time I took the tiller at

the last minute, ready to switch off the engine, while James sprinted up for'ard ready to take over from Vernon, who got the chain through the bow fairlead and secured it back to the mooring cleat successfully. We felt triumphant.

Once the boys were bathed and fed and our supper under way, we drank our cider and beer sitting on cushions in the well; the cat prowled round us, while the river and its reeded banks turned to gold, then bronze, before fading to a dreamlike silvery grey. Unaware of it at the time, that weekend was the happy zenith of four years' sailing. At twenty-five I did not bother to analyse feelings or emotions in depth; so tranquil and confident was I in my deep, all-embracing love for James, simplistically believing that without a doubt, it was the same for him. There would still be great and exciting sailing journeys to come, but already, a few months later, subconsciously, slowly, I became aware of the great gulf between us.

I could not, would not, admit to it; but looking back, how abysmally boring my companionship must have been. We had no newspapers on board, so that my knowledge of what went on in the world was nil; therefore, I had no conversation, other than the day-to-day happenings in the boat and the boys.

That evening though, all was peaceful happiness. Tilly purred as she sat in my lap until we went below to eat, having lit the riding light on the mast. Very early next morning, James and I went ashore in the dinghy with the metal milk jug. We had spotted a farm from the boat which seemed much further away when it came to walking! They had just finished milking and filled our jug direct from the warm frothing buckets. It was going to be another hot day and it was exciting to be ashore in a strange place, which, because of landing in the dinghy, felt like a foreign country. Luck was with us as a baker's van passed us doing his deliveries, so we bought enough fresh bread for the two remaining days. We did not talk, content to listen to the different bird song of the dawn chorus – different to the mewing, crying call of the swooping, hungry gulls so familiar on board. As we rowed back, the peaceful silence was rent by excited shouts and calls from Michael and Peter in the well and the delicious smell of frying bacon greeted us when we climbed on board, hungry as hunters after our long walk.

When the sun rose higher, a cat's paw of breeze ruffled the river's glassy surface, bringing a grin to James's face. 'We'll sail out past the Needles and have a look at Yarmouth on the way,' he said. I thought of my father and step-mother, 'Yes, next

time we must go and see them. He should have forgiven us by now for the blizzard incident.'

The entrance to Yarmouth seemed wide and easy and we made a mental note to go in there the next time; as James said, 'This wind is too good to waste – we must try out her paces at sea, not bottled up in the Solent – too crowded for me.' We barely heeled over, so neither Sarah nor I felt seasick. This was exhilarating, storybook sailing. Above us the Needles soared, menacing and impressive as we sped past them, helped by the tide, which nearly caused us a very close shave with a buoy, before we were truly at sea again, sailing on a close reach to starboard.

James was supremely contented, deciding to teach us all the song, *In the hills of West Virginia*. (Copy of song printed on page 79). His expansive, enthusiastic moments were rare, but so infectious we would all bubble over with the joy he felt. It did not matter how much noise we made, with no one but the waves and seagulls to hear us. The song was simple, fun to harmonize in the chorus lines and we were soon word perfect. We sailed west until the tide turned, when we went about and retraced our way back to the safe shelter of the Beaulieu River for one last night. Three days, three idyllic days we were blessed with that Whitsun of 1951, for even on the Sunday as we returned to Hayling Island, *Elsa* was wafted along, not driven by gales. Sarah and Michael acquired a delicious honey-coloured tan; James, Peter and I were brown as coffee beans, while Vernon, who never took off his shirt, looked pale by comparison. He had been so quiet I wondered if he had enjoyed the weekend, but he assured us in his slow Canadian drawl, 'It's been great, just great.' I suppose with five of us all making a lot of noise, he could not compete, but he warmly said, 'I sure would like to crew for you again – she's a grand old lady.' I winced and hoped that *Elsa* would not feel hurt at the allusion to her age.

With Sarah there, James and I could go ashore together in the evenings at weekends. Occasionally, we went to the cinema, dining in a little restaurant afterwards. This was such a treat for me and only the second time since our marriage that we had been able to do so. There was always a new sailing venture to plan and discuss and I never really noticed any change in his kind remoteness.

One Sunday in June, when we were not going to sea, James thought that Michael and he would sail the dinghy round to a beach further down the island, where Sarah, Peter and I would meet, having gone by bus with the pushchair and a

picnic lunch. Michael was only four, and very excited at this grown-up adventure and waved goodbye importantly. The wind was forecast as 'light airs, variable. . . .' A safe day to introduce a toddler to small boats. The rest of us had been sitting on the beach for some time, scanning the harbour where so many dinghies bobbed about, but not seeing ours. We wondered if we had got the right rendezvous; then we lay back, too lazy to worry unduly. After an hour, small doubts crept into my mind, despite the perfect weather. Perhaps Michael had fallen overboard. We had no lifejackets and in those irresponsible days never even thought of them. Finally, the tiny sail came into view and we rushed into the water to help beach her. 'What happened? Why were you so long? I asked, 'I was beginning to be afraid. . . .' A scowling infuriated James stopped me short, 'We had to tack the whole way. Michael wouldn't sit still. Kept asking when we were getting to the beach – most annoying.' Relieved, I said, 'Oh James, he's only four – you mustn't expect too much at that age.' A small smile started in the corner of his wide mouth as he admitted, 'I know – but what *really* finished me was when he said "Daddy – it's quicker by bus!" ' At that Sarah and I became quite hysterical. We laughed till the tears ran. But James's pride had ben hurt and he did not see the humour or aptness of his son's accusation.

It took Sarah's presence to make me realize how little laughter there had been in our life. Our sense of humour differed widely.

A teasing wind increased, stopping any sunbathing, forcing us to put on jerseys; the family excursion was not a success. Michael chose to return with Sarah and me by bus, leaving his disgruntled but relieved father to sail home alone! I was especially glad of Sarah's company when James was away for a week or a fortnight at a time, on exercises around the Scilly Isles.

Was it during that summer that he fell in love? I could only guess with an intuitive seventh sense – refusing to acknowledge any change in his remoteness – talking to Sarah about him as though by confessing my love for him, it would preserve it – crystallize it.

I must have bored her with my accounts of his sailing prowess, recounting, too, snippets of my four years in occupied France without my parents. Having never been close to them, James replaced all family affection for me; he

was the brother I never had, the father I barely knew. He was the first and only man I had loved utterly and – admittedly – obsessively.

Another long weekend was due in July and for once I was not dreading it. James wrote long letters with instructions for its preparations. I could hardly wait for his return, for reassurance that he must still love me; yet I contained my too eager rapture when he finally stepped on board after an absence that had been longer than usual. I told him how much my father was looking foward to our visit, 'James – they want us *all* to have lunch with them at Norton Cottage – Vernon too – isn't that kind?' There was no affection between the two men and James merely grunted, 'Yes, that's all right – but we mustn't waste too much sailing time with them.' Next he asked, 'Have you got the full spare gas cylinder and the petrol and paraffin?' I reassured him. He was more withdrawn and remote than ever, only coming to life when dealing with the boat – absent-minded. His love-making was perfunctory, without the passion and warmth we had known – yet I wanted him so.

However, there was no time to brood, with many preparations. I tried to conceal my hurt from Sarah. When spoken to he would nod absent-mindedly, 'Good. I'll go and charge the batteries. Vernon is coming on board first thing in the morning.' Sarah and I groaned inwardly, for though harmless and innocuous, poor Vernon did have a personal problem of BO which in the narrow confines of the boat offended us. He obeyed James slavishly though, if ineffectually and was always available.

The forecast was good, with a Force 4 to 5 southeasterly, making the passage over the bar in the narrow entrance quite exciting, even at slack water, high tide. Sarah and I clung on to the children as *Elsa* plunged up and down for a few long minutes in the treacherous shallows, until once at sea, her flapping sails filled, steadying her as we heeled gently over. Despite Spithead itself being slightly rough, we had an exhilaratingly fast sail on a broad reach into the Solent, with the wind astern.

I managed to hide my slight queasiness, putting the boys in their bunks until we reached sheltered waters. James was in his element, loving the feel of the responding boat as she sped through the playful waves, her rounded bow smacking into them. His watchful eyes concentrated on every ripple of canvas or change in direction of the streaming, fluttering RNSA burgee. A man of the sea. A man apart. He called to me, 'Take the tiller for a bit – she's easy to handle here – keep her

full and taut. I want to free one of the hanks on the forestay.' She was just manageable for me with the steadying line round the great tiller and I thrilled to feel the powerful surge of 1,500 square foot of sail, as for half an hour I revelled in my position of skipper. Slipping back into the well, with his cat-like agility he said, 'It won't be easy in Yarmouth – there's a strong breeze so I'll jolly well sail in – no engine.' Vernon interrupted, 'Gee – how will we stop?' James grinned, fixing him with his steely gaze, 'We'll down sails the *minute* we're in the entrance and rely on our momentum to carry us on to the right jetty.'

We were going to be in good time thanks to the following wind and I was relieved to think we should not be late for lunch. My other unpredictable worry was Peter's behaviour. He could be utterly enchanting, with a smile to charm the proverbial birds off the trees, or he could be unbelievably naughty.

In no time at all we were approaching Yarmouth. Both boys stayed in the saloon as Sarah, Vernon and I stood by for action. 'Right,' yelled James as he pushed the huge tiller over, 'Down sails.' Vernon wound down the winch, while Sarah and I gathered in the great folds, arms flailing wildly trying the squeeze the wind out of them. Several things then happened simultaneously. From the end of the main pier, the harbour master hailed us through his megaphone, asking us to tie up to No. 1 jetty. Heavens! We were nearly on it! James yelled to Vernon, 'Take the for'ard line. Jump in the dinghy. Row like stink to the jetty and secure it. Take a couple of turns, *Stop* us! Vernon seemed slow as a tortoise to my quivering nerves, stumbling at last into the dinghy. However, what none of us had realized was his inability to row. He started to go round in circles, with *Elsa* drifting, carried by her own momentum, on a certain collision course with some of the smartest, wealthiest yachts with which the harbour seemed to be filled! I reacted quickly for once. Screamed at the hapless Vernon to come back on board, as I tore up for'ard, barefoot; hauled on the line and jumped down into the dinghy in his place. James could not leave the tiller. Rowing like fury with very little distance left to go, somehow I chucked the line up to a languid yachtsman who, thank God, at least knew what to do, even if he *did* look like someone out of *HMS Pinafore*. *Elsa* swung round, bearing down on the trot of yachts with the minimum of crunching. By this time I was back on board, fending off, feeling furious with Vernon and curiously elated by my own performance!

A smart yachting cap, followed by a blue blazer with brass buttons appeared in the companionway of the hapless boat

we were tied up to, making 'tut-tutting' and 'what have we here?' noises. Even his Dunlop plimsolls were immaculate. I must admit we all looked like dishevelled gypsies, but somehow felt vastly superior, wondering out loud whether any of 'these toys' every put to sea! At that moment, the boys erupted into the well, full of pent-up excitement; Michael asking in a loud voice, 'Where are we? I'm very hungry.' The blue blazer's wife, also sporting a yachting cap, lots of make-up, a foulard tied just so and wearing perfectly tailored white slacks, with red nails clasping a glass, peered at us. She muttered darkly: 'Oh my God, – *children!*' and disappeared below. James apologized, not altogether sincerely, for bumping their precious paintwork which brought about a complete change of attitude in blue blazer who became too friendly, too quickly, inviting us to drinks. I explained that we were lunching with my father who lived on the island, but that we'd love to that evening.

The whole cavalcade of us had to troop across four yachts before reaching the jetty itself, a slow process as Michael and Peter had to be lifted over each one. Thank goodness most of the yachts were empty as the owners would have been busy drinking in the famous hotel by the ferry-boat pier. We decided to do likewise after telephoning Norton Cottage to ask if they could meet us in the car. Sarah stayed outside with the children, while we wriggled our way to the bar full of similarly dressed yachting fraternity, talking loudly about spinnakers and racing tactics – a totally different world to ours.

Soon my father appeared, cheerful and affectionate, his anger over the December incident temporarily forgotten. Their cottage was quite near and he ferried our party of six in two trips. We were all given an affectionate welcome by my step-mother and the boys tore round the garden, ecstatically happy to have so much room to run around in. This became slightly unpopular when one or or two flowers got trampled on and Michael tried hard to catch one of the Leghorn hens. A delicious lunch had been prepared for us all, so praying silently for good behaviour I placed a boy on each side of me, with Sarah on the other side of Peter, the rascal. In fact all was well, until towards the end of the meal, a winning smile on his face, Peter decided he wanted to sit next to his father on the other side of the table, which he proceeded to do by climbing from chair to chair, behind the back of those sitting on them. This was not popular either. Poor James sat embarrassed, while my father frowned, muttering, 'Spoilt brat,' beneath his breath. He was right. My step-mother

though thought the whole incident highly amusing and was sweet about it. Thanking them profusely for giving us all such splendid hospitality, we removed Peter and ourselves before any further catastrophe occurred. We invited both parents on board for tea, but they suddenly had a lot of gardening to do, leaving James visibly relieved!

That evening, the liquid hospitality from the boat next door was lavish; sailing yarns were swapped and we sat on deck in the warm night full of wellbeing. Most yachts had their riding light lit, so we lit ours too and they gave the harbour a fairytale appearance; a myriad of flickering bobbing lights, like Tinker Bell's in *Peter Pan*. Even Vernon cheered up, becoming quite talkative, insisting on giving a rendering of *In the hills of West Virginia*. We joined in, switching to *We'll rant and we'll roar like true British sailors*. Definitely a cheerful evening. The next morning we were up early and away without waking our neighbours who were no doubt sleeping it off.

SPANISH LADIES

FARE WELL AND A-DIEU TO YOU FAIR SPANISH LAD-IES FARE WELL AND A-DIEU TO YOU LA-DIES OF SPAIN FOR WE-VE RE-CEIVED OR-DERS TO SAIL TO OLD ENG-LAND BUT WE HOPE IN A SHORT WHILE TO SEE YOU A-GAIN

WE'LL RANT AND WE'LL ROAR LIKE TRUE BRIT-ISH SAIL-ORS, WE'LL RANT AND WE'LL ROAR A-CROSS THE SALT SEA UN-TIL WE STRIKE SOUNDINGS IN THE CHANNEL OF OLD ENG-LAND OH FROM USHANT TO SCIL-LY ITS THIRTY FIVE LEAGUES.

Giving the Needles a wide berth, we sailed in leisurely fashion back to Chichester. The original plan had been to sail round the island, but the wind was still South-East, which would involve endless tacking, with quite a choppy sea caused by the onshore breeze. As we tied up alongside our jetty we all agreed it had been *nearly* as perfect as the Whit weekend.

James was off again in *Plover* for another two weeks, but with the anticipated summer leave period to look forward to, time did not seem to stretch too endlessly – when he was not near it was easier to imagine all was as it used to be – at that stage ignorance was still bliss. He intended to ask Vernon and one other to accompany us, for we were going back to France – to Cherbourg this time and *Elsa* really needed three men for a long journey. While he was away the weather was perfect, enabling Sarah and me to sunbathe every day once the chores were done. Sometimes we would take a picnic tea and the pushchair; catching the bus again to the beach on the southern tip of the island, which was pebbly, but enjoyed by both boys playing on the water's edge.

This time, with two of us to prepare for the long fortnight's sailing it seemed like child's play. We chatted away, about nothing in particular, but with her ready sense of humour, Sarah transformed the drudgery into exciting anticipation. James wrote to say the 'third man' would be a naval officer called Wilkie. Sarah and I speculated, 'At least he can't be as dreary – or smelly – as old Vernon!' she said laughingly. There was not much else in the letter to satisfy my longing for him – the warmth and love of his earlier letters had vanished. There was no hint of anything untoward when he returned at the start of his leave. He kissed me, excited at the prospect of some *real* sailing, 'Instead of playing at it in the Solent duck pond!'

We were too busy with our own side of preparations to exchange more than a few sentences; mealtimes were riotous and at night our lovemaking had recaptured some of its magic and warm intensity – for me at any rate. Both crew arrived the next day, Vernon completely overshadowed by the enormous, ebullient Wilkie who played rugger for the Navy, *and* for England! A second row forward – a real scrum half, enormously tall and broad, with huge muscular arms and legs. Immensely cheerful, he teased Sarah and me good-naturedly all the time; the boys adored him and the size of his appetite matched his build. Even Vernon seemed to come alive occasionally, eyes crinkling behind the thick glasses.

The summer of 1951 was one of the kindest I can remember, for when we set sail on 1 August a light Nor'Nor' West was

blowing; offshore and ideal; even the sun shone, unaffected by the scattered cotton wool clouds. With his fair hair and blue eyes, Wilkie was like some Norse Viking, a tower of strength who filled the saloon with his bulk. We were all in the well as we sailed through the Solent at a spanking speed, eagerly discussing plans for our time in France.

The sun shone on glittering sea horses, but the wind was cold, despite it being 1 August, and we all snuggled into our seaman sweaters. A doorstep of bread, butter and cheese, followed by an apple completed lunch; Sarah and I decided the washing up could wait till we got to Cherbourg! The motion was definitely uncomfortable below and none of the men were going to volunteer to do it! Up on deck we felt fine and I scanned the horizon eagerly for my first glimpse of France – the land of my teens – the country I loved best.

An old French fishermen's song kept going round and round in my head and I went up for'ard to sit on the cabin top so that I could sing noisily by myself. I felt very happy. *'Hardi les gars, Vire au guindeau....'* The blue misty line on the horizon thickened, before I could say anything, James had sat down beside me, giving my shoulders an affectionate hug, 'We'll be in Cherbourg by this evening at this rate,' he said, really thrilled with *Elsa's* performance. I smiled contentedly, 'I can't wait.'

FRENCH FISHERMAN'S SONG

There would be a lot to do once we were in harbour, so I went to see if Sarah and Michael were all right. Both of them were fast asleep in the after cabin, so having checked that Peter was also dreaming his wicked schemes I decided to copy them. As usual after my short sleep I felt ghastly down below, so unobstrusively I clambered up in the bows to blow the dizziness away before putting the kettle on.

The bow wave always had a mesmeric effect, each wave different as we surged forward, spray thrown up in sparkling cascades; the bowsprit seemed to plunge one minute and soar the next, while the net beneath it dipped into the restless sea, scattering a million rainbow drops of salt water. The combined hiss and muffled roar of the depths, coupled with the whine and singing of the wind in the rigging, brought back to my mind in a flash past sailing trips. A day such as this made up for so much.

Feeling cold, drenched with spray, but less seasick, I bravely went below, where James lay peacefully asleep on the settee, confident that his crew could come to no harm in mid-Channel. As always, my heart turned over, beat faster with tenderness, love and admiration. I knew already how one-sided this emotion must be, but just to be allowed to continue was all I thought I wanted in life. Tea safely brewed, I carried a mug over to Sarah, who had just pushed back her hatch exclaiming, 'Goodness – we're nearly there Wilkie!' He and Vernon were keeping watch together, delighted at our speed. As I handed her the tea I said, 'This is *her* sort of wind; she's not very good at tacking – mostly goes sideways close-hauled!' They laughed. 'We'll have to wake the skipper soon to check our position on the chart.' Quickly and protectively I pleaded, 'Not just yet – he's so fast asleep.' Wilkie promised, 'No – we'll give him a bit longer – but my guess is he'll wake up instinctively when he's needed.' Remembering the blizzard I nodded without saying anything.

Sure enough, James woke with the easy practice of naval officers, so used to sleeping for short spells at any time of the day or night. In the well he quickly scanned the approaching coast, dashing below to check our position and landmarks on the chart. Speaking to Wilkie and Vernon he said, 'We're being carried a bit off course by the tide but the wind is shifting so if we go about on a short leg, we'll make up the leeway.' Slowly we clawed our way back up the coast to be in the right position for the final approach to Cherbourg. The coastline was unfamiliar to us all, yet reminded me of some stretches of Devon and Cornwall, a few dramatic cliffs dominating a mainly flat crescent-shaped bay.

Soon the long *digue* or breakwater etched itself clearly against the background of the town, a seemingly continuous line with no apparent entrance.

For what seemed like hours we remained tantalizingly close, sailing fast through the water, but due to the tide, making no actual progress, until finally slack water allowed us to go about again, hugging the massive sea wall as we entered the sheltered waters behind its great arm. James wanted to sail as far as possible before starting the engine. A customs launch approached and hailed us. I was grateful again for my ability to speak French easily, asking them what James wanted to know; conducting our conversation as they cruised alongside. Yes, we could go into the inner harbour where the fishing boats and some other yachts lay; in return I promised them we had nothing to declare, but hoped to acquire something before our return home! As they sped on their way, they told us how to enter the inner harbour. Now – at last – we lowered the sails, started up the engine, nosing our way cautiously.

Skilfully James manoeuvred the stately, unwieldy Boeier in among the fishing boats, whose skippers stared at us unbelievingly. France again! How deeply satisfying and fulfilling to be back. A couple of gesticulating deck hands called to us, 'Mettez-vous là, près du quai – personne ne vous dérangera.' There was only just room to edge our way in, hoisting the bowsprit in order to prevent it crashing into the wheelhouse of the trawler ahead of us. Wilkie and Vernon threw our line ashore easily, for we were level with the quay, it being high tide. James stopped the engine and Sarah and I put out the fenders.

I knew that Wilkie and Vernon were longing to go ashore and drink in some *estaminet* or café as soon as they had had supper, so we set about preparing the steaks I had kept as a treat. The crew wanted Sarah to go ashore with them, but she was tired after the long day's sailing and promised to go another night. James said he would go for a short while, but did not dare leave the boat for too long, in case some trawler wished to claim our berth. I too was dead tired.

My sleep was so deep that I never heard the men return, barely waking when James gently got into the double bunk, kissing me goodnight on the back of my neck. Leaving him to lie in, I forced myself out of the cosy warmth at the usual crack-of-dawn time, to prevent Michael and Peter noisily waking up the supine Wilkie who would be sleeping off a litre or so of vin rouge in the saloon where he lay snoring on the settee. Confronting me was a vast metal and enamel sign, at least a yard long, propped up against the table. Defiantly, in red letters on a white background it stated, *'Defense de*

traverser la Voie. Propriété de la SNCF.' (Forbidden to cross
the railway line. Property of the French Railways.) A smaller
sign lay drunkenly at the other end of the table, advertising
some bistro in the town. Part of me, which felt suddenly
much older than the two men, found it both funny and
childish and I smiled to myself. However, I knew that the
French Police would not appreciate the drunken humour of
two British yachtsmen. The railway sign was too large to have
been brought back unobserved, its theft assuredly reported to
the police and *Elsa* was hardly inconspicuous. Anger quickly
replaced my momentary amusement and I brusquely woke up
the bemused Wilkie, 'Wilkie! How *could* you do such a thing.
We are visitors – guests in a foreign country. What will the
French think of the English if people like you do things like
this. . . .' Slowly he woke up, completely nonplussed and
puzzled by my outbreak of temper.

For a moment he could not think what I was talking about;
his hangover was evident as he clutched his head, 'Oh, my head!
What's the matter? What have I done!' I turned the sign round,
speaking very crossly: 'You have stolen this from the railway
– and that is extremely serious. You should be ashamed of
yourself – at your age.' He tried to laugh, but the effort hurt,
as he asked, 'What does it say?' I translated it, and continued
berating him, until everyone had assembled in the saloon. Sarah
tried to lift it and found it too heavy, 'How on earth did you
manage to carry it all the way back?' she exclaimed. Unabashed,
Wilkie cheerfully said, 'Oh, we took it in turns!'

Vernon's hangover was worse than Wilkie's and he looked
ghastly. I was remorseless and ordered them to take both the
signs back straight away – before breakfast. Wilkie's expression
changed when he saw I was serious, 'But how can we – I've
no idea where I took them from!' Losing my temper again, I
just told them to return it to the station master and apologize
profoundly. At that moment footsteps could be heard on deck.
Two gendarmes appeared looking extremely annoyed. The theft
of the two signs had been reported at first light and the men's
riotous though cheerful tipsy behaviour the night before, had
not gone unnoticed. Summoning all the charm I could, holding
Peter in my arms, in order to appear as pathetic as possible; I
pleaded the cause of the two young men. Luckily the gendarmes were pro the British Navy and when I explained that for
these two naval officers this was their first holiday in France
since they were boys before the war; the glorious red wine had
swiftly gone to their heads, unaccustomed as they were to
drinking any. Long and persuasively I talked, until finally they
agreed not to prosecute, merely to caution them with a dire

warning not to repeat the behaviour. I gave my word to keep an eye on them! As one of them pointed out, 'If someone had been killed, crossing the railway lines illegally, it would have been the fault of the two drunken Englishmen. The Entente Cordiale does not cover everything!' By this time, Wilkie and Vernon were standing like two little boys caught stealing apples, visibly impressed by the rapid conversation in French which they could not follow at all.

Finally, James offered them *un coup de rouge* to set them up for the day and we all drank to the said Entente Cordiale. With smiles and handshakes all round they departed, escorting Wilkie and Vernon, carrying the signs, to show them where they came from. I did feel sorry for them with their hangovers, staggering beneath the weight of the SNCF sign. 'Never mind,' I called after them, 'Breakfast will be ready when you get back – eggs and bacon!' They merely groaned.

Once the decks had been cleared of the clutter of tangled ropes and sails and sluiced down, James lowered the dinghy to teach both men how to sail her. The inner harbour was empty except for a few fishing boats and one or two yachts, making it ideal for dinghy sailing. Sarah and I put the washing lines round the rigging and caught up with the chores of washing and housework, before taking the pushchair and both boys shopping. To me it was sheer undiluted joy to be on French soil again. How could I ever have left it? The *charcuterie* shops were especially tempting, with *rillettes*, pâtés and *saucissons*, completely unknown in England at that time. Our mouths were watering, but prices were high, so we were restricted by our meagre foreign allowance. Fruit and vegetables however were cheap and plentiful, with delicious, fragrant tomatoes, huge as melons and misshapen. Once we had bought *baguettes* and filled our bottle from the cask of wine in the *épicier* our baskets and the pram were over-flowing. Fresh fish for the hot evening meal could be bought from the trawler astern of us.

For five days we lay peacefully moored in the harbour, though James longed to put to sea again. Meanwhile I had telephoned to friends in Paris whose country cottage was not far away, near Ouistréham. This inspired him, 'Why don't we sail round there – it's not far – and there is the Orne Canal just above the port, where we can tie up to the bank.' It seemed a happy compromise, involving only one day's sailing to get there. I rang the Bertucats to arrange a day to invite them on board.

We just managed to scrape together enough francs to have a farewell dinner before leaving Cherbourg; Sarah stayed on

board with the little ones until the end of the delectable seafood meal, when James and I returned to the boat so that she could take our place, joining Wilkie and Vernon. The wine and food inspired lovemaking with an unforgettable abandon. We were happy and at peace that night.

The weather was changing though, with the wind becoming more westerly, bringing clouds and a threat of rain. James want to sail with the turn of the tide next day, around midnight, which meant that Sarah and I could stay below, as with three men they would not need us on deck. I hated leaving the calm anchorage, though the noise and bustle of the harbour, necessitating occasional shifting of berths had been a nuisance at times. I was fast asleep and barely noticed *Elsa* slipping her moorings, but the familiar queasiness at 6 a.m., as I tried to get dressed while she pounded through a moderate sea, made me wish I had laid down fully clad.

Gulping down some Kwells I lurched up on deck before daring to put a kettle on. James was at the tiller, looking happy for the first time since we tied up in Cherbourg. The Cotentin Peninsular protected us from the worst of the westerly, as it was offshore and we seemed to skim over the slight sea, borne along too by a strong current. The dawn was just breaking, lighting up the low line of coast some miles to starboard. James pointed at some mammoth black structures which appeared to rise in isolated clumps out of the sea itself, 'Look!' he said; 'Quick – get Sarah and Vernon – that must be the remains of Mulberry Harbour.' We were too far out to see clearly, but imagination and vivid memories conjured up the long-awaited miracle of the Allied landings. I had been eighteen and in Paris when they had taken place, in June 1944, after four years of Nazi-occupation and remembered with a shiver of exultation what that news had meant. Now, it was six years ago – a lifetime away, and I was twenty-six. None of it mattered though any more; emotionally I felt that my life had not started until I met James. I stared at the distant, vast edifices. Never had we sailed so fast – a good nine to ten knots – it took one's breath away.

James had not got a detailed chart of Ouistréham itself and did not know how damaged the entrance might still be, nor what wrecks might still lie submerged. The entrance did indeed prove to be tricky, though the lighthouse stood out boldly, guiding us into the crowded lower harbour. After such an exhilarating sail, James was loath to lower the sails, but with no room to manoeuvre under canvas, he was forced to start the engine while we clawed our way past some of the bigger vessels lying there, avoiding any damage by skilful use of boathook and

fenders. We only tied up for a short period, as it was very crowded, preferring to glide on up the Orne Canal to a quiet, undisturbed, solitary berth beside the tow path.

Soon we were secured to two stout bollards. There still remained a week of the summer leave and Wilkie and Vernon asked if they could go to Paris. James agreed, laughing as he said, 'Pity I can't come with you – but someone's got to look after the boat!' Then seriously he said, 'You must be back by the tenth – in case we get the right sailing conditions – my leave is up on the fourteenth. Just make certain you have recovered from any hangover and don't get arrested will you!' They went off like two happy schoolboys and I wondered how they would get on as they only had a smattering of French between them; but then, many French people spoke English reasonably well.

Sadly, the weather stayed overcast with rain showers, typical August weather! The Bertucats came to tea, with their old parents who lived nearby; their expression of surprise, mingled with admiration when they first saw *Elsa* turned to consternation and dismay when Michael and Peter appeared in the well. Old Madame Bertucat lifted her hands in horror as she exclaimed, 'Mais non! Ce n'est pas raisonable, ma petite Tonia, avec les bébés!' Luckily Michael could not understand what she was saying, or he would have been extremely annoyed, aged four, at being called a baby. Down in the saloon, neatly swept, with woodwork and brass shining, they were once again full of praise. Sarah had produced our only six cups with the matching teapot, and the *pâtisseries* were the best that Ouistréham could provide. I had known José Bertucat during the war, when his fiancée had just finished her studies at the Cours Montaigne where I was at school. We had a lot of news to catch up on, so Sarah showed the parents round the boat while we chatted. They could hear the thud of tiny feet on the deck, and occasionally Madame would put her hand to her heart exclaiming, 'Mon Dieu!' expecting every minute to hear a splash. I tried to explain how careful and accustomed to the boat both the boys were, having known no other life, but she never relaxed until the small horrors came below, complaining that it was wet outside.

Our little battery wireless could not get the BBC meteorological reports, but I listened each morning and evening to the French equivalent, the Météo, giving details of the weather for Normandy and the Channel; each day repeated the saga of westerly gales and rough seas. It was worrying, for with a stationary 'low' there was little likelihood of an improvement before we would need to set sail.

Wilkie and Vernon dutifully returned from Paris on the 10th, exhausted and penniless, but enamoured of the beautiful city as I knew they would be. They were relieved that the gales prevented us from sailing on the 11th, for they were able to catch up on some sleep. Meanwhile, the water tanks were filled, the washing lines taken down by James and surreptitiously put up again by Sarah and me as we endeavoured to keep abreast of the endless washing. Stores of milk and bread kept having to be renewed and James warned us, 'I think you two had better lash down anything breakable, we may have an uncomfy crossing.' Knowing his talent for understatement I felt both frightened and worried.

The wind stayed constantly in the West, with no South in it; finally on the 12th we had run out of time. Dark grey clouds blew raggedly at an alarming rate across the wet, grey sky as we slipped our moorings just after dawn. Sarah and I stood briefly in the well, holding on to the cabin top while the rain and gale whipped at us; staring in horror at the ugly, grey, tossing and swirling seas just outside the comparative shelter of the Ouistréham harbour mouth.

The men hoisted the sails, lowered the starboard leeboard and James lashed the restraining rope round the tiller, for it would be hard to control in those seas. Lovingly and furtively I glanced at his stern, good-looking face, aware that his intense concentration made him become one with the boat. His piercing blue eyes noted and took in every detail as he called out rapid but clear instructions to Wilkie and Vernon. He very seldom wore a sou'wester and the rain made his hair curl tightly; how I envied him those curls! The black oilskin he was wearing glistened; he looked piratical, positively revelling in the challenge ahead, as he bent forward to turn off the engine with a brief, 'Won't need that this trip.'

Then, with a sickening plunge and roll, we were part of the fury. No transitional period. Sarah and I exchanged glances, and she pushed back her companionway hatch, staggering down the steps to her cabin, while I made by way to my bunk, carefully holding on, in order not to be thrown over. The wind and seas were coming straight from the Atlantic, a great long swell, topped by furiously breaking waves. When we were in the trough of one of the swells, the waves seemed to tower above us engulfingly; the next moment *Elsa* would swoop and soar on to the crest, allowing us a view of seemingly endless grey troughs and crests; spume and waves hurtled at each other, like animals scrapping. An awe-inspiring, seasick-making sight.

All that day, with two men at the helm, James fought to

keep her close-hauled and heading North; but crab-like and stubborn, *Elsa* went her own sweet way, inventing new motions with each wave, sometimes pitching and nearly standing on her head, simultaneously achieving a drunken roll. Squally showers reduced the visibility, as the men strained their eyes for the flicker of a lighthouse beam. With the turn of the tide it was impossible to tell what progress *Elsa* was making, torn between the Force 8 westerly gale and an east-flowing tide, resulting in steeply pitched seas. Every few hours Sarah mastered her seasickness and came over to the galley to make a hot drink for the drenched crew. Even this was a major effort, working one-handed, holding onto the cooker for support whilst carefully judging the moment to pour the boiling water onto the wedged teapot or mugs. The men grabbed their own mugs and a handful of biscuits, for Sarah would have been flung across the saloon if she had tried to carry one up into the well.

James came into our cabin, sipping the hot tea gratefully; dripping water from his oilskin as he sat on the edge of the bunk. He looked so tired and pale, but completely confident, 'Vernon is on watch at the moment. We seem quite safe out here in mid-Channel. I don't know where we are, but when it gets light we'll try tacking in closer to shore.' I felt a surge a fear, 'Have we got to be out all night James?' Firmly he answered, 'Of course, the open sea is the only safe place.' Finishing his tea and biscuits, he said, 'I'll go and see Peter now – save you getting up – and give him some milk – if there's any left, and a biscuit.'

Suddenly the movement became more violent, making it difficult not to be thrown out of my bunk. I saw James turn hurriedly and hasten up on deck. I literally felt so ill that at times I did not care what happened, but a gnawing guilt and fear for the boys and for Sarah, so innocently involved in this insane tumultuous journey, caused me to pray incoherently and wildly. Soon he reappeared, looking concerned and apologetic, 'Darling we just can't carry so much sail. No point anyway and it might split, so I'm afraid we've got to lower the mainsail – I've told Sarah. She's coming up on deck. Come up as soon as you can.' Fear galvanized me into forgetting my wretched sickness, as I struggled into my boots and short duffel coat, weaving my way across the saloon in a zig-zag sprawl and up into the well. Sarah was there, looking calm and determined, showing no sign of any emotion or fear. (She later told me that I gave her the same impression!) Wilkie and Vernon stood close to James as he wrestled with the tiller, shouting to make himself heard above the thunderous roar, clearly explaining what each of us had to do. He would steer, keeping her as steady as

possible, while Wilkie lowered the straining 1,500 square feet of sail with the winch. Vernon would haul in the slack of the main sheet, as Sarah and I gathered in the folds to the best of our ability, standing on the cabin top or in the catwalk.

We crept along the slippery deck, drenched with spray, unable either to speak or hear each other, flung about like rag dolls as we endeavoured bodily to throw ourselves onto the wildly flapping and billowing mainsail. The starboard catwalk and side were frighteningly steep as *Elsa* heeled over in her impetuous surge forward, forcing Sarah and me to cling on for dear life. The darkness of the night became blotted out by the terrifying claustrophobic blackness of the sail which cavorted and cracked like a live creature, reducing to nil our puny efforts to encompass it. We gasped for breath as our arms vainly fought to dominate the engulfing folds. Many times it seemed that the sail would win and force us over the side as we crouched in the catwalk, clinging on to any handhold for sheet survival. Finally, after what felt like an eternity of terror, *Elsa* eased her mad careering through the night, proving that the mainsail must at least be down, even if not gathered in. Sarah slowly emerged from the folds, drenched, cold and trembling and crawled towards me. By the time we reached the well we felt exhausted but somehow exhilarated by the fact that we had won a battle against overwhelming forces.

She crept back into her cabin to change her soaking wet clothes and crawl into her bunk again, where Michael's warm little body would soon cause her shivering to cease. *Elsa* seemed to sail just as enthusiastically under her foresail and jib, so that with the worry and tension of a possible rent mainsail behind us, James showed his relief, 'Well done, darling' he said quietly, through lips grown stiff with salt water and cold, 'Wilkie and Vernon will tie it up. Go back to bed but put the kettle on, on your way if you can.' Thankfully I climbed down the steps, peering into Peter's cabin at the bottom. He lay fast asleep, his fluffy blue dressing gown enfolding him like an envelope, a half finished biscuit in one outflung hand, and I envied him the dreamless innocent sleep. I managed somehow to hold on to the kettle to prevent it spilling. Before it had boiled, James came down, lurching across the saloon and casually wedging himself by the galley, 'That was a great job you and Sarah did. *Elsa's* fine now – riding the gale easily. I think it's easing off. I'm going to sleep for an hour. Wilkie's on watch and Vernon's dozing in the well.' Reassured I slept too, until one of the men quietly opened our door, whereupon he was instantly wide awake, 'What's it like? Feels quieter,' he said as he struggled into wet

boots. 'Yes. It's nearly dawn and the gale has eased a lot.'
Vernon drawled in his laconic voice. I joined the men in the
well. Dawn had risen, the gale had ceased, backing from West
to South-West, so that even under foresail and jib alone, we
had clawed our way on the port tack to within sight of land.
I felt as elated and relieved as the men must have done. James
scanned the coast with field glasses, dashing down to the
saloon to check on the chart and Reed's Almanac. He told us,
'I'm not absolutely sure where we are. I think we've been
blown off course and further east than Chichester harbour.
We'll go in close and investigate before the tide turns.

I knew the men must be ravenous by now and promised
them all I would cook a huge breakfast as soon as we rounded
the end of *any* pier or jetty; it did not matter which or where!
Meanwhile, I offered to boil yet another kettle. Wilkie went
for'ard to hoist the mainsail in order to speed us towards an
unfamiliar stretch of coastline. Soon the steadying influence
of the mainsail was felt as *Elsa* heeled over gently, gathering
speed, so that when I next appeared on deck, the entrance to
a small harbour was clearly defined. Hopefully we would
soon have our longed-for breakfast.

Just then I heard the more powerful throb of the customs
launch as they drew alongside. This was too much, just as we
were about to prepare breakfast, so I tore up on deck leaving
Sarah scrambling the eggs and making toast; leaning over the
side, I implored, 'Oh, *please* go away and come back after
breakfast – we haven't had anything to eat for twenty-four
hours – caught in a gale you know,' and tore down below again
just in time to prevent the high chair toppling over as the two
brothers engaged in mock battle, full of pent-up energy. Totally
surprised by a surely unprecedented request, the customs
officers obligingly drove off saying they would see us later.
James was angry at my apparent discourtesy, but secretly
relieved I felt; Sarah and the crew roared with laughter.

Elsa nosed her way slowly up between the piers, riding the
southerly swell gently as James decided where to moor her.
By this time the boisterous infants had wolfed a huge
breakfast and finished the milk, so Sarah offered to go ashore
as soon we we tied up in order to get some more. We had gone
some way up the long entrance, finally reaching a quayside
where some fishing boats were tied up. Gruff greetings were
exchanged as someone caught our lines: 'Bad storm last
night,' from the fishermen, answered by the laconic James
with, 'Yes, bit rough. Had to lower the mainsail.'

He still did not admit that he had no idea where we were
and surrepetitiously asked Sarah, as she went off with the

milkcan, to look at the Post Office and find out the name of the harbour! She was amused at this, but also awestruck by his incredible feat of navigation. By the time the men had secured our lines and tidied up some of the clutter, I had made a huge saucepan full of scrambled eggs, which, accompanied by the still delicious French bread was devoured by them in an instant, just before Sarah returned with the milk and the triumphant news that we were in . . . Littlehampton!

It was Sunday, summer leave was up the next day, meaning that James and the men would have to return to the ship. Thoughtfully he looked at us both, 'I'm afraid you'll have to stay here for a week – we can't possibly get round to Hayling Island today. In fact we three will have to leave later this afternoon.' At first I was dismayed, 'But James – there's such a shambles on deck. How can we get ashore? What about water? . . .' James calmed me down, 'Don't worry, Wilkie, Vernon and I will tidy the decks and put the cover on the mainsail. Then I'll see about a gangplank. Though only Michael will be able to go ashore with one of you. I'll rig up a hose too.' Once again I was deeply grateful to have Sarah on board, for without her I could not have got ashore at all.

The week flew by, and when James and Vernon returned the following Saturday we had an idyllic sail round to Hayling Island. In a ladylike and dignified manner, *Elsa* rounded Selsey Bill, giving it a wide berth, but inside the Looe Channel marked by conical buoys. We entered Chichester harbour just before slack high water, leaving the black can buoys to port and the red ones to starboard, eventually tying up at our old berth. Michael was beside himself with joy at finding his precious car and various toys hidden away in the boatyard and especially happy when Tilly was fetched, gently purring, graciously allowing the children to hug and stroke her. It always took at day or two to forgive James and me for leaving her behind, during which she studiously avoided sitting on our laps or rubbing herself against our legs.

Now – looking back – with not many days left for this exorcizing – that was the last carefree time. Doubts and suspicions there were, but nothing definite – ripples and light airs of fear – but not for a while yet, the threatened gales and storms portending finality.

CHAPTER TEN
Land's End to Liverpool

Sarah had now had her summer holiday, spending a fortnight with her mother in Cheshire. How I missed her as I struggled to be everywhere at once, taking both children on the bus for the shopping, extricating the pram from the sail locker, precariously half dragging and half lifting it across the gangplank. The bus stop was quite a long way from the boatyard, with an infrequent service. As the remainder of the ship's company were now on leave, James had to double up on his duties which meant him staying on board *Plover* overnight twice a week, and I hoped and prayed no gales would blow at night while I was on my own. Mostly we were lucky; the rigging merely tapped the mast peacefully as I lay in our bunk, fearfully waiting for the menacing whistle and shriek denoting a rising wind blowing through the shrouds.

At the time the lack of friends did not seem strange, for the party-giving, social scene had not yet evolved and we had no drink on board, except for the odd bottle of plonk – and yet looking back there must have been brother officers and their wives who would have enjoyed the novelty of a simple meal aboard – even if it did mean 'walking the plank'. No. James must obviously have wished to keep his other life apart, avoiding any confrontation.

The days were full of movement and excitement; the boat herself was in some mysterious way, alive and an uncertain, fickle friend. Her moods, like mine, depended on the weather and I loved to make her look as beautiful as she deserved. When the wind blew though, she scolded noisily through creaking mast and boom; a loose block rattling perhaps; eventually losing her temper and shrieking like a harpie as the gale buffeted around her, causing her to strain at the ropes as if she wished to escape. The kind people in the office were friends too, though James never invited them on board.

Sarah returned and September loomed with the equinoxial tides and gales. We were delighted to see her as we prepared to settle into a winter routine. James was away at sea for weeks at a time and I could never have coped single-handed with the capricious vagaries of September. At spring tides when the gale blew from the South-East, causing an even higher flood tide, the wavelets would cover the jetty and *Elsa* would strain at the lines holding her off, as though she wished to perch up on the jetty itself. Our hull would bump against the wooden stanchions, needing only a couple more feet of water for *Elsa*, with her shallow draught to float partly up on it – a repetition of the situation up the Medway. Curiously the worst storms always seemed to happen at night and when James was away.

Michael, meanwhile, grew more adventurous in his precious pedal-car. One cold autumn day, Sarah and I were polishing the ship's bell and binnacle, when we saw something which made us freeze into immobility. About fifty yards away, along one of the narrow jetties, young Michael was busily pedalling his car. . . .The jetty, intended for dinghies in the summer, was the same width as the toy car. It had no hand rails, and he was rapidly approaching the end – surrounded by water. Neither of us dared to move or shout across, for fear of distracting him, but my heart was in my mouth as Sarah clutched my arm. Nothing could save him if he fell into that icy water, sitting in the little red car, for even if we dived in to swim across, he would have been dragged down. It would take too long to run round from our own jetty and up the little one he was now coming to the end of – rapidly. Prepared, nevertheless, to dive in, we stared in hypnotised horror, which changed to amazed disbelief at the simple outcome. Having reached the end of the jetty, he paused for a second, then unconcernedly stood up, holding the little car's sides, turned right round and calmly pedalled back to the other end. Sarah tore round to meet him and explain, with just the right amount of stern reprimand and fear, never, *never* to ride out along any of the jetties – ever again. He agreed, commenting, 'No, I won't. It was very hard turning round. I'll show you what I did!' and gave her an on the spot repeat performance! She managed not to smile, pointing out that indeed a false move might have made him fall in, and *lose the car*!

The cold spell was followed by an anticyclone, bringing clear bright weather, set fair for several days. There was no question of any serious sailing, but *Plover* was holding a party in the wardroom for all the officers and their wives.

She was back in Portsmouth and as James had a long weekend, he thought it would be a brilliant idea just to sail round and tie up alongside. This seemed safe, for it was so close; accordingly we slipped our moorings early one Saturday morning. It took only a few hours to sail round Southsea front, close enough clearly to see Eastney Fort and Southsea Castle and into Portsmouth harbour. Michael's eyes were round with excitement at the sight of so many big ships, *Plover* being one of the smaller ones; even so she dwarfed the roomy Dutch barge. Gently James nudged her alongside, while Sarah and I hung out the fenders for fear of scraping the little minelayer's smart, grey paint.

In no time we were secure, feeling very proud indeed of our seamanship and our connection with one of HM ships. Later on a ladder was lowered for us. By this time I was beginning to feel apprehensive and shy about meeting so many strangers, who probably all knew each other well, living next door to each other in naval quarters. Sarah bustled about putting the children to bed, by which time it was dark, though the ship's decks were brilliantly lit.

I put on my one pretty dress – steel grey, mid-calf length, with a black velvet collar, and tried to tame my brown hair, full of tangles due to the salt air. James absent-mindedly told me I looked fine and kissing the boys goodnight I prepared to climb the ladder with an expectant thrill at the thought of my first party on board. The usual naval generosity with drinks ensured a relaxed camaraderie, shyness melted, and the plain wholesome dinner seemed delicious purely because someone else had prepared and cooked it. Sheer disbelief was registered by the few other wives on learning that we lived and sailed on a boat – with small children. Glances were exchanged and though a few obvious questions were asked, the subject was dismissed as '*too* original' and 'too quaint'. I was relieved when the conversation became general even if I could not join in with my views on world affairs, naval policy, amenities in Portsmouth, restaurants or politics, as I had none. Even if we had had a newspaper on board, I would not have had time to read it, so that I felt inadequate and ignorant. Why had James not insisted on bringing me a daily paper and encouraged me to talk about something other then *Elsa* – sailing – *Elsa* – sailing ad nauseam. There was no one there that evening capturing James's attention – that must be why I had been included in this party. There would only be one other such evening – with electric and traumatic consequences.

The rest of that evening was fun though, for some of the

officers did enjoy sailing and wanted to talk about it. We were the last to go and the Captain accompanied us on deck where a cold starlit night made me shiver, especially when I leant over the side to where *Elsa* lay, bathed in moonlight, far below. Terror struck me, but I must not show my fear of the long climb down. James went first so that he could guide my feet back on deck from the ladder. We tip-toed to our cabin so as not to wake Sarah and the boys. James's loving caresses were all I could wish for. Maybe he loved me too – maybe it was just the wine.

Next morning, with a light northerly breeze his ambition to leave under sail was fulfilled. He hoisted the mainsail before casting off, but it did not fill till we had drifted a little way from the lee of the ship's side, then encouraged by cheers from a handful of officers and ratings lining the rails, I hoisted the foresail and jib on the winch and we stood about, ready to sail though the entrance to Portsmouth harbour. With an off-shore, ideal soldier's wind the sea was calm and *Elsa* glided through the cold, briskly sparkling Solent, close-hauled (for her) on the starboard tack, the Isle of Wight clear-cut to the South.

Tilly joined us on deck for lunch, stalking carefully from stem to stern, skilfully choosing a warm sheltered spot in which to commence the lengthy licking and grooming ritual before curling round to sleep. While Sarah prepared lunch I sat on the after cabin top beside James. He was deep in thought, as always, miles away, and I longed to ask him what he was thinking about, but I knew how much the question irritated and bored him. I knew too by now that I never *would* know. Instead, without being able to stop myself I did the next thing most likely to annoy him, talked about the dinner party on board, 'It was fun last night – I enjoyed meeting everyone, it's a pity we can't meet up more often.' His eyes were expressionless, but he made an effort to respond, patient over the interruption to his wide-ranging thoughts, 'I'm glad – in fact I thought it rather boring – they're a pretty dim lot, leading uninspired lives.' I began again, relishing our comparative privacy, as I vainly tried to mend one of Peter's precious cars, whose rubber wheels were always coming off, 'This is perfect – why can't we always have an offshore wind?' Quite rightly this did not merit a reply. Soon we would be off the tricky entrance to Chichester harbour; the short idyllic opportunity for talking peacefully would be over. As though sensing this, James spoke quietly, 'Sorry to be so absent-minded, but there's an opportunity for a splendid long sail – two in fact – next year. I only heard

about the appointment a short while ago.' Though fearful of the 'long sail' he mentioned, encouraged by his concealed enthusiasm, I pressed him for details. He went on, 'Well, my time in *Plover* comes to an end next Easter. I'm being sent up to HMS *Ariel* – the electrical school at Warrington in Cheshire for a few months. Rather than be separated all that time we could get a crew and sail up there during the Easter leave and back down again in the summer one – what do you think?' Perhaps this would stop his preoccupation with whoever it was – it might all blow over – and anything – *anything* – rather than months of separation. The horrific memories of the past sailing nightmares faded deliberately, in the same way that one forgets the pain of childbirth. I agreed without reservation, 'Yes – I'm willing – but that would mean all round Land's End and up to Liverpool? What about the boys? It's too far for them – really it is. . . .' He answered carefully, 'That is what I was thinking about. We might ask Sarah if she could take them up to her mother in Cheshire while we sailed up there, then they could all join us once we'd found a pleasant berth.' 'James – that's a brilliant idea – ask her now – do.' But as always in a boat, events move rapidly, stopping any further conversation. We were off the entrance, the tide was right, but with a northerly breeze there was no hope of sailing into the harbour, so Sarah and James lowered the sails and winched up the leeboard while I kept her steady, at the tiller. The engine responded straight away, throbbing noisily into life, waking the boys – who were not really asleep, and were told they could come into the well if they promised to stay there. Tilly woke too, stretching, yawning, jumping down into the well, rubbing against our legs, purring with relief at the proximity of land. Slowly we progressed, manoeuvring the obedient *Elsa* into her old position. Tilly jumped a glorious cat-like leap across the last few feet of water, sauntering along the wooden jetty, her tail held high.

We resumed the interrupted conversation. James repeated to Sarah what he had told me and I added my entreaties. Always considerate and helpful, and no doubt remembering the acute discomfort of the return journey from Ouistréham, she immediately promised to ask her mother if she and the two boys could stay in Cheshire for two to three weeks over Easter and again in August. Later, when we were preparing supper while James collected the milk and any mail from the boatyard office, Sarah looked at me searchingly, 'Tonia – what an awful long way to go. I think you're mad. Thank goodness you're not taking the little ones. I'm sure mother will be delighted to have us.' I thanked her in advance,

warmly, 'I know – it will be grim. Four men to feed and no you to help me – but he loves it so. I'm so grateful to you for offering to have them and, of course, it'll be lovely for your mother to have you at home – despite the "horrors" ' (James's name for them). Gaily I added, 'Goodness – I hope you won't be landed with them for ever!'

Dim, unformed thoughts crowded into my over-imaginative mind. I reasoned that though I truly dreaded and was afraid of the 'wild tempestuous seas', my agreeing to the sailing trips, trying to hide my fears, would perhaps increase James's love for me – would bind him to me through the link of the sea – a logical, uninspired reasoning which has ever since made me mistrust my judgment.

During the Christmas leave, Sarah went home to spend a few days with her widowed mother, writing a delightfully reassuring letter to say that it was all fixed up for the boys to stay for both periods.

James decided he would need a crew of three for the long journey – two on watch at a time – and this took some time to find. Meanwhile, I made endless long lists of provisions, for as James said, without children on board we could stay at sea for days at a time – a dreadful thought! At least they would be happy and well looked after, for the warm-hearted and kind Mrs Murphy, Sarah's mother, was looking forward to having them.

All this time I longed for some sign of affection, friendliness or even recognition of my willingness to undertake such a hazardous journey, involving cooking for four men. In vain. To all intents and purpose he was wed to *Elsa*. Exerting an immense amount of self-control I forbore to ask him what he was thinking about, but over supper one evening, when we had drunk some wine – a rare treat – my tongue was loosened and I could not stop myself once again asking the age-old question, 'James *do* you still love me?' He would not look at me, but answered, 'Yes – of course.' Foolishly I persisted, 'Promise you'll tell me if you stop loving me – I must know. . . if there's anyone else. . . .' Again the non-commital agreement to do so. It was as usual totally unsatisfactory. I should have made a direct accusation earlier – but then, where would it have got me. There was nowhere I could go if I *did* go – why *should* I go? *Elsa* was my home too. Much better to feign acceptance of this hopefully temporary situation and hope that whatever it was would blow away. I was thwarted and a prisoner in my own home. My attempts had not cleared the air as I had imagined, merely increased the awkward tension between us.

*My mind raced back and forth like a caged beast. The tragic
unfairness of his lack of love for me hit me anew as I asked
myself for the thousandth time, 'Would any other woman
have put up with those sailing conditions? Would any other
man have felt and acted thus?' What a wicked, devilish
waste of years. . .and love.*

Towards the end of March, with the help of the boatyard, we
put the boat onto some blocks so that James, with some of
them, could carry out the yearly scraping and rubbing down
of the steel hull with wire brushes before putting on a coat of
antifouling and paint. Afloat once more, we painted her sides
from the dinghy; the same deep rich green, set off by the
vivid curved yellow line of the rubbing strake. She looked
regal, and comforted me in my loneliness.

I asked James about his new crew, Geoff, Jimmy and Stan.
He knew little if anything about them, apart from the fact that
they liked sailing, having done some – in small dinghies! –
and that Stan was an engineering officer, 'Useful for looking
after the engine, if we have to use it.' Jimmy also was a naval
officer and young Geoff was a medical student who had
heard somehow of this forthcoming 'exciting adventure'.

During the last few days before Sarah left with the boys, we
listened avidly to all the weather forecasts. There were no
long-term forecasts in those days, but we prayed for an
anticyclone or at least a ridge of high pressure. Mid April had
been warm and sunny which forced one to think it could not
last. We would miss Michael's fourth birthday at the end of
April, but I knew Sarah would celebrate it with a cake for him.
Peter was now two and a dreadful handful; I wondered if she
would be able to manage him. Of overriding importance was
my determination to try and make James notice me, and
appreciate what I was doing for him.

He drove Sarah and the boys to the station; both of them
were far too excited at seeing trains for the first time to be sad
about leaving us behind; that evening our motley crew were
joining us so that I had no time to miss the 'horrors'.

I had decided to allocate the cabins in order of seniority,
giving Sarah's to Stan, Jimmy went into Peter's, and young
Geoff had the uncomfy bunk in the bows by the paint locker.
They seemed friendly and cheerful, though they must have
wondered what they had let themselves in for. Stan's opening
remark had a familiar ring to it and did not endear me to him,
'I don't like cats.' I spoke sharply, 'You won't see much of
Tilly, she sleeps through most of the sailing – and she doesn't
like everyone either.'

It was swiftly obvious that I would get little help from any of the three self-satisfied young men as I washed up and dried up alone. During supper I had tried to joke about chores, 'I've even got a left-handed potato-peeler!' Though they responded light-heartedly I understood it would be a chore to be avoided, 'Oh well. . . if it's a lovely sunny day and I can sit up on deck. . .' and, 'Of course I'd like to – but when I'm not on watch I'll probably be asleep. . . .' I went to bed, leaving the four of them poring over charts.

At first light we were all up, filling up with water and petrol. Thankfully it was a fine morning with a light East-South-East wind, Force 2 to 3, a rising barometer and a good forecast; only the merest niggling fear remained. I was back in the galley when we left Mill Rythe for the last time. The engine shuddered into life, helping James to steer away from the jetties while the sails were being hoisted, quickly filling, lending wings to her measured, obedient progress. It was a beautiful day to be sailing through the Solent, (the next and final time I would see it would be for the Spithead Review) and James switched off the engine as soon as we were clear of the entrance, remarking that it was not running as smoothly as usual. I too had noticed a vibration unfamiliar to its usual quiet throb. For me it was ideal sailing weather; not so for James who would have preferred more wind. A few yachts and sailing dinghies showed off their paces after the tedious winter overhaul, swiftly sailing past and round us like mischievous ducklings while *Elsa* unmoved by their butterfly dexterity and swallow-like antics, sailed steadfastly on. It was too cold to sit up on deck after the midday meal was cleared away, leaving me a free hour or two; yet I was loathe to lie down below as this accelerated the nausea. Tilly had been fed and for the hundreth time I speculated on cats' immunity from seasickness.

James decided to put into Weymouth to mend the engine, and was impatient and cross at the waste of precious time; though with so little wind he knew the engine might be vital for entering harbour. For me it was a sentimental return to familiar sailing ground. After going about, an easy reach on the port tack took us past the entrance to the enchanting Lulworth Cove where we had been so idyllically happy. I glanced at James, willing him to remember it too, but with the three-man crew standing by, plus the knowledge that he was all intent on the approach to Weymouth, weighing up in his mind when and if to start the engine for the sharp turn to port past the breakwater, I bit back any remark. He did point out to them the silver, gleaming froth and spray in the

distance, denoting Portland Race, saying that if we listened very hard we would hear its thunderous roar. Dutifully they did so and were suitably impressed, though at that distance, unless you knew it intimately, the vision was not frightening.

In Weymouth, a young engineer removed the slatted grating over the engine room, talking incomprehensibly of corrosion, carburettors, faulty petrol feed, dirty plugs, distributor heads, leaking batteries and so on. As it was late, the engineer, having stripped down the engine, promised to be back with the necessary new parts very early next morning. James emphasized the need for an early start, with a West-flowing tide to take us round Portland Bill. 'Beastly engine,' he muttered, 'Always letting one down.' I pointed out to him that on the whole it had behaved remarkably well, adding shyly; 'Do you remember that fiendish starting handle in *Pat?*' He smiled, the blue eyes warm and amused, 'Will I ever forget it. My thumb has never been the same since!' I went on, as he replaced the engine covering, 'I was thinking about the time we moored here, in *Pat.*' He was afraid that I might become sentimentally mawkish, just when he had so much on his mind; looked fleetingly yet affectionately at me, remarking casually, 'Yes, Weymouth hasn't changed much, but it looks a bit smaller from a bigger boat doesn't it?' I bit back all I wanted to say, all the reassurance I needed and longer for him to give me; reasoning that I could show my admiration and love by doing all that was required of me as efficiently as possible. One day surely he would tell me what I wanted to hear. One day.

Still the weather held, a slightly stronger East-South-East breeze, Force 3 to 4, making James itch to set sail, miserable at the waste of time. Finally, the engine responded to the care lavished on it, starting instantly, throbbing quietly and smoothly. The tide was right and we cast off, heading South on a long tack to take us well outside the Race. Stan, Jimmy and Geoff stood on the cabin top, once the sails were up and the engine stopped, holding onto the shrouds, mesmerized by the awesome, growling fury of the Race.

When we were at least two miles out we went about, giving the area a wide berth, helped along by the tide as well as a fair wind. This was copybook sailing; none of us felt sick.

We were some miles off Start Point when the tide turned and as the wind was not strong enough to give us many knots, we spent an age between Prawle Point and Start Point. The men settled down to their watches – James with Geoff, and Stan together with Jimmy. The following day, as the sun warmed us, we revelled in *Elsa's* effortless motion through

tamed and gentle waves, tide and wind with us. Occasionally the bowsprit would dip, shaking drops of spray off the net. It was too beautiful for the two off watch to stay below and sleep; our spirits soared as we sat in the well. On days like that we felt like Christopher Columbus, Drake, every king and every explorer that had lived and sailed, discovering distant lands. James felt this buoyant mood too, and in one of his rare boisterous humours, as we sailed within sight of the famous Eddystone Lighthouse, taught us all the rollicking song, *My Father is the keeper of the Eddystone Light* – and he slept with a mermaid one fine night. . . .'

EDDYSTONE LIGHT

One night by the light of the flickering glim,
As I was a'readin' of the evening hymn,
I heard a voice call out 'Ahoy!'
And there was my mother a'sittin' on a buoy.

'Oh! What has become of my children three?'
My mermaid mother asked of me,

'One was exhibited as a talking fish
And the other was served on a chafin' dish'.

The moonlight flickered on her seaweed hair,
I looked again and my mother wasn't there
Her voice came echoing through the night,
'To HELL with the Keeper of the Eddystone light!'

We sang at the tops of our voices with no one but the sea, sun, wind and sky to hear us. We sang other naval songs too; *In the spring she wore a purple girdle*, and the traditional, *We'll rant and we'll roar like true British Sailors*. We sang until we were hoarse and it was time for me to get lunch. We did not sing again. Had we done so, it would not now be such a poignant, happy memory.

IN THE SPRING (Another nautical sad little ditty)

In the spring, she pushed a perambulator
She pushed it in the spring time and in the month of May
And when they asked her why the hell she pushed it
She pushed it for a sailor who was far, far away.

Behind the door her father kept a shotgun
He kept it in the spring time and in the month of May
And when they asked him why the hell he kept it
He kept it for a sailor who was far, far away.

In the spring she planted purple violets
She planted in the spring time and in the month of May
And when they asked her why the hell she planted
She planted for a sailor who was six feet down

Six feet down – six feet down – She planted for a sailor who was
Six feet down

After another day or so we put into Newlyn in order to fill our water tank and to pander to my request to buy fresh bread, milk and fruit to speed us up the west coast into St George's Channel.

For once I did not feel guilty at wanting to go into harbour; night was approaching and none of us wanted to sail round the famous Land's End in the dark, missing its magnificent desolation. We were in luck too, for we tied up astern of a trawler with a tremendous catch of mackerel, ensuring an excellent supper.

We motored out of Newlyn on a brilliantly sunny morning – early, to catch the West-flowing tide – listening to the forecast. The sea was a rippling mirror, clear and translucent, of an indescribable emerald blue. I emptied the gash bin over the side and called to the men in astonishment when huge, evil-looking fish surrounded us, turning on their backs, showing their smooth white bellies as their gaping jaws eagerly snatched at the rubbish. They were basking sharks; three of them glided gracefully and playfully alongside us for a few minutes only, until the rubbish was eaten. We would never have seen them if it had not been for the glassy calm. Anxiously I peered at the falling barometer before installing myself in the well to watch and experience sailing round Land's End.

The sails hung limp and lifeless – no whisper to stir them. James resigned himself to the humiliation of having to use the engine until we were well off the Lizard. We felt a sense of wonder at the thought of nothing between us and America except the Atlantic, whose slow, great swell, like rolling Sussex Downs, cradled us in its long sweeping roll. Inexorably the tide bore us past the impressive Wolf Lighthouse, to the bleak westernmost Bishop Rock Lighthouse. Apart from a French crabber, gently drifting like ourselves we seemed to be alone in this vast world of sea and I was deeply grateful that it should be so peaceful. We hailed the crabber and I spoke to him in French asking if he had had a good catch. He answered cheerfully, somewhat startled at being spoken to in French from a Dutch Boeier!

The day was slowly clouding over, with a slight breeze, enabling us to go about and sail up the coast towards the Bristol Channel; close enough to admire its rugged beauty. Longships Lighthouse was too far away for us to appreciate its solitary grandeur. The wind slowly increased, still from the South-West, as the barometer continued to fall rapidly. I tried to ignore both facts.

Elsa needed at least a Force 5 to speed her heavy, rounded steel hull along, pounding and surging through the turbulent cross seas of the Bristol Channel, caused by conflicting tides and wind. Hastily I swallowed my Kwells, letting them take effect on deck before attempting the big evening meal. James looked at me anxiously. He was at the tiller which was bucking and kicking savagely in the now heavy seas, 'I'm afraid we're in for a bit of a blow tonight – but at least it's going the right way.' I told him I could not get a sound out of the old battery wireless, which did not surprise him as we were too far away from any transmitters to pierce our steel hull, especially as we had no aerial of any description.

He pointed out Lundy Island, a dark grey lump in the distance, nearly lost in the gathering grey gloom of dusk. 'Are you all right?' he asked gently, and I nodded, unable to speak for fear of showing my cowardice. He went on, 'We were lucky to come round Land's End in such ideal conditions.' Gradually the wind increased, white horses appearing on the waves' crests and the mainsail bellied out, the sheets straining. A squall of rain hit us and I dived below for James's oilskin. The motion of the boat was different to any I had known. The seas coming from astern caused her to plunge down into a trough where for a while she was held by an undertow, before climbing, stern first, up the next following sea! This had come about in less than an hour and I would have to hurry with a hot stew supper while I was still able to. As usual, wedged in the galley, I felt abysmally sick, but somehow found and opened the right tins, feet well apart for balance as we rode this roller-coaster sea. The shrouds and rigging round the mast over the galley, slapped and whined and shrieked, which could only mean one thing – this was a full-blooded gale. Struggling into the well, leaving the stew firmly wedged against the rail round the cooker, I called to James that they could help themselves, but that I was too seasick to cope.

I went to my bunk, fully dressed, too frightened to rest, creeping back into the well, my heart in my mouth as I watched the three crew skid and slide in a precarious manner on the cabin top while James luffed her up the merest fraction

to spill some of the buffeting gale out of the sail. The wind was whipping the white caps off the peaks of the waves, now five or six feet high, hissing and rushing past like express trains, even making the same noise. I crouched in what little shelter there was aft of the well. It took the men ages to tie all the little reef points, but it had the desired effect. With only the binnacle light in the well to emphasize the black fury of the night it seemed impossible to believe that it was only a few hours from the calm of Land's End.

All night and all next day it raged, more terrifying still in broad daylight with miles and miles of towering white waves. The horizon was bounded by *Elsa's* position. On top of any particular wave one glimpsed this petrifying vista, then plunging down into a chasm once more, they reared all-engulfing about us. Down below I became increasingly aware of another noise which had joined the cacophony. A slip-slopping noise of bilge. I knew there was not much water in the bilge so it puzzled me. Our shallow draught was only three feet. Really panic-stricken now, I opened the locker under the settee and to my horror saw and smelt the evil, oily bilge water, lapping round the tins and gear stowed there. My first thought was that we had sprung a leak, rapidly followed by, 'We will sink!' I scrambled back on deck as fast as I could to tell James, so intent on keeping the straining *Elsa* sailing as safely as possible he had not noticed anything untoward. He exclaimed, 'My God. The engine will be flooded.' Leaving Jimmy and me to steer our wild unplanned race, he tore below to confirm what I had suspected.

Some of the seas we had taken on board had found their way to the bilges, but there was more than that warranted. He rigged up the pump, 'We'll pump out what we can then perhaps I can see where it's coming in.' Once the pump was primed the men took it in turns, for it was hard work. Slowly it dawned on me all the damage the stinking, oily bilge water would have done. I wailed, 'Oh James, all the blankets and clothes in the locker under the bunks. . . ?' He nodded at me sadly, as I alternated between rage, tears and terror at our plight. For an hour or more the bilge streamed out over the side, until James reckoned the level would be low enough for him to make some inspection.

This necessitated pulling back the saturated carpets prior to lifting the boards – a soul-destroying job, enveloped by the foul smelling stench, in a tossing boat behaving like a newly-broken colt, as she lunged and wildly plunged. After searching the hull in each cabin he came up on deck to reassure himself and the helmsman on how *Elsa* was

handling. Still he found nothing, until he suddenly remembered the sterngland, wishing that he had done so earlier. Down into Sarah's damp cabin he went, hoping it would not be impossibly difficult to find. Ripping everything up again, he found it at last, the water seeping in where the propellor shaft entered into the hull. He repacked it with grease and shredded rags, staying down until he was satisfied that no more seas were coming in. By now *Elsa* looked as though she had been ransacked, prior to being sent to the breaker's yard. My spirits sank when I realized the enormity of the task that faced me, once the gale had subsided.

Certainly I was getting my sealegs after two or more days continuously at sea and gradually too, the tumultuous waves were lessening their ghoulish game with us, affording us an essential respite. Eventually the gale blew itself out, leaving us wallowing in lumpy seas, which would take some time to calm down. The sun came out. Suddenly from one extreme to another, we found ourselves in what is known as a 'dead calm' – a dreadful misnomer. The wind dropped completely, leaving poor *Elsa* at the mercy of a wayward swell underlying the leftover waves with no direction or purpose, causing her to roll, pitch and wallow worse than any drunken sailor. The racket was deafening as blocks and tackle banged against each other and the sides, accompanied by the thudding of leeboards, a strange reeling motion in which even James had difficulty in keeping his feet.

Afterwards, James suggested that everything should be brought up on deck to dry off; making the exhausted crew groan and swear volubly. Slowly we dragged the dripping mattresses, cushions and carpets up into the glorious sparkling blue day; spreading then over the cabin top until there was not a spare inch. James hoped no stray plane or helicopter would inspect our ugliness too closely, for our appearance was that of the scruffiest jumble sale on record, ruining our usual seamanlike look.

My despair and misery were absolute, for most of my clothes were ruined; the few pretty dresses, not in constant use, were stowed out of the way in the lockers, as were the few blankets and sheets. Over the years the oily stains would fade away, but at the time, when possessions were few and precious; to me it was a catastrophe.

At midday, James got a good sight with the sextant and was able to pinpoint our position on the chart. We were some miles off Caernarfon Bay, nearly in the Irish Sea, with Holyhead our nearest port. How long it would take to get there depended entirely on the wind, for the engine was

utterly dead. We had removed the engine room grating to try to let the healing sun dry it out; from time to time Stan would half-heartedly clean a plug, endeavouring to mop the parts he could reach, but it would need dismantling before any life could be coaxed back into its cold, wet insides. The battery also was sodden and flat. Becalmed on a lessening sea, we now tentatively prayed for a fair wind, not however tempting fate by whistling for one!

Eventually a fresh westerly blew up, enabling us to make for Holyhead. The reef points were shaken out again and soon the rugged coastline of Anglesey was visible; we sent up a small ragged cheer. The South Stack Lighthouse stood out clearly, but the harbour and port were unknown to us which made our entrance hazardous. In order to maintain steerage we had to keep the mainsail up yet ready at a moment's notice to lower away. James's masterly handling steered her safely into the outer harbour, where a long jetty at right angles forced us to go about, in order to enter the inner harbour. Almost immediately we were waved to a berth alongside the pier, just astern of a trawler. It was obvious that despite lowering all sails in record time we had too much way on to stop. Simultaneously, Geoff and I realized our bowsprit was going to smash into the wheelhouse of the trawler; we sprinted up for'ard, jumped from our bows to its stern and leant with our combined weights and grim determination against the end of the bowsprit. At the same time Stan and Jimmy got a line ashore; we were safe but trembling from our exertions. The delay caused by a broken bowsprit, plus damage to an irate Welshman's trawler could have been devastating – possibly ending our trip prematurely, for time was running out on us as usual.

Soon we heard the lilting, soft Welsh voices as a few fishermen gathered to inspect the exotic foreign bird suddenly landed in their midst. Delighted to stop the herculean task of straightening the chaos below, I hailed them from the well to ask if they had any fish for sale, soon joined by James asking for the name of an engineer. Fish they had a'plenty, which they tipped all fresh and scaly-glistening into my dish, unwilling to take any payment until persuaded. James strode off, to see the mechanic – a long walk to the end of the pier and the town.

Half-heartedly the crew helped me to replace the carpets and finish off tidying up on deck. They were tired out and so was I.

It took two whole days to nurse the engine back to life, finally having to dismantle it completely. During all that time,

the two engineers spoke quietly to each other in gentle, slow, sing-song voices, never once losing their tempers, despite the intense irritation they must have felt at their initial failure. One of them would just say, 'Well Dai, we'd better just try this,' or whatever the new idea consisted of. We were amazed, dumbfounded at their forbearance. The end of the trip was in sight, but the weather was atrocious. It rained continuously on the two long-suffering Welshmen as they struggled, blowing in under the canvas cover we had draped over the boom to give them some protection. Visions of an abortive trip haunted me, moored here, on my own until James could wangle a long weekend and continue the journey. I longed too to see the boys again and wondered what devilment they were getting up to in Mrs Murphy's house. Tempers became frayed with the crew at a loose end, playing poker and eating endless meals – cooked by me!

Then, suddenly, one morning the rain stopped, the barometer crept slowly up, blue sky peered between grey clouds which rapidly dissolved into wispy white ones and best of all, an ideal, Force 3 to 4 West-South-West breeze blew up and James made the decision to sail that day – engine or no engine. 'At least let's get as far as the Mersey,' he firmly stated. The two placid engineers returned for their third day, forlornly pressed the starter as a gesture and nearly fell over in astonishment as the engine pounded into life. We all scurried round in excitement, congratulating the two miracle-workers, while James asked them for their bill. That was the crowning touch to their good naturedness, it was as low as they could make it and we felt tearfully grateful to them both.

The crew filled the water tank, unfurled the sails and stood by in readiness to cast off. Spring turned into early summer as we sailed merrily along – yes, merrily – all gales forgotten, thankful to have the tide and wind with us as we approached the tumbling seas off the Skerries, where the hidden rocks marked by conical black buoys caused swirling mini tide-rips mimicking Portland Race. The playfully wicked seas leapt around us like flames and Geoff was quite worried, though I assured him that this was far less frightening than the gale we had experienced a few days ago.

We even sailed between tall, black forbidding rocks, flaunting our sailing prowess, encouraging Geoff to polish the brass bell and binnacle in preparation for our triumphal entry up the Mersey. It took his mind off the maelstrom around us! Suddenly we were through it – a sharp dividing line ruling the start of orderly waves, rolling sensibly along. One gentle night's sailing, taking a long leg out, would bring

us into Liverpool Bay early in the morning.

Crosby Lighthouse was our first glimpse of the entrance, then swiftly we weaved our way between black boat beacons, with red flashes marking the east side of the Crosby Channel and the red conical buoys with a white flash on the west side. There were gloomy bell buoys too, seeming to herald doom. In no time at all we were struggling in vain to keep abreast of a seven-knot ebb tide in the Mersey.

Ships and coal barges jostled for place, crowding the busy river and we hastily started the engine in order to make some headway. James decided to approach Runcorn at the head of the Mersey and anchor while he went ashore to find out exactly which locks and canals would take us to the Weaver and Acton Bridge. We had made it. With a day to spare! He was gone a little while and on his return shyly and diffidently presented me with a beautiful little brass anchor to make up for the ruined clothes and chaos below. Immediately I felt both touched and guilty; moved that he should have understood and sympathized with my distress, when I was at fault for having made such a fuss – though secretly I would have loved a promise of the pretty things replaced.

We motored on up the Mersey until we came to Runcorn and the Western Point Docks (Weston Mersey Lock in 1952). There we entered our first lock – a strange even frightening experience suddenly to be hemmed into a narrow confine with water gushing out, leaving an impression that we were sinking. Lines grew taut, requiring adjusting; then just as abruptly all was still; the next lock gates opened and we were through into the Weaver Navigation. A mile or so further on we came to Weston Marsh Lock where we repeated the performance, thereby transferring to the River Weaver proper. All was calm, orderly and countryfied, affording such a contrast with the turbulent passage up the West Coast.

Weston Marsh had contacted the Sutton Weaver swing-bridge who kindly opened their bridge in order to let our seventy-foot mast slip through. The island formed by the Weaver river and canal was completely unspoilt, consisting of grass, marshy land and trees, with a few cottages on the river edge. Thankfully, slowly, we glided past, mooring just below them, near to Acton Bridge. The journey of many hundreds of miles came to a gentle halt, with not a day to spare. Weaverham would be our shopping centre for the summer. Tilly, looking thin and dirty, bounded ashore before we had secured our warps, grateful to be on dry land again – like her mistress.

CHAPTER ELEVEN

Misery on the Mersey

It was a strange disembodied summer, tucked away so far from the sea, emphasized by the lack of tides in the still, dank waters of the canal. Only one or two cottages stood on the little island where we moored, all in a claustrophobic valley, steamy hot, vibrant with mosquitoes.

Mrs Murphy drove Sarah and the boys back to *Elsa* at the first opportunity. They hugged me briefly, then devoted all their time to Tilly and exploring the grassy bank which was to be their new playground, provided someone was on deck to supervise. Tilly had been shaken by the long, rough sail, hardly eating anything, but so immensely relieved to see grass and land again and the boys, she responded enthusiastically; licking them with her rough tongue, butting her head against their legs and consenting to be installed in a cardboard box pulled along with string. My relief at seeing Sarah was enormous as I confessed to her, 'I hardly dare show you your cabin – *or* the rest of the boat. Everything got soaked – it was dreadful.' I knew her response would minimize the damage or work involved and I was right. As she stepped down into the saloon, wrinkling her snub nose she merely said, 'Mmm – pongs a bit doesn't it? Never mind. We'll soon clear it up.'

The heat became oppressive, producing a very nasty smell from the canal itself, along which, from time to time, floated the swollen bodies of drowned, disintegrating animals; black and unrecognizable. There was no question of swimming in it, so James bought the boys a round rubber dinghy, which when filled with water doubled up as a swimming pool. Shopping was a nightmare for poor Sarah, who had to cross from the island to the far bank by a little bridge, climb up to the main road just before Acton Bridge and catch a bus into Weaverham. If the boys were ashore I had to watch them

carefully, for they would venture to the far end of the island, where lurked a nasty swamp. We knew nothing about it, until ear-splitting screams sent me racing towards the boys, to find Peter up to his waist in oozing, slimy, muddy water, anxiously watched by Michael, unable to help. It took ages to clean him off and the smell lingered for ages!

Each morning Michael and I did 'lessons' for a short while, for he was just five and would be going to school in the autumn, when we sailed back down to the Hamble. Luckily reading was easy for him and we spent boring moments following the adventures of Andy-Pandy and Looby-Loo. Arithmetic eluded him however; whether I used oranges, or bricks or toy soldiers, he could not see why two of them joined by two others made four! My patience gave out and we stopped doing 'maths'.

Soon, with Sarah to encourage and inspire us, we aired and dried the cabins, stacking the tins neatly back in the lockers, washing the oily stains out of the carpets as best we could; opening all scuttles and hatches in order to get a through draft. Then Peter developed a cough. At first I thought it only a summer cold, but slowly it worsened, unaccompanied by a runny nose, and I recognized, from my own distant child-hood, the long, indrawn breath of whooping cough. The vaccine did not exist as yet and when Sarah went into Weaverham, she telephoned a doctor's surgery to ask if there was any special treatment or medicine for the boy to take. He was apologetic but assured her there was nothing he could do for it. Remembering my own whooping cough, aged seven in Egypt, when I felt I would suffocate at the end of each long drawn-in 'whoop', followed by sickness and nosebleeds, I was very apprehensive, especially as we had no doctor of our own nor any telephone near us; the cottage on the island did not possess one. Within ten days, Michael caught it, though luckily not as badly as Peter. Sarah had not been home for weeks, not wishing to leave me alone with the boys, for James was frequently on duty; but finally I persuaded her to go.

The horrendous whooping cough, as though waiting deliberately for that precise moment, attacked viciously. Peter lay there, wan and exhausted from repeated coughing fits, finally unable to get his breath at the top of the 'whoop', his little face blue as he fought for breath, eyes frightened and imploring. I felt helpless, powerless, but lifted him gently, my arm round him, with a hand pressed to his hot, damp forehead. That crisis passed and he was sick, but before he could have another, similar attack, I left young Michael in charge, with strict instructions not to leave the boat, and I ran

to the nearest telephone box. I had seen one on the main road, but it must have been over half a mile away. I ran until I felt my own lungs would burst and looked up the number of the doctor Sarah had phoned. Still out of breath I pleaded with him to come and see Peter; faint with relief when he agreed to do so. As I gave him directions on how to get to *Elsa*, I could sense his surprise over the telephone. Then I sprinted all the way back to the boat, my heart in my mouth, to find them peacefully playing, during one of the many respites. Perhaps that one, gasping, horrific 'whoop' was the climax for him, as I do not recall another quite as bad. In revenge both James and I started 'whooping'. Somehow I had not expected to get it a second time, which, combined with sleepless nights proved utterly debilitating.

HMS *Ariel* proved a very different social atmosphere to that of a ship, holding various 'mess nights' and parties. It was impossible for me to attend any of these, for it would have been unfair on Sarah to leave her alone in case of a repetition of the 'whoop', coupled with my own exhaustion due to sleepless nights. Apart from the mad dash to the telephone, I never left the boat for the whole of that summer. James enjoyed one or two of them, attended by WRNS officers and QARNS, making me acutely jealous, certain by now that one of these attractive, unattached women had ensnared him.

On one particular night I lay awake for a long time, waiting for him to come back from a party, eventually crying myself to sleep, only to wake up, still in horrified solitude in broad daylight at 6 a.m. I dashed over to Sarah's cabin, choking back the tears, 'Sarah – he's still not back. He must have had an accident. What shall I do?' Sarah, though worried, spoke reassuringly, 'Look - I'll get dressed and go ashore and telephone HMS *Ariel* to find out – go back to bed for a bit – you look ghastly.' Before she had finished dressing, a rather pale James came across the gangplank – with his arm in a sling. I rushed to him. 'What's happened? Your poor arm – did you have an accident?' He tried to quieten me, in his habitual undemonstrative fashion, 'No – not an accident. At least not a car accident.' Anxious and curious I pressed him with questions, 'Well then, how? Tell me.' Seeing he would get no peace until he told the whole story, he admitted the truth, 'It was a game in the wardroom. We'd all had rather a lot to drink – someone tried to stir me up with a broom-stick.' I was horrified, 'Oh, no! Are you badly hurt?' Grimly he answered, 'No – I've told you. It's nothing much. The collarbone is slightly cracked.'

No longer worried or frightened I was furious with him, 'How the hell could you get mixed up in such a silly game at your age? How stupid!' Wearily and uninterestedly he merely grunted, 'Oh shut up – I tell you I'm all right – just tired.' No. I was *not* going to shut up. 'You are utterly irresponsible and I'm fed up with just sitting here cooped up in the boat while you go off and have fun – and how are you going to sail back down to the Hamble with a cracked collarbone?' In icy tones he spoke – as to a stranger, 'That's enough, Toni.' But by now I had worked myself into a state of blazing temper, my jealousy flaring out of control, made worse by the many times I had repressed my feelings over the disastrous sailing trips, and the whooping cough; I lashed out with all the venom I could muster. I did not feel sorry for him, for he had been having a great time, a tremendous time – with no thought of me, 'You are *so* selfish – don't you realize I'd give anything to get off this damned boat for half an hour or so?' Determined to stay patient, calm and cool, for Sarah was not far away in her after-cabin, he said, 'You wanted to come up here so that we could be together. I'll be perfectly capable of sailing back down and we'll get a crew of three anyway. Leave me alone I want to lie down. It hurts and I'm tired.' I felt no sympathy, burning with rage and blinding jealousy. The old saying 'better the devil you know . . .' conflicted with the fact that a certainty is easier to confront than faceless suspicions; but I hovered between the alternatives. *Did* I really want to know, or remain optimistic? Would constantly ignoring 'it' make 'it' go away?

The atmosphere on board *Elsa* was tense and unhappy in that unnatural, steamy hot valley, stagnant water around us and me tired and ill. James and I quarrelled and argued. He wanted to put to sea again, proposing a long weekend sailing trip to the Isle of Man. Willingly – for once – I agreed, thinking that once he was sailing, HMS *Ariel's* attractions might be forgotten – momentarily at least. It was settled, with just one extra for crew and taking Sarah and the boys.

All was fixed for three weeks later, during which time the 'whoops' slowly diminished, leaving us listless and pale, with me actually welcoming the thought of bracing healthy sea air. I resented the proximity of unattached women at the base, *Ariel*, glamorous and untrammelled by children, I resented the boat which was becoming a prison – but I banished that image for I loved *Elsa*.

I resorted once more to a repetition of that most undignified, unworthy procedure of asking him whether he loved me. Not believing the half-hearted 'Yes'. I was ashamed of my

inability to curb the unsatisfactory, probing questions, yet incapable of stopping them. He would read the paper, bored by me. For once, yes, I was eager to sail. The weekend scheduled for our trip, in mid-July, was unpredictable, with strong winds and grey skies, though being so far from the sea it was hard to visualize what it would be like. One of the officers from *Ariel*, Phil, joined us for the trip; his blond bearded appearance was cheerful and he was a great tease, enjoying playing with the boys – a rare treat for them as James never did.

The Isle of Man lay about seventy-five miles North-North-West of Liverpool, in the Irish Sea, which with prevailing South-West winds should only take us just over a day, or night, depending on when we sailed, leaving us one or two days to explore Douglas. The boys were tremendously excited, having forgotten how restricted their playing became once we put to sea. We left very early one Friday morning, hoping to arrive in Douglas early on Saturday. For the initial part of the trip we allowed the boys to play in the well. What we had not anticipated was the immense amount of scurrying about there would be involving Sarah and me once we reached the locks, with only one crew instead of the three on the way to the Weaver. We found ourselves pushing off with boathooks, putting out fenders and throwing warps ashore; trying to be in three places at once, by the merest chance I glanced automatically towards the well, having secured the line – and saw only one boy. I tore along the catwalk, and my eyes caught sight of the frantic scrambling five year old, trying to climb up the side of the lock where we lay. As the water rushed out of the lock to lower us for the next stretch of water and we dropped down, he was convinced we were sinking and was determined to save himself. Sarah was nearest and I yelled: 'Catch Michael, I'm coming,' and jumped down to dash across as Sarah reached him. I dread to think what would have happened if he had fallen in that maelstrom of water.

The barometer was falling and grey scudding clouds, matching the grey outlines of the Liver Buildings, chased each other, blotting out any remaining blue sky and the sun. The Mersey was rough and the strong seven-knot tide churned into waves by the gusting wind made James decide to anchor for the night and go ashore first thing in the morning for a detailed weather report. It would be madness to set sail in the Irish Sea if a gale was imminent. I did not even have to try and convince him of this. The anchorage, some way off from the shore, was very exposed, causing *Elsa*

to pitch and roll, tugging at the anchor chain inducing an incredibly uncomfortable motion.

During the evening the wind dropped slightly and we went up on deck to a transformed scene. The lights of Liverpool glittered and were reflected in the wide, wide river; the Liver Buildings softly outlined against a fairly lurid sky, denoting stormy weather, but looking romantic.

But next morning saw no improvement, and at dawn, James and Phil lowered the dinghy so that they could row ashore. It would take the two of them taking turns to row across the swift current and I watched, fearfully, as the little dinghy appeared to drift downstream until it got out of the main force of the current. They were ashore a long time, causing us acute anxiety as we swung with the tide, frightened that once the ebb was strong we should end up at sea minus the captain and crew. Neither Sarah nor I mentioned this at the time: each of us hoped to delude the other that all was well. Lunch was ready by the time they reappeared as a small dot near the shore. James's and Phil's arms were exhausted with the exertion of rowing against tide and wind. A gale was forecast; it would be suicidal to put to sea. Both disappointed and relieved we retraced our complicated journey through canals, locks and bridges.

It would not be long in any case, before we were due to set sail for the Hamble and Portsmouth, where HMS *Ariel* was being transferred.

I realized with a sickening lurch of heart that I now could never get him back from the undoubted lures and charms of the woman – still nameless – at *Ariel*. They would be meeting up again, unhampered whenever he was on duty after our return to Portsmouth. Dear God, I could not win. No, that was a defeatist attitude – I would try.

Phil was willing to crew for us, promising to ask if anyone else would join the gallant *Elsa* on her return journey, carefully not mentioning the appalling gales and struggle on the way up! With only a few weeks left, the variable weather would have plenty of time to change – yes – and change back again.

Each weekend Sarah went to see her mother, taking advantage of our proximity to Chester. She also met someone who became very fond of her; the feeling was reciprocated and I feared that soon she might well leave the boat. For her the atmosphere on board was upsetting as she was fond of the boys and me.

Each moment of every fraught day was a bustle of physical activity. Gradually the 'whooping' died away, and a little

colour apppeared in the boys' cheeks, despite the unhealthy, germ-laden atmosphere of the canal. The closed-in feeling induced a sense of claustrophobia in me, where my thoughts and fears ran round my head like rats in a cage, erupting now and then into more scenes of shameful jealousy. I only stopped short of asking for names. James had repaired and replaced any damaged gear and rigging during the boring summer weekends – never once did he play with the boys or take us out. The only time I was on the road was during my mad dash for the telephone. He renewed worn clevis pins, halyards and cleats, paying special attention to the rudder and transom which had taken such a battering on the way up.

I knew that this summer had been a disaster. At first sight the berth had seemed ideal, in country surroundings, but utterly marred by the growing tension in our relationship, the stifling heat and smell from the canal, our whooping cough and James's cracked collar-bone – now mended. Now all pretence of affection or lovemaking had virtually ceased. We lay carefully not touching in the narrow double bunk – my body and feelings yearning.

A week later, after an uneventful return journey, we tied up safely at Bursledon, on the Hamble, and went ashore to settle our berth and explore the ample facilities. James was very preoccupied and as we returned to the boat I asked him what the trouble was. 'The trouble is the old car. It's on its last legs – and it's absolutely essential for toing and froing.' This was indeed a blow, but surely we could buy a second-hand one? He thought this a bad idea, 'It's only exchanging the devil you know for one you don't.' I thought hard, then hesitatingly said, 'Surely, if I help too, we could at least buy a *cheap* new car?'

Meantime Tilly consented to appear on deck, haughtily stalking the length of the long wooden jetty, until she found the delicious familiar smells of a boatyard, where shavings, sawdust and mouse deliciously intermingled.

CHAPTER TWELVE

Mental Hurricanes – Sailing Hurricanes

That evening, left on our own, exhausted and drained, I made my final bid. With the farcical and mistaken idea that I could perhaps bribe or buy back his non-existent love for me, I offered to sell my grandmother's few jewels in order to buy him a new car. After all, if he did not have a car he would be obliged to live permanently at the shore base, *Ariel*, and she would have him all to herself. There were two or three valuable brooches with lovely big diamonds, but in old-fashioned settings and they had sat in the bank all these years. I did not feel as guilty as I might have if I had had daughters, yet ruefully and regretfully I proceeded with the business of selling them. He bought a Mayflower – such a pretty name. His gratitude was short-lived.

Meanwhile the cheerful return of Sarah and the boys helped the constant pain of heartache. Michael and Peter approved of their new playground, racing along as I had feared, without looking where they were going, and for several days I stood on deck to make sure they reached the boatyard safely; but, so sure-footed were they by now, that never once did they stumble or fall in. Sarah regaled us with tales of Peter's wickedness – how he had locked himself in the bathroom at her mother's house, which meant she had to climb a ladder and get in the window to open the door. She was so happy at this time, having become engaged to a charming Army officer who descended on us occasionally from Oswestry in a Land Rover to take her home for the weekend. They wanted to marry quite soon and I dreaded the thought of the boat and the boys without her.

A little school was found for Michael which he could get to by bus. I only had to cross the main road outside the boatyard, put him on the bus for a short ride, where he would be met at the other end.

Despite the comforts of the present berth, I was uneasy, unhappy, sensing impending disaster. Fully aware that pestering him with questions aggravated him, nevertheless I could not help myself – a hidden demoniacal force made me. I now was certain that he was in love with someone in HMS *Ariel*, rendering us and even *Elsa* unbearable to him. I felt so powerless, praying for a miracle. Poor Sarah, too, felt the tension in the cramped quarters, an unwilling witness to our pathetic arguments. The boat became a prison.

For a while in September, the hustle and bustle of getting Michael ready for school momentarily superseded my personal worries. He was quiet and acquiescent, not liking the idea of school, for at heart he was a 'loner', but accepting the inevitable with obedient reluctance. Leaving Sarah with Peter, I went on the bus with Michael for the first few days to introduce him to the school and the bus. This nearly caused a disaster, for Tilly, who liked to follow any of us going for a walk, tried to come with us on the first day and I only just spotted her in time before we crossed the busy main road. Picking her up, Michael and I ran back to *Elsa*, where Sarah shut her in Peter's cabin, making a mental note to do so each morning. Peter was lost without his beloved older brother, demanding 'lessons' too, which I started in an amateurish fashion and, though not quite three, he took to drawing letters like the proverbial duck to water. It was true that with only one child during the day, there was not enough for Sarah and me to do. Even when the winds blew and the equinoxial gales and tides did their worst, *Elsa* lay snugly in her berth, for this was far more sheltered than any previous mooring. The lines holding her bows off needed checking certainly; miniature wavelets would smack against her bows and she strained at the restricting lines, but there was never any danger of floating up on to the jetty as there had been at Hayling Island.

Sarah told us she would be leaving at the end of October; though happy for her, I knew we would miss her dreadfully.

Before she left I went shopping on my own, into Fareham on the bus, to buy an evening dress for a grand Christmas party being given for the wives and HMS *Ariel*. James could not avoid taking me for the invitation had been sent to me. This would be the catalyst surely. It was the first time in many years that I had bought any clothes, there being no need for them on board. Now, pathetically too late, I wanted something glamorous to transform me from Cinderella into a fairy princess. The glowing wine-coloured velvet of a halter necked dress tempted me and I hung it lovingly in the minute

cramped cupboard, taking care not to crush it, sandwiched between an oilskin, my one winter coat and a couple of dilapidated skirts.

Sarah's fiancé drove down to collect her and her belongings and we all helped to carry her bits of luggage along the jetty. I held back the tears as I kissed her goodbye and gave them their wedding present. She had shared so much, had become part of our life, always good-natured, full of fun and common sense; never at a loss or in a panic. She knew and hated the uncertainty of what was to come, grieving deeply for me, but helpless to avert an outcome I could not yet acknowledge. Because of her presence, which necessitated a code of conduct, somehow the inevitable had receded, but henceforth I was alone.

As a favour, the elderly woman who lived in one of the yachts offered to look after the boys for the evening of the fateful dinner and party at HMS *Ariel*. James collected me that evening, resplendent in uniform, cheerful at the prospect of a party, talking to Michael and Peter as he said good night to them, entreating them to be good, which left them speechless as he rarely spoke to them. Sarah had often remarked on this, but I had defended him on grounds of tiredness, or preoccupation. The dress was not commented on; but the prospect of the evening was a heady excitement, with a drinks party followed by dinner. Seated at a vast table covered in finest linen, silver and crystal, all was such a contrast. The wine was intoxicating – a sedative to my misery and I wanted James to know how much I was enjoying the evening. I saw him further down the table and across from me – saw his transparent, charmed happiness – saw his eyes look meltingly, not at me. . .and knew. I looked across the table at the woman next to him who returned the melting look. The impact of that initial confrontation exploded like a dum-dum bullet in my heart, mind and soul – entering so easily, nearly painlessly through my eyes, only to spread and corrode, devour and ravage all emotion and senses. The lovely glittering party turned grey, dissolved into bitter ashes and on the way home, at last, I asked point-blank and with a thudding heart, having learnt her name, 'Are you in love with Judith?' Looking straight ahead, hands gripping the wheel, he merely answered, 'Yes.' I let out a cry, for it hurt so to have it at last admitted to my face. I wanted to open the car door and end it all. . .but, of course, that particular, suicidal, fleeting moment was quickly overcome by the thought of the boys. I would have to live with this knowledge – be patient, philosophical – hope it was a passing affair.

So – relentlessly, inexorably, the sea-saga moved towards its Wagnerian climax. The pathetic love story and its finale a very pale accompaniment to what the sea still held in store – as its farewell.

That Christmas, with James home for a fortnight, I could nearly believe all was normal – in the daytime – but at night in our bunk he never touched me. He appeared relieved at not having to pretend any longer, reconciled and engrossed in preparing the boys' presents. We hid Michael's red tricycle in a quiet corner of the boatyard, where James painted the old red car for Peter. *Elsa's* hull and rigging needed a thorough overhaul in readiness for the Easter leave. I ventured to ask where we might be going. Thoughtfully he said, 'I'd like to go to St Peter Port again and Brittany – perhaps Dinard or Cherbourg.' As though we were two strangers speaking I said how much I'd love to see France again. He went on, 'I thought I'd ask Celia to come, when I send a Christmas card. I know she'd love it. She hasn't seen *Elsa* since we sailed her round together in 1950.' I knew what a tremendous help she would be as there was no Sarah, yet at the same time I resented, in advance, the glaring contrast between us. . .competing as it were with two women.

However, the trip, planning for it, the sailing itself, being together and doing what he liked most, would – might – help to bring him back to himself and to us. We would have to find someone to look after the children.

The boys' stockings hung at the foot of their bunks, the boat gleamed with polished wood and brass and the stove shed a warm glow. Try as I might, nothing could dispel the approaching menace, for once the festivities were over, the forced cheerfulness gave way to an increased aloofness. Normal life was poised on a knife-edge, where I took care not to disturb the unreal calm by twisting that knife.

We heard from Celia by return. She was overjoyed at James's invitation and 'couldn't wait' for Easter, offering to bring lots of cold food for the trip. We made enquiries about the children and heard of a very kind woman who took little ones in to board for just such occasions. We met her, a calm, motherly person, appalled at the idea of two little ones at sea, assuring us that she would look after them as if they were her own. She showed us the room they would share, mentioning that there might be two or three other children for them to play with. The set-up seemed ideal and I was greatly relieved.

February was intensely cold, but many chores kept me warm. When the gangplank was slippery with ice and nearly

vertical at low tide, it was an extremely tricky operation holding a heavy coal hod in one hand, and for the evening operation, a torch in the other! I heaved a sigh of relief each time my slithering, skidding feet reached the deck. Sometimes the hose from the stand-pipe to the tank would be frozen for days at a time, putting severe restrictions on the use of water on board. Both boys suffered from colds, sore throats and earaches and on the one occasion the doctor had to come on board to give Michael a penicillin injection he was both astonished – and to my surprise – full of admiration! It had never occurred to me that I was doing anything out of the ordinary.

At last, March winds brought the indefinable spring smell to the air, making the seagulls mewing and calling a happier, less forlorn and menacing sound. The Hamble suddenly became alive with the seasonal yachting fraternity strolling up and down the jetty in a hale and hearty manner, not too smartly dressed at this time of the year, humping tins of paint and varnish, smoking pipes and looking slightly askance at the lines of washing round our rigging!

Without being too disloyal I could not help thinking longingly of a bath, with taps and gushing, plentiful, hot water, instead of the little rubber hose which took the trickle of hot water from the gas water heater to the bath in the galley. What a joy it would be just to pull out a plug instead of having to pump away every inch of the boys' bath water in the little sit-down bath.

There had been no more parties in *Ariel* since Christmas, but before the Easter leave period started in early April, the WRNS gave a fancy dress party. Naturally, I was invited, and thought dreading the inevitable confrontation I got quite excited at the idea. We discussed costumes. James was dubious, 'I don't think I'll bother to dress up.' I had an idea, 'You can't go in uniform – why don't you wear my old faded coral Breton sailor's trousers and smock?' He had forgotten they were among the bilge-soaked clothes in the lockers. It was agreed; he would get a big beret and some old fish netting. I decided to go as a gypsy, 'Swirling skirt, tight blouse, a flower in my hair and bare feet.' He interrupted me, 'You can't go in bare feet.' I was determined, 'Of course I can – my feet are as hard as nails running about on deck – and I'll take one of the glass balls I fished out of Folkestone harbour as my crystal ball.'

A kind old lady came to look after the brothers and I felt light-headed with the determination to enjoy myself. As James had a beard he really did look like a Breton

fisherman. He wore the Dutch wooden clogs we had bought in Dordrecht as a finishing touch.

It was a wonderful, relaxed evening, everyone enjoying themselves in a heightened, abandoned way, sheltering behind their disguises. The band played boisterously, rhythmically and to my sheer delight, suddenly struck up an old-fashioned polka. James even asked me to dance and we clumped around the floor, he in his sabots, with me leaping agilely on my bare feet, breathless with excitement and joy. Perhaps all was well after all. I read the captain's palm, telling his fortune with mock solemnity, foretelling his promotion to admiral and ten children! I was so proud when James won first prize for his Breton fisherman's fancy dress and received his prize from the captain's wife. Though I knew no one at the party except for a few remembered faces from the last one, I chatted away happily for I did not see James again – until a glimpse revived the painful stunned shock as I saw him talking to Judith and smiling with the verve and dynamic enthusiasm of that evening at Christmas time. Suddenly, all was over again – my lip bitten till it drew blood, to stop myself from crying out – from crying.

I wanted to hide with my inconsolable grief. With only a fortnight to go before the Easter cruise I did my best to bury the ache, to forget everything in the preparations. Michael was on holiday so that both boys came to Fareham by bus when I went shopping, luckily, as it happened, for sheer tiredness often sent me to sleep on the return journey, when Michael would wake me up at our Bursledon stop. They helped on deck too, taking little buckets and cloths to wash down the sweeping curve of the cabin top. I was busy in the galley when Michael came running down to say there was a man on board. As we never, *ever* had visitors, this puzzled me; climbing into the well I was greeted by a photographer from the *Tatler* – no less. I posed decorously on the hatch combing while the boys carried on with their self-conscious washing down. The resulting picture was excellent, but I had been removed! Sad!

Another crew had been found and this time James reckoned that two men would be plenty as Celia would be there. Two officers from *Ariel* were willing and able – Ted and John. Tilly had to go to her cattery, for we were going to France – a relief for both of us, for cleaning out her box was a hateful chore and she hated rough weather.

Celia was enchanted to see us all, bubbling over with excitement at the prospect of two whole weeks' sailing, contrasting starkly with my apprehension. She had not seen

Peter since he was a new-born baby; now he was just three and she laughed affectionately at his incomprehensible jargon – he still left all the talking to Michael who translated for him. Then we drove the two down the road to Mrs Appleby, where Peter clung to me, sobbing, while Michael, nearly six, tried hard not to. She assured me that they would be perfectly all right as soon as I had gone and I knew she was right, yet I felt a dreadful pang and lump in my throat as I hugged them goodbye, leaving quickly so as not to prolong the tears. At the cattery, where we left Tilly, she gave us a dirty look before sitting down with her back to us.

John and Ted were waiting for us when we got back, sitting on the jetty. Unfortunately the weather forecast was not good, the general synopsis including a rapidly approaching area of low pressure which would cause a confrontation of two fronts as the weakening area of high pressure we had been experiencing became engulfed. Slowly we motored *Elsa* past the sleeping craft moored to the jetty, down Burlesdon creek in a fresh Force 3 to 4 southeasterly, which veered and backed constantly, echoed in the high shifting clouds at different levels.

In order to compete with Celia I took two Kwells, determined to remember to top them up at regular intervals, no matter what the warning said on the packet about over dosage.

Ceila had volunteered to do any cooking in rough weather, for which I was both grateful, yet stupidly resentful. Once past the Needles we went about in order to get plenty of searoom for, with an on-shore wind, that was important. Both Ted and John were quick, sure-footed and able to anticipate all the skipper's gruffly barked orders. Despite the Kwells and a stiff tot of rum, it took all my dwindling reserves of willpower, plus determination to match Celia, before I could go below into the sickeningly familiar, pitching, tossing galley. Even then, once lunch was heating I leapt back up on deck, shamefully leaving her to dish it up. I could tell that both Ted and John were feeling a bit below par, which left just the exuberantly cheerful brother and sister team revelling in our staggering progress through steeper seas now that the tide was flowing against the wind and waves.

However, the barometer crept up a point and the odd squally showers eased off – I tried not to worry about the old adage, 'When the rain's before the wind, then your topsail halyards mend . . .', by reasoning that it had been windy all along. Suddenly, without any warning, the wind backed, blowing from nearly due East, increasing violently to Force 6,

gusting 7, while gradually the clouds sped away revealing a hard blue sky which transformed the sea to a cold emerald green, topped by vicious white horses, spume and spray. We were carrying too much sail and before the danger became too great, James lashed the tiller which Celia and I tried to hold and keep a firm footing, while the three men lowered the mainsail. This did slightly reduce her mad lurchings, but by now the terrifying shriek of the gale in the rigging made it impossible to make oneself heard.

It had all happened so suddenly we were stunned. The sun made a cruel mockery of our wild cavorting plight. Surely it would die away as quickly as it had flared up? Yet hour after hour dragged by, increasing our danger. Both staysail and jib were lowered with much difficulty by James and Ted, holding on virtually with their toes, shaken like rats by a terrier, as *Elsa*, driven too fast, plunged her bowsprit and bows deep into the rapidly increasing troughs and mountainous tops of the waves. The leeboard was hoisted right up, for fear of it smashing against the hull, then we were sailing under bare mast and rigging alone, still racing sickeningly fast through engulfing seas which threatened to break over our stern. We all crouched in the well, holding on for grim death, powerless and unbelieving, as the scream of the gale increased to an even shriller pitch, coinciding with the tide turning again, forcing the height of the following seas to a dizzying thirty feet or so from trough to crest. James realized that he must quickly get the sea anchor over the stern to slow us down, or else we would surely and certainly be swallowed and engulfed by the yawning, hungry, endless waves that bore down on us relentlessly. By now it was at least Force 8, gusting *hurricane* Force 10 and 11. Bravely two of them fought their way into the for'ard cabin for the drogue (the sea anchor made of canvas in the shape of a cone, used to slow down a vessel in such conditions). We attached one of our thickest, longest, spare mooring ropes to the stretchers, keeping the wide end of the cone open, lashing the other end to one of the winches beside the mast, then James threw it over the stern from the well where we sat or stood, knuckles white from holding on so tight – helpless as condemned men in a cage.

The rope jerked taut and we held our breath and prayed that it would have the desired effect. Up till then I had been too frightened to look out over the stern, frozen into immobility; but I forced myself to stare for a long horrifying moment at the magnificence of the following seas as they cascaded down on us – rolling on like some irate

mythological army, rank upon rank of death-inflicting steel scimitars. From the tiny hollow shell of the well, one had to crane one's neck back to see the tops of waves at least half the height of the seventy-foot mast. I held my breath in awe and terror. Forgetting the situation between us, I grasped and clung to James, shouting to make myself heard above the screeching gale, 'James – whatever happens – I love you – please – do you?' He would not – or could not answer.

If the deadly green waters had crashed down on deck, *Elsa* would have been swamped; her steel hull filling and sinking instantly. Piercing through the terror exploded the sheer unbelievable beauty of those rearing jade monsters, glistening in the savage sun. As the drogue and ropes became saturated and heavy, they slowed down the run-away *Elsa*, and she then began to float like a seagull, climbing up, up, up the mammoth sea, perching for a split second on the crest before beginning the slithering descent into the depths again. We paid out more lines and incredibly she continued to bob like a cork, serene, unperturbed and safe.

The movement, of course, defied description. Dimly heard crashes floated up from the galley. Even James, for the first and only time in all those years sailing, was sick – just once. Only Celia was immune; saving the strength and lives of the three men by braving the heaving galley to make drinks. I retched and retched on an empty stomach, too frightened to go below to get more Kwells, dizzy and faint with exhaustion, clinging onto the gunwale, spent and useless, praying that it would cease.

As night fell, the extraordinary phenomenon of a near hurricane in mid-Channel did slowly, slowly abate to a normal Force 7 gale. I staggered below to my cabin, forcing myself to swallow a handful of Kwells, falling half conscious onto my bunk. My tongue and mouth hurt, my stomach and whole body ached; shamefully, I wished I was dead. I presume that being unable to drink or eat I became totally dehydrated, a condition I was ignorant of in those days. Faintly I was aware of Celia looking in to see how I was, and asked her if they were all coping. I felt too dreadfully ill to care what happened. The men got no sleep that night as they nursed the valiant *Elsa* through a storm-tossed wet night, but I dozed fitfully, drugged and shocked. The thought uppermost in my mind being one of relief that the boys were not on board too.

By dawn next morning, the gale had eased to Force 4 or 5 and had shifted again. But where were we? James could not hazard a guess at dead reckoning, for the complications of

wind, tide and drifting, plus the effect of the sea anchor made nonsense of any calculations. The day was overcast but clear; carefully we scanned the horizon, not knowing whether we were nearer to France or England. We were under sail again by this time, the men having hoisted them at first light and we felt sure that sooner or later some headland would miraculously appear. Yes, there, on the horizon. Two barely perceived faint smudges, only seen when not looked at directly, but catching the eye as we scanned the merging of grey sea into grey sky. As we were still heading West, and the smudges were ahead but to port some miles away, it could only be France.

Shaking out the reef points, the men set sail in earnest towards the welcome landfall; James rushed continually below to consult the chart and it soon became obvious the two smudges were the headlands of Roscoff and Primel Trégastel. We had been blown about one hundred miles off course, but could now enter Morlaix, despite not having a detailed plan of the harbour entrance, by carefully navigating the wide yet potentially dangerous rocky mouth of St Pol river.

Forcing down yet more Kwells, feeling faint and weak, after the excitement of finding out where we were, I collapsed once more onto my bunk. Soon we reached the rock-strewn entrance, though I saw none of this, for now my heart leapt wildly and I could not breathe and lay there like a stranded fish, gasping for air. I sobbed at the shame of my feeble collapse, not feeling seasick any longer now that we were in the calm waters of the river estuary. The beacons and buoys marking the channel in the fairway were easy to follow – Duon Roche, Stolvezen, Le Cochon Noir and Pierre Noir.

The clattering of feet and clicking of winches told me the sails were being lowered, and the wonderful, salutary chug-chugging of the engine proved that it had weathered the incredible storm, for amazingly we had shipped no green water. Cautiously and with great care James steered *Elsa* up the Tréguier Channel, between the Ile Louet, the Tour de la Lande and the Ile Noire.

I tried to sit up but my wildly beating heart and breathlessness sent me crashing back. Eventually Celia appeared, sorry to see my state, but exulting in the safe landfall and triumphal progress into Morlaix. Kindly, she brought me a mug of tea. Then, thankfully, at last I slept, too weak to move, waking only as joyful clatters and thuds meant that finally we were safely secured alongside a jetty or wharf. James left me alone to sleep and rested all afternoon on the

settee in the saloon – while I longed and yearned to be comforted by the feel of his arms around me. By degrees my heart and breathing returned to normal, but leaving me still shaken and feeble and appalled at what a brief glimpse of the saloon disclosed. The carpet was once again saturated by endless tramplings in wet boots, soaked and dripping oilskins and upset teapots and mugs. I would tackle it next day.

That evening, sadly, I was not strong enough to go out with all of them to a bistro in the town, for I could not even walk that far. Celia and James were ebullient in their success and, miserably, I thanked her for all she had done during the whole twenty-four hours; hating being left behind alone on board and unreasonably hating them for their triumph. I cried with rage and misery – surely they could have waited till next day to go and gloat ashore. I would not have dreamt of leaving Celia on her own had the roles been reversed and their selfishness cut me to the core. I should never have taken such a massive overdose of Kwells, but I had been desperate.

They did not return until the early hours of the morning, having well and truly wined and dined and wined again. Back to normal myself by morning, I fought my way through the debris and clutter in the galley in order to get breakfast and heard of their riotous party.Two fishing boats had been lost in the whirlwind hurricane and the diners in the bistro had been tremendously impressed by our survival, duly fêting the party and plying them with generous bottles of wine. Celia, in particular, had been acclaimed, quite rightly, for her courage and fortitude, which only increased my loss of self-respect – I hated them both.

All this while, James and I had not exchanged more than a casual remark; anger flared inside me. I could not *help* being seasick *and* terrified and I more than made up for my inefficiency at sea by my efforts in harbour. We would have a celebratory lunch on board. So, while they went shopping for the delicious local bread, cheese, fruit and wine, I began a mammoth spring-clean below deck. First of all though, in order to dry the sodden carpet the three men had to haul it up on to the jetty, where a fitful sun, dodging grey clouds, soon dried it. I scrubbed the floorboards, wiped the greasy bespattered paintwork in the galley, hung up all the damp trousers jerseys and oilskins on deck; brushed and dusted, washed up all the pots and pans in the overflowing sink and felt very virtuous. Then I prepared and laid lunch while waiting for the four to return.

Hours later they arrived having revisited the friendly bistro for a few more *coups de rouge*. Cinderella stayed plain

Cinderella. I had thought to have plumbed all depths of despair and self-pity during the war years in France – but this was far worse. It was a very low ebb to reach.

Brother and sister were naturally delighted to be together again, so much to talk about now that the sailing crisis was over, so many reminiscences. That afternoon the sun shone hot and strong and the three of us went for a walk over the Breton heather, while the two crew slept off their midday vino. As Celia and I waited for James on the quayside, unable to contain my pain at his deception, I told her everything, about Judith, and that James loved her and no longer loved me. She was incredulous, but not in the least sympathetic – her devotion to her brother would not allow any criticism of him, 'Don't worry Tonia, it will pass – it can't be serious.' That was all. The walk, with each of us locked in our own thoughts, and far apart, was strained. After a while, I caught up with James who was striding ahead and tried to talk to him, 'I know I couldn't come out to dinner last night, but I do think its pretty mean of you to celebrate again today without me. Why didn't you come back for me after shopping and at least take me out for some wine?' Bored by my remark he grunted, 'Well, it was rather Celia's efforts we were celebrating. . . .' Stung to bitterness I interrupted, determined not to cry, 'But, for heaven's sake, I had spent the whole morning clearing up the beastly mess left from the sailing – I mean its wonderful of Celia to have done all the cooking at sea, but I've worked hard too – and *it's not my fault I'm seasick,*' I shouted. He shouted back, 'Oh stop pestering me.' I persisted, goading him, 'Well, I bet no other woman would put up with all this sailing – not even your precious QARNS nurse.' Clenching his teeth he hissed, '*Shut up.* Go away – leave me to walk on my own.' Celia did not want to talk either, so, my mind in a turmoil, I made my way back to the boat.

Though it was raining the next morning, the prevailing southwesterly was back, which was exactly what we needed to sail to St Peter Port. So we motored back down the lovely river and this time I sat on deck, feeling at one with the gentle grey drizzle – heart-broken to be leaving France, without having even been into Morlaix – heart twice broken at the irretrievable situation.

Two days later we arrived back in England. Michael started the summer term; Peter proudly walked to the bus with us, wanting to go to school too, missing his brother and demanding more and more 'lessons'. Each morning I woke with a heavy heart, coupled with the human gift of hope without which life would be unbearable. It seemed as though

I was at the eye or epicentre of a hurricane myself. Perhaps if I kept very still it would blow over or past me without damaging or flattening me.

Summer's blue skies and warm sun mocked me for my hurt was very raw. Having no car, afternoon walks with the boys were restricted – either down to the end of the jetty admiring the sleek aristocratic yachts – empty most of the time, despite the caressing breezes and scorching sun – or around the yard and dusty path. *Gypsy Moth II*, Sir Francis Chichester's tiny, exquisite yacht lay moored a few boats down from us and my admiration knew no bounds. How could he, all alone, face the implacable, ruthless oceans?

We saw little of James for he was often very late back, or not at all – nights when he was *not* on duty. He was taking Judith to the New Forest in the new car, Oh, the irony, the bitter humiliation of it. How did I know? Quite simply because when he was on board, he would be covered in mosquito bites, tossing and turning in the bunk, unable to sleep – hot and restless. So I asked him, brutally outright – half knowing the answer – how he had got so bitten by midges and mosquitoes. Cruelly he told me, 'We went to the New Forest.' The 'we' went through me like a knife – I was no longer the other half of 'we' and 'us'. I screamed at him in hellish fury and despair, 'How could you – and in the car I bought for you.' On and on I went, losing all control, until he hit me, not hard, but enough to send me sprawling. We were aghast and shocked at our behaviour. This could not go on.

One evening he told me that we had been allocated an anchorage for the Spithead Review in June. Even though the date was only a month away, the tension of his overwhelming presence, when I knew he was longing to be elsewhere finally broke me. I pleaded, wept, implored – spoke of my great love for him, the boys, and finally *Elsa*. I did and said all the wrong things. He did not say much – just looked straight through me with eyes as cold as the sea.

Summoning all my remaining dignity, aware of the finality of what I was about to say, with hatred giving me courage, I spoke through clenched teeth, 'Leave then – go to *Ariel* and be with her. I cannot and will not share you, knowing you hate being here. Goodbye, James.' Without a word, he packed a zipper bag, while I sat in Sarah's old cabin – forcing myself not to call him back – emotionally and physically drained, limp as a rag.

I could hear his footsteps on the gangplank, then recede along the jetty. Just in time Peter's voice called out from his cabin where he was having his rest, just in time to stop me

doing something irrevocable. Together we went to meet Michael at the bus stop, coming home from school.

The whole of the preparation of *Elsa* for this joyous Review was perforce done by me. When anger won over distress I would get in the dinghy, laboriously climbing down into it with a pot of yellow paint to touch up the rubbing strake, pulling myself slowly round the boat. I washed the green hull too and gilded the sardonically grinning dolphin. No one would notice I knew, but this was *Elsa's* occasion and she must look her party best. My thoughts were in a turmoil, emotion dominating common sense as I reflected that the Spithead Review might well be *Elsa's* swan song.

She would have to be sold for I could never take her to sea. Where should the boys and I go? When I reached this point my jangled nerves and reasoning dissolved into hot tears and great sobs that shook my body.

The sea saga is over. The remembering of it has proved how indelibly those years will be etched in bitter memory. But I have the boys, and I have Tilly.

D1612470